Contents

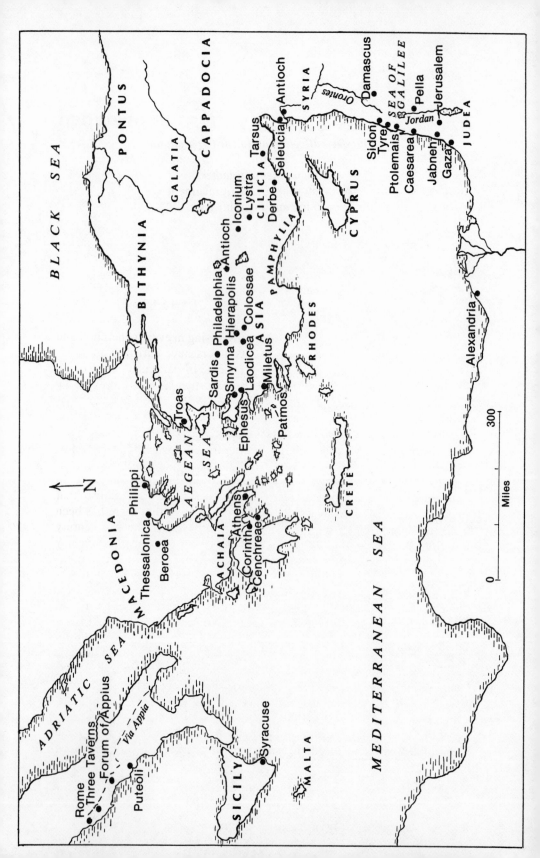

Foreword

In a few years the community of those who believe in Jesus of Nazareth as the unique revelation of God will celebrate a bimillennium. Their history began with a few Palestinian Jews who perceived in faith that God was in Christ Jesus reconciling the world to himself, and has continued through two thousand years of preaching and teaching till today they constitute a billion people of every nation, race, and tongue. The challenges presented by such a propagation in time and place have forced Christianity to face new questions arising in every generation and culture. These thought-provoking encounters have enriched the tradition by a growth of doctrines and practices. In particular, the Roman Catholic Church, the largest of all the Christian bodies, has explicitly acknowledged that the Spirit of God active in the first believers and their proclamation of Jesus continues to guide Christianity to new insights into the revelation given through Israel and Jesus Christ.

Inevitably, however, thinking Christians will ask about the connection of two millennia of accumulated tradition to the insights and practices of the first Christians for which the New Testament is our guide. In my judgment, neither of two simple answers responds adequately to that question. On the one hand, it is incorrect to deny that there has been Christian development in doctrine and practice since the first century (either because such development cannot be intellectually or creedally tolerated, or because of the contention that all subsequent doctrine was already known in the first century). On the other hand, perception is lacking in the response that there is no genuine relation between the New Testament and the developed Christianity of subsequent centuries (either because such developing tradition is entirely wrong, or because it is quite foreign to the New Testament). I would contend that a solid relationship exists, but one complicated to the point that both biblical scholars and theologians have devoted much study and writing in their attempt to decipher it. Frederick Cwiekowski strives in this book to summarize the results of those investigations for the non-professional readers.

I admire his attempt because I think he has dealt intelligently and faithfully with the essential aspects of the earlier Christian tradition

enshrined in the New Testament and with subsequent Christian tradition. A systematic theologian by training, he shows *an informed awareness of the complexity of church developments* since the first century and
is respectfully cautious in stressing their validity. (Roman Catholics
should admire his fidelity to church doctrine as he diagnoses it.) But he
has also familiarized himself with *a broad span of New Testament research.* (And on this score perhaps I am strongly prejudiced in his favor,
for he adopts a centrist approach, relying on what one can reasonably
substantiate in the biblical data, rather than on radical hypotheses based
on silence or unverifiable reconstructions—an approach I myself have
adopted.) In presenting these two components, one cannot have certitude. Certain developments of the later church are amply attested in
tradition and teaching; others much less so. Certain aspects of the first
century church are very clear; others less so. Consequently, scholars
loyal both to the New Testament and to the church with its great Christian heritage will differ honestly, even as I do from Father Cwiekowski
on a few points of phrasing and emphasis. However, I know no popular
book that in so short a compass has covered the biblical background for
christology and ecclesiology as well as he has here. Let those who require unanimity or certitude wait for another attempt; in the past there
has *never* been unanimity or certitude on the material discussed here,
and I suspect there never will be. Let those who are interested in a very
intelligent and respectful survey that could win a high degree of centrist
agreement read this book with gratitude.

Raymond E. Brown, S.S.
Auburn Distinguished Professor of Biblical Studies
Union Theological Seminary, New York
Epiphany 1987

Introduction

During the past few decades Christian self-understanding has been greatly helped by increased knowledge about the New Testament writings, about Jesus, and about the early church. We have benefited from studies of the language of the New Testament, for example, and from a better knowledge of the thought world of the first century; historical and archaeological studies have clarified some of the background to the New Testament writings. Through the careful research of specialists we have greater access to the religious and cultural milieu of the first century. Recently some scholars have sought to use the tools and methods of sociology as a means of shedding further light on the ministry of Jesus and the development of the early church.

This is not to say that we can now produce an exact historical account of Jesus' ministry or of the life and mission of the early church. Available sources do not permit us to carry through such an undertaking, however much we might wish that such could be done. But recent studies give many insights nonetheless into the rich and complex development that is part of our Christian beginnings. We are able to sketch the main outlines of the ministry of Jesus; we can be confident that scholarly reconstructions of events in the early church or in the life of a particular church are fairly accurate. The work of scholars in this area continues still and we can expect that in years ahead yet further advances will be made.

This book is born of the desire to make available to a greater audience an overview of recent scholarly work on the beginnings of the church. While the topic is of interest to many, not all have the time or the opportunity to read the many works in which scholars discuss the growth and development of the early church. The account of the beginnings of the church offered in this book presents the highlights of our current understanding of the period which extends from Jesus' ministry to the end of the first century. We thus span the period of the first, second, and the beginning of the third generations of the Christian church.

The first two chapters deal with background material. Chapter One gives a general view of the pre-critical understanding of the church's beginnings. The chapter shows why Roman Catholics in particular held to this view, and why they have good reasons now to approach the study of the early church in another way. Other Christian readers will find this chapter a help not only to understand the Roman Catholic experience in dealing with this matter, but also to see some of the basic issues that enter the current scholarly discussion of the topic. Chapter Two gives an overview of the Greek, Roman, and Jewish worlds in which our account of the early church unfolds.

Chapter Three deals with the public ministry of Jesus. It looks at his mission and those elements of his ministry which had an impact in shaping the church after his death and resurrection. Chapter Four deals with the earliest post-resurrection communities and the early Christian mission. This chapter treats the first two decades of the Christian church. Chapter Five looks at the church of the fifties and early sixties of the first century A.D. It draws upon the letters of Paul, our first written sources among the New Testament writings. The sixth chapter discusses the significant changes that took place from the mid-sixties to the end of the seventies. This period is marked by the death of the great apostolic leaders and the church's efforts to carry on without their direct guidance. Here we draw upon the Letter to the Colossians, the Letter to the Ephesians, and the Gospel according to Mark. It was at the end of the sixties that the Jewish War took place. The war ended with the Roman occupation of the city of Jerusalem and the destruction of the Jewish temple. We review these events and, in the following chapter, look at the development of Judaism after the war.

Chapter Seven deals with the eighties and nineties of the first century A.D., a time of important literary productivity for the early church. Through Matthew and John, the pastoral letters and the Letter to the Hebrews, we get a view of Christian communities in various locations in the Mediterranean world. In Chapter Eight our historical account concludes with a look at the church as we see it at the end of the first century and the beginning of the second. The Book of Revelation helps us here, as do two sources which are not part of the New Testament: a letter of Clement of Rome and the letters of Ignatius of Antioch. A final chapter, Chapter Nine, offers some reflections on what our understanding of the early church might be saying to us today.

While it is hoped that this book will be of service to Christian readers generally, the book is deliberately attentive to the Roman Catholic experience of understanding the church's beginnings. There have been significant changes in the way all Christian churches have come to view the historical character of the New Testament writings; this, of course, has had a marked impact on the way the historical beginnings of the church are understood. Roman Catholics also have in their tradition a series of formal doctrines which concern Christ and the founding of the church, its sacraments, and its priesthood. For Catholic readers, at times the presentation in this book is led to discuss the relationship between these dogmatic statements on Christ and the church and the findings of current biblical and historical scholarship. I do not find that modern scholarship conflicts with these dogmatic statements. It does help us to see those statements in a more nuanced historical perspective than was previously the case, and to recognize more clearly the development that took place from the time of Jesus' ministry to the end of the New Testament period.

> It may help Roman Catholics to keep in mind that when we discuss the origins of the church we are dealing with both continuity and development. The dogmatic statements of the councils stress, for understandable reasons, the element of continuity between Christ and the church. Current biblical scholarship contributes to our understanding of that continuity; it also helps us appreciate the presence of development in the life of the early church. Together, both the church's dogmatic statements and contemporary biblical scholarship contribute to our understanding of the church's beginnings.

For the past twenty years I have taught in a Roman Catholic seminary; it has been my happy lot for most of those years to teach courses on Christ and on the church. Early in my ministry I also began to teach groups of lay people, in Catholic communities and in ecumenical settings; I see that work as an extension of my seminary teaching. It is in that same perspective that I see this book. In teaching seminarians I have found that biblical scholarship sheds invaluable light on church doctrine. I have learned, too, that it is perfectly possible to make an intelligent and responsible combination of scholarly progress in understanding with the best of traditional church teaching. It is in the desire to share that discovery with the growing body of Catholic laity who are keenly interested in their religious beliefs, and who, with Christian believers generally, are interested in their religious beginnings, that this book has been written. It is my hope that other Christian groups may also find this work useful, not only in the overview of biblical and historical studies which it provides, but also in the help it might give to understand the Roman Catholic experience in dealing with an issue of vital interest to all Christian believers.

As I bring this work to conclusion I realize my profound indebtedness to those who have been so much a help to me in understanding the Bible and the world from which it came. The names of authors whose works I have used appear in the text or in the list of suggested readings at the end of the book. In a more personal way I am deeply grateful to Raymond E. Brown, S.S., who most graciously read the manuscript and offered many very valuable suggestions. I thank Frank J. Matera and Thomas R. Hurst, S.S., for their assistance on sections of the text. My thanks, too, to Howard P. Bleichner, S.S., and to Vincent M. Eaton, S.S., both of whom read the entire manuscript and made many helpful suggestions. The limitations of the final text I accept as my own responsibility.

For research assistance I am grateful to David P. Siemsen and the library staff at St. Mary's Seminary and University in Baltimore; to the Dominican Fathers at the Ecole Biblique in Jerusalem; and to the director and staff of the W. F. Albright Institute of Archaeological Research, also in Jerusalem. I appreciate the stimulus to my work that came from students at St. Mary's Seminary in Baltimore and at the M.R.E. Program of the University of St. Thomas, Houston. I am grateful for the personal encouragement I received from Thomas F. Schindler, S.S., Sarah Sharkey, O.P., and from the members of my family. My thanks, finally, to Lawrence Boadt, C.S.P., editor at Paulist Press, for his kind assistance and gentle patience.

The quotation from *Vatican Council II: The Conciliar and Post-Conciliar Documents,* Austin Flannery, O.P., general editor, is printed with permission of the Costello Publishing Company, Inc. The quotation from *I Clement* comes from *The Epistles of St. Clement of Rome and St. Ignatius of Antioch,* James A. Kleist, S.J., editor, and is printed with permission of Paulist Press. Citations of the biblical text are taken from *The Oxford Annotated Bible,* Revised Standard Version.

Chapter One

A New Understanding

A dramatic shift is currently taking place within the Roman Catholic community concerning the way in which the beginnings of the church are understood. After a look at the basic outline of the understanding of the church's beginnings—an understanding dominant until recent times—we will review some of the assumptions about New Testament writings and the Roman Catholic directives which supported and promoted that understanding. An examination of some of the recent developments in New Testament studies will prepare us for the understanding of the beginnings of the church as presented in the succeeding chapters of this book.

The Pre-Critical Approach

The basic view of the church's beginnings which until recently was held by most people, in catechetical works, in volumes on the life of Christ written before 1950, and in many expressions of official Church teaching was the result of a pre-critical approach to understanding the beginnings of the church. The approach is called "pre-critical" because it did not apply modern critical methods in its use of the New Testament writings which formed the principal basis for this understanding. This approach has sometimes been called a "blueprint approach" because of its presupposition that Jesus, in his lifetime and in the period after his resurrection and before his ascension, set up a detailed blueprint of the basic structure of the church.

This view even today has a strong influence on the minds of many when the topic of the church's beginnings is thought about or discussed. This older understanding performed a useful service in the face of sometimes hostile attacks on the church but the exigencies of recent developments require us to examine its presuppositions. The overview which follows is not taken from a single source; it represents, rather, a composite whose various elements are taken from current presentations which exhibit this approach.

The church, in the old view, had its beginnings in the public ministry of Jesus of Nazareth. Jesus, always possessing the consciousness of his messianic dignity, taught during his lifetime that he was the Messiah and, at least in some veiled way, communicated that he was the true and natural Son of God. Jesus' disciples, further, professed their faith in Jesus' divinity during his lifetime. Authentic historical records (Mt 14:33 and 16:16) were regarded as the basis for such a view.

Jesus saw himself as one sent by God with the mission of instituting an organized church, a new and divine religion distinct from Judaism. He set up this new religion through his preaching, his miracles, and his calling disciples into a new community centered about himself. Jesus intended to found a church as a society which would continue on earth for centuries to come. He taught a determined body of doctrine applicable to all times and to all people. He dissociated himself from official Judaism: he opposed the Jewish religious leadership of his day and drew a line between his followers and other Jews.

From among his followers, Jesus chose twelve apostles and gave them special training to carry on his teachings and way of life. To one of these, Simon, Jesus gave a new name, "Rock" or "Peter," and said that he would build his church on that rock. The historically authentic record of this primacy given to Peter was thought to come from an eyewitness, the evangelist Matthew, one of the Twelve and the first of the gospel writers. Another of the Twelve, and therefore also an eyewitness, was Zebedee's son, the evangelist John, the author of the fourth gospel. Both Matthew and John were companions of Jesus for about three years, eyewitnesses of Jesus' preaching and miracles. During Jesus' earthly ministry the roots of the structures and offices of the new church were clearly implied, even if these were further developed by the apostles after Jesus' ascension. In at least some presentations of this precritical understanding, Jesus' disciples, at the time of his death, felt that they did not belong to official Judaism any longer but saw themselves united by a new religious leader and by new religious principles. Before his death Jesus had instituted the sacrament and sacrifice of the eucharist and the sacrament of orders, and the apostles saw themselves as priests in this new religion.

After Jesus' resurrection, as this understanding has it, Christ formally appointed Peter to be shepherd of his entire flock (Jn 21:15–19). To Peter and the other disciples, a group constitutionally erected as an apostolic and ecclesiastical hierarchy, Christ gave a synthesis of the church's operational program and a teaching investiture: "All authority in heaven and on earth has been given to me. Go therefore and make disciples of all the nations, baptizing them in the name of the Father and of the Son and of the Holy Spirit, teaching them to observe all that I have commanded you . . . " (Mt 28:18–20).

This, basically, is the outline of the pre-critical approach to understanding the beginnings of the church. It was until recently the dominant view in the popular mind and was presupposed in official church documents. More recent expressions of this approach sometimes show greater sensitivity to developing biblical studies, but elements of this outline still appear in some writings and discussions about the beginnings of the church.

The Rationale Behind This Earlier View

If we are fully to understand the reasoning which is behind this approach and see why it still has a strong influence within Roman Catholicism, we must back up some and look at the context out of which it emerged. Two principal factors led to the view we have just looked at. The first was the reaction toward historical and biblical studies which was taken in the church's struggle with modernism in the first decade of the present century. The second was the approach toward historical studies taken by many Catholic writers and preachers in their efforts to explain and defend the faith of the church in the period between the church's condemnation of modernism (1907) and the 1950s.

It is best to see the account which follows as an account of people dealing—and at times struggling—with issues that were very important to them and to their religious self-understanding. An awareness of Roman Catholicism's encounter with modern biblical criticism may help Roman Catholics to better understand themselves as they deal with other questions now facing them. The Roman Catholic experience also sheds light on the struggles within other Christian churches which now are facing the same issue of trying to understand the scriptures.

The Modernist Period

It was only in the years after the First Vatican Council (1869–1870) that Catholics began to deal seriously with the methods and results of the critical biblical scholarship which had been undertaken by many Protestant scholars in Europe since early in the nineteenth century. The various aspects of these biblical studies involved the efforts: to obtain as accurate a text of the Bible as was possible (textual criticism); to reconstruct the historical setting behind the texts and the events of which they spoke (historical criticism); and to understand the various literary forms—e.g., poetry, wisdom literature, prophecy, historical narrative—in which the biblical text was written (form criticism). While much of this work had lasting value, not a little of it was undertaken with presuppositions that opposed the dogmas or the institutional structures of the Roman Catholic Church.

Even in the presence of such hostility Leo XIII (1878–1903) did not oppose the involvement of Catholic scholars in these new approaches nor did he wish to stifle the progress of biblical studies within the Roman Catholic Church. In 1893 he issued an encyclical letter "The Study of Holy Scripture" (*Providentissimus Deus*) on the study and use of the Bible. The pope's stand was nuanced and cautious. In 1902 Leo XIII set up the Pontifical Biblical Commission which gave a limited measure of encouragement to the new methods of biblical studies. During the final years of Leo's pontificate, however, developments took place which led his successor to take a different approach.

The turn of the century and the first years of the 1900s saw various efforts within Roman Catholicism in France, in Italy, and (in a small way) in England, urging reform of the church and of the church's doctrine with a view of adapting them to modern needs. These efforts, later very loosely labeled *modernism,* had various objectives and had little, or at best limited, contact with each other. While the questions and the studies of the clergy and laity involved in these efforts were in many respects legitimate, there were also, unfortunately, imprudent claims, over-simplifications, and sometimes wild exaggerations and errors which could only provoke a negative reaction. Some of the writers used pseudonyms as they sought to test the waters with their new conclusions. This strategy was interpreted by others as camouflaging attacks on the church. While the writings of the modernists involved questions of philosophy and theology and the social role of the church, our principal interest is on the issue of biblical sources and the relationship between biblical texts and the church's dogmas, structures, and apologetics.

Alfred Loisy

The writer who served to bring this biblical strand of the modernist movement to the fore was the French Catholic priest, Alfred Loisy (1857–1940). Loisy was convinced that the new biblical studies could be a great blessing to the church. He saw in the use of critical methods a means of distinguishing the essence of the Christian faith from what he regarded as the outdated teachings and structures of the church of his day. Further, Loisy held that the dogmatic formulations of church teaching have to be continuously adapted to changing patterns of thought.

The church's teaching authority, in Loisy's view, had the responsibility of judging succeeding historical expressions of faith in the light of the original, i.e., apostolic, religious experience. This position allowed him as a scholar to carry on his historical studies as he wished, and led to his indifference to any opposition between the findings of biblical or historical studies and official church positions.

It was in response to a French translation of the widely popular German work of Adolf von Harnack that Loisy in 1902 brought his own studies to public attention. Harnack (1851–1930) was one of the most prominent Protestant historians and theologians of the nineteenth century. His best seller *The Essence of Christianity* argued that the basic ideas of Jesus—the universal fatherhood of God, the community of humankind, and the infinite value of the human soul—were gradually, in the course of Christian history, covered over by dogmas and structures which distorted that basic message. Harnack argued that critical historical studies enabled us to extricate the essential ideas of Christianity from later developments. The book was obviously a challenge to the Catholic Church which emphasized church tradition and dogma and which argued—especially since the time of the polemics of the sixteenth century—that the church's basic structures were founded on Christ's institution and that its dogmas were unchanging.

In responding to Harnack, Loisy wanted to show that sound historical studies did not lead to Harnack's conclusions. He hoped at the same time to gain within the Roman Catholic Church acceptance of the critical approach. Such approval would also endorse his efforts to find in the gospels a means of promoting church renewal. The title of Loisy's book was characteristic: *The Gospel and the Church* (*L'Evangile et l'Eglise*). It was published rather hurriedly, in the same year as the translation of Harnack's work.

Loisy's book provoked a strong and largely negative reaction. His arguments were interspersed with passing comments that the gospels were not historical documents but testimonies of faith; that Christ himself did not anticipate later developments in the church, etc. The reasoning of the book provoked questions from sympathetic critics but also misunderstanding from some readers and opposition from church authorities. Loisy's work was condemned by the archbishop of Paris in 1902. However, in the following year, encouraged by some who were sympathetic to his views, Loisy sought to clarify the statements of his first book. He replied to his critics in a second book, *Reflections on a Little Book* (*Autour d'un petit livre*). (It was also in 1903 that Leo XIII died and Pius X was elected pope.) Loisy's new volume was presented in part as "an outline and historical explanation of the development of

Christianity." But, by the author's admission, this study was guided by the principles that the exegete and the historian must prescind entirely from preconceptions about the supernatural origin of the scriptures. The scriptures must be interpreted in the same manner as any other historical document. He took for granted that there was a profound development not only in the formulation but also in the meaning of the Church's dogmas as well as in the organizational structures of the Church. Loisy's defense of his positions became hardened in this second work. He argued for a strict division between faith and dogma on the one hand and historical and biblical criticism, Loisy's interests, on the other.

The Condemnation of Modernism

Loisy's publications were but one part of the complex movement called modernism. While relatively few priests and lay persons were directly involved in the writings of the movement, many saw a grave threat to the well-being of the Church in the implications of the various modernist positions. In 1907, under the direction of Pius X (1903–1914), the Office of the Holy Roman Inquisition (its name was changed to the Holy Office in 1908) published a *Syllabus Condemning the Errors of the Modernists* (*Lamentabile Sane*), in which sixty-five statements on biblical and theological matters, all taken from the works of Loisy, were "condemned and proscribed." If one were to assume, especially in an uncritical way, that the opposite of what was proscribed or condemned was the correct understanding, one quickly recognizes similarities with the understanding of the church's beginnings given earlier in this chapter. Because of that, it will be useful to note some of the errors cited by the statement of the Holy Office.

Concerning Christ's knowledge: #32: "It is impossible to reconcile the natural sense of the gospel texts with the sense taught by our theologians concerning the conscience and the infallible knowledge of Jesus Christ." And #34: "The critics can ascribe to Christ a knowledge without limits only on a hypothesis which cannot be historically conceived and which is repugnant to the moral sense. That hypothesis is that Christ as man possessed the knowledge of God and yet was unwilling to communicate the knowledge of a great many things to his disciples and posterity."

Concerning the founding of the church: #52: It was far from the mind of Christ to found a church as a society which would continue on earth for a long course of centuries. On the contrary, in the mind of Christ the kingdom of heaven together with the end of the world was about to come immediately." And #55: "Simon Peter never even suspected that Christ entrusted the primacy in the church to him."

The syllabus of modernist errors was followed on September 8, 1907 by Pius X's encyclical, *On the Doctrines of the Modernists* (*Pascendi Dominici*). The encyclical labeled modernism "the synthesis of all heresies" and argued that the many roads of modernism led "to atheism and the annihilation of all religion." The encyclical applied the term "modernism" to the complex of heresies which were thought to be the logical conclusion of heterodox elements or trends within the movement. One of the trends thus proscribed was the new discipline of biblical criticism.

To counter any modernist leanings among the clergy and specifically among seminary professors, the pope in 1910 required all clergy to take an oath against modernism, the first part of which included a statement on the value of the rational and historical foundations of faith and the foundation of the church by Christ. The third article of the oath states: "I hold that the church, the guardian and teacher of the revealed word, was *immediately and directly founded by the true historical Christ himself during his life among us,* and that it is built upon Peter, the prince of the apostles, and upon his successors" (italics added). When one recalls that the decisive and resolute opposition of Pius X to anything associated with modernism followed so soon after the teaching of Vatican I (1869–1870) on the universal jurisdiction and teaching authority of the pope, it is not difficult to understand that the pope's reaction had a strong impact that would last for decades.

The Pontifical Biblical Commission, 1905–1915

The anti-modernist stance found in the condemnations in the syllabus of modernist errors and the oath against modernism received further support from the directives of the Pontifical Biblical Commission between 1905 and 1915. The commission was established by Leo XIII in 1902, the year of the publication of Loisy's *The Gospel and the Church.*

The decisions of the commission were issued in the form of affirmative or negative responses to long and often intricate questions. The decisions have largely historical interest for Roman Catholics today since they have been implicitly revoked by later decisions and other directives. The decrees of this early period were generally extremely cautious regarding critical developments in biblical studies. In those years and for decades to follow the rulings served to stifle Catholic research in the sensitive areas with which we are dealing.

In the commission's decisions concerning the New Testament great attention was given to questions of historicity and authorship. A directive on Matthew's Gospel (1911) taught that Matthew the apostle wrote the gospel bearing his name before the destruction of Jerusalem (A.D.

70). Further, the commission insisted on the historical accuracy of several passages of key importance in an understanding of the beginnings of the church: Matthew 14:33 was seen as "the apostles' profession of faith in the divinity of Christ" before the resurrection; Matthew 16:17–19 was seen as "referring to the primacy of Peter"; and in Matthew 29:19–20 we have "the form of baptism given to the apostles together with the universal mission of teaching." We can see in these directives strong support of the view outlined at the outset of this chapter.

A decree given four years earlier (1907) concerning the fourth gospel also insisted that the author of the gospel was one of the apostles, John, and that the discourses of Jesus in this gospel, so evidently different from Matthew, Mark, and Luke, were nonetheless Jesus' own and not the theological compositions of the writer. These particular directives bear on our study in two ways. First, Jesus is portrayed in the discourses of the fourth gospel as having a very vivid awareness of his own divinity and clearly speaks of that divinity to others during his public ministry. Implicit in this is the idea that there could be no limits to Jesus' knowledge about the needs of the future church. Second, the Jesus of the fourth gospel sees himself and those gathered around him in clear opposition to the Jewish religion of their contemporaries. Both of these elements figure in the view of Jesus and the church outlined earlier in this chapter. Statements of the modernists by contrast held that the author of the gospel was not himself an eyewitness to the historical Jesus but rather a distinguished Christian witness to the life of Christ at the close of the first century, and that the discourses of Jesus in the fourth gospel were "theological meditations" of the evangelist rather than strict historical records of Jesus' teaching.

Three other decrees of the commission have a bearing on our account. The commission taught (1912) that Mark's gospel was written by a disciple and interpreter of Peter and that Luke, a physician, the assistant and companion of Paul, wrote the third gospel. Further, both authors used "trustworthy sources, either oral or already written." Concerning the Book of Acts, the commission directed (1913) that Luke used "most trustworthy sources . . . accurately, honestly, and faithfully" so that "complete historical authority may by claimed for him." Further, the commission held that the Book of Acts was written not later than the first Roman imprisonment of Paul (ca. A.D. 63). Finally, the pastoral letters, 1 and 2 Timothy and Titus, were said (1913) to be written by Paul himself between his first imprisonment and his death (ca. A.D. 63–66).

Apologetic writing in the decades after the modernist crisis made much of the historical character of the New Testament writings. While the commission's directives were not constantly quoted, the stress on the historical character of the New Testament writings (some seen to be written by eyewitnesses to the events of Jesus' life) remained a powerful influence on later writings about Jesus and the beginnings of the church.

Further confirmation of this tendency came in 1920 when Pope Benedict XV (1914–1922) issued an encyclical (*Spiritus Paraclitus*) to observe the fifteenth centenary of the death of the great biblical scholar, St. Jerome. The pope's letter was influenced by the difficulties in the years prior to its publication. Strongly insistent on the complete historicity of the Bible, it remained negative toward advances in biblical studies. In the 1920s leading Catholic biblical scholars were still given little freedom in publishing their work.

Modernism never took hold in the United States. At the beginning of the century American Catholic scholarship was in its infancy and tended more to reflect European scholarship than to pursue its own work. A paradigm of the American situation is seen in *The New York Review,* a publication begun in 1905 by St. Joseph's Seminary, Dunwoodie, New York. The *Review* featured essays by European intellectuals, some of whom were later regarded as Modernists, and by some American scholars. The publication was severely criticized after it printed a series of articles by a professor at St. Bernard's Seminary, Rochester, New York, on the human knowledge of Jesus, and an advertisement of a book by George Tyrrell, an Englishman and former Jesuit who was regarded as a modernist. Though the archbishop of New York initially defended the *Review* and explained that the advertisement appeared through an oversight, the journal ceased publication in 1908.

In Europe critical scholarship went underground; in the United States it was stopped just as it was getting underway. Only in the 1930s and 40s did Catholic scholarship in the United States revive. The Catholic Biblical Association was founded in 1936. In 1940, *Theological Studies,* published by the Jesuits at Woodstock, Maryland, picked up where *The New York Review* left off in 1908.

Catholic Writing After Modernism

In the years after the struggle with modernism many Catholics wrote responses to those who either challenged the traditional understandings of the church's dogmas, teaching authority and structures or dismissed them altogether. Not surprisingly, the attitudes and approaches were defensive and, as often happens in polemics (and not infrequently also in apologetics), some of the assumptions of the "opponents" were accepted as starting points. The most important of these assumptions had a direct bearing on the understanding of the church's beginnings. It was assumed by both sides that scientific history was the only legitimate means for studying the human past, and, in our specific case, the beginnings of the church. This approach to history was born in the nineteenth century's efforts to make the study of the human past as scientific and as rigorous as physics or chemistry. The objective of historical study was to learn of the past "as it had really been," in the famous expression of the historian, Leopold von Ranke (1795–1886). Anything that smacked of reconstruction or reflection was cast aside. This approach to history, with its exaggerated and exclusive emphasis on the factual, was called "historicism."

Catholic writers made an effort to explain and defend the church's beginnings in the face of those who argued that a scientific study of history undermined Catholic claims about its own foundations. But Catholic writers did so in works which assumed the same understanding of history as their opponents. Catholics argued that biblical sources were eyewitness reports, strictly factual, written by disciples who intended to record the history of Jesus and of the early church. Catholic writers today refer to the Catholic apologetics in the decades of the 20s, 30s, and 40s as an "historicist apologetic."

In the light of more recent understandings, there were two very serious flaws in the assumptions of this historicist apologetic. However laudable in its intent, this effort accepted the same understanding of history as the opponents of the church. Also, in the heat of argument, it misunderstood the nature of the biblical sources. The gospels and the Acts of the Apostles were accepted as accounts of eyewitnesses (Matthew and John) or of those who were companions of eyewitnesses. (Mark, it was assumed, was Peter's companion; Luke, the companion of Paul.) In this framework it was assumed that the accounts of these authors were strictly factual, and therefore susceptible of providing the kind of proof needed to answer critics within and outside the Church.

Many Catholic writers regarded these assumptions as implicit in the directives of the Pontifical Biblical Commission of 1905–1915, and in the syllabus of modernist errors, the encyclical of Pius X, and the oath against modernism. Rarely are these official documents invoked today—we will mention one notable exception in a moment—but the spirit of their approach still lingers in some presentations of the beginnings of the church based on the texts of the New Testament.

The recent instance where some of these earlier documents were cited was the working draft of the proposed constitution on revelation in 1962. The story of the change from that draft to Vatican II's final Constitution on Divine Revelation in 1965 documents a dramatic shift. These developments explain as well why current critical Roman Catholic biblical studies approach the New Testament in a new way. The church's official guidelines are based on this changed approach. So too is our understanding of the church's beginnings.

Recent Scholarly Developments

Since our understanding of the beginnings of the church depends almost completely on the New Testament, a change in our approach to the New Testament writings and how we read them calls us to a re-examination of understandings based upon the scriptural texts. It was in the early 1940s that the Roman Catholic Church undertook a major change in its official approach to understanding the Bible. In 1941 the Pontifical Biblical Commission, in a letter to the Italian hierarchy, spoke against attacks still being made on a critical study of the Bible. In 1943 Pope Pius XII (1939–1958) issued what has been called the *Magna Carta* of modern biblical studies in his encyclical letter *On Promoting Biblical Studies* (*Divino Afflante Spiritu*). The letter was issued to commemorate the fiftieth anniversary of Leo XIII's encyclical on the study of scripture. Although Pius XII praised the work of Leo XIII and Benedict XV, he allowed and encouraged a freedom for scholarly research not envisioned by either of his predecessors. The pope's stress on recognizing the different types of literature in the Bible was probably the greatest single contribution of the encyclical. This recognition allowed the student of the scriptures to deal in an honest and forthright way with the obvious difficulties which come from reading the biblical texts from a consistent historical viewpoint. This recognition and subsequent developments in the same direction were to have a profound impact on later efforts to reconstruct the story of the church's beginnings.

Two other authoritative statements must be mentioned before we come to Vatican II. In 1955 the secretary and the sub-secretary of the Pontifical Biblical Commission issued a clarification about the status of the commission's 1905–1915 decrees. They did this in a review of a new edition of a collection of church statements about scripture (*Enchiridion Biblicum*). Part of the review read as follows:

> . . .as long as these decrees propose views which are neither immediately nor mediately connected with truths of faith and morals, it goes without saying that the scholar may pursue his research with complete freedom and may utilize the results of his research, provided always that he defers to the supreme teaching authority of the Church.
>
> Today we can hardly picture to ourselves the position of Catholic scholars at the turn of the century, or the dangers that threatened

Catholic teaching on Scripture and its inspiration on the part of liberal
and rationalistic criticism, which like a torrent tried to sweep away the
sacred barriers of tradition. At present the battle is considerably less
fierce; not a few controversies have been peacefully settled and many
problems emerge in an entirely new light, so that it is easy enough for
us to smile at the narrowness and constraint which prevailed fifty years
ago. (Cited by E. F. Siegman, "The Decrees of the Pontifical Biblical
Commission," *Catholic Biblical Quarterly* 18 [1956], p. 24.)

Thus Catholics were free to pursue their studies and to adopt new positions according to the methods of modern critical studies, as, for example, on the gospels' authorship of which we will see more in a moment.

The decidedly positive attitude to critical biblical studies seen in the
pope's 1943 encyclical letter and in the 1955 statement of the Biblical
Commission still encountered some resistance in the years before the
council opened in 1962. In the opening years of the pontificate of Pope
John XXIII (1958–1963) certain Catholic biblical scholars in Rome were
the object of severe criticism and two prominent professors were removed from their teaching positions at the Pontifical Biblical Institute.
In 1961 the Holy Office issued a warning against ideas which called into
question "the genuine historical and objective truth of sacred scripture."
The largely negative tone of this document issued on the eve of the
opening of Vatican II engendered a pessimism among some scholars as
to what would be the council's position on biblical studies.

Scripture Studies and the Second Vatican Council

When the bishops of the Catholic world gathered in Rome in the fall of
1962, they received among their working documents one entitled "On
the Sources of Revelation." The text reflected the continuing tension in
the church concerning biblical studies. The proposed draft had been
drawn up by theologians of the pre-conciliar Theological Commission
whose president was Cardinal Ottaviani, the secretary of the Holy Office. Many of the bishops of the council argued that the draft did not
incorporate recent developments in biblical studies and excessively restricted the research of scripture scholars. The draft text actually cited
the anti-modernist documents of the 1905–1915 period as its authorities.
On November 20, 1962, a vote was taken to determine whether the draft
should be sent back to the commission for a basic redrafting or whether
the discussion should continue on the existing text. Of the 2,209 bishops
voting, 1,368 voted for a redrafting of the document, 106 votes short of
the necessary two-thirds to carry. On the next day, November 21, Pope

John exercised a prerogative which was his as president of the council. In view of the fact that fully sixty percent of the council's bishops found the draft basically unacceptable, the pope directed that the draft be withdrawn and rewritten by a mixed commission made up of bishops of both the Theological Commission and the Secretariat for Promoting Christian Unity (established by Pope John XXIII in 1960 and placed under the direction of Augustin Cardinal Bea, a world renowned biblical scholar). The pope's decision on November 21 marked a turning point of the council.

The 1964 Instruction of the Pontifical Biblical Commission

It was to assist the conciliar debate on the proposed constitution on revelation that in 1964 the Pontifical Biblical Commission with the approval of Pope Paul VI (1963–1978) issued its "Instruction on the Historical Truth of the Gospels." Because the gospels are such key sources in our understanding of Jesus and his part in the beginnings of the church, it will be useful to take note of the commission's statement.

A careful reading of the document shows that the Biblical Commission was really far more concerned with the character of gospel truth than with simply reasserting the historicity of the gospels. The part of the instruction (Part IV) which has a direct bearing on our study is its guide "concerning the reliability of what is transmitted in the gospels." It is in this context that the instruction speaks of the "three stages of tradition by which the doctrine and the life of Jesus have come down to us." Stage one of the tradition, the farthest back in time, deals with what Jesus said and did and what the disciples saw and heard. Two things are stressed: what the disciples saw and heard prepared them to be witnesses of Jesus (not biographers or historians); that Jesus "followed the modes of reasoning and of exposition which were in vogue at the time" and "accommodated himself to the mentality.of his listeners." These are the words of the instruction; they allow for limits in Jesus' worldview even if they attribute this to his accommodating himself to his hearers. The question of Jesus' understanding of himself and his mission was very much an issue in the modernist period. We will deal with it in Chapter Three.

The second stage of the tradition leading to the composition of the gospels constitutes the period when the apostles and other first generation Christians, many of them eyewitnesses, proclaimed and explained the life and words of Jesus and especially his death and resurrection. Several points of the instruction should be noted. First, somewhat in passing, the instruction states that "after Jesus rose from the dead . . . his divinity was clearly perceived." This is the first time an official Roman Catholic document makes such a distinction; it indicates that during Jesus' lifetime the disciples did not clearly perceive his divinity. This contrasts with the insistence of the Biblical Commission's decree in 1911 concerning the historical authenticity of Matthew 14:33. That decree described as historical the apostles' profession of faith in Jesus' divinity before the resurrection. The 1964 instruction recognizes a shift in our understanding of this sensitive issue. The instruction continues: "The apostles passed on to their listeners what was really said and done by the Lord with that fuller understanding which they enjoyed" after the events of the resurrection and the coming of the Spirit. With this "fuller understanding" the apostles interpreted Jesus' words and deeds "according to the needs of their listeners." It is very significant for our study to recognize that during this period of oral preaching the account of Jesus' public ministry was interpreted in the light of the post-resurrectional interpretation and understanding of Jesus and his mission. Such a recognition will help us in our reading of the biblical text. Finally, in the preaching on the apostolic community, many modes of speaking were used: catechesis, stories, testimonies, hymns, songs of praise, prayers, and other literary forms used by people of the time. Some of this preaching and teaching, we know, was put down in writing.

The third stage of the tradition comes with the actual composition of the four gospels. The instruction uses the term "sacred authors" instead of "apostles" (second stage) for those who wrote the gospels. This reflects the current view that none of the gospels as we have them was written by an apostle or an actual eyewitness. In the past Matthew and John were thought to be apostles and eyewitnesses of the historical Jesus. The instruction also makes important observations about the process and the method by which the evangelists edited the primitive traditions, passed on by word of mouth and in some cases in written form. (The study of this phase of gospel composition is called "redaction criticism." It is the most recently developed element in the critical study of the Bible.) "From the many things handed down they [the evangelists] selected some things, reduced others to a synthesis, (still) others they explicated as they kept in mind the situation of the churches." The instruction indicates that the authors of the gospels selected, synthesized and explained what they received in order to address the situation of the churches for which they were writing. This analysis of the Biblical Commission on the formation of the gospels is the common assumption of critical biblical scholars in our day. An awareness of this process is an indispensable factor in interpreting the gospel texts. Its application has a profound effect on our understanding of the church's beginnings.

The commission's 1964 instruction is an important moment in the story of Roman Catholic endorsement of modern critical methods in the study of the New Testament. A synopsis of the instruction's teaching was incorporated into the 1965 *Dogmatic Constitution on Divine Revelation* (article #19) promulgated during the fourth and final session of Vatican II. It is this understanding which is the official teaching of the Roman Catholic Church. The directives of the 1964 instruction and of the 1965 constitution of Vatican II as well as the spirit and method of biblical study which they endorse constitute a basic guide in the presentation of the church's beginnings; that presentation will be undertaken in the subsequent chapters of this book.

Two additional notes. Among the sixteen documents of Vatican II, four are constitutions; the remaining texts are called decrees or declarations. While all the texts express the teaching of the council, the four constitutions are, as it were, "constitutive" of the faith and practice of the Roman Catholic Church as the council saw them. It is very significant that the teaching of the 1964 instruction on the interpretation of the gospels is included in one of the council's constitutions.

In the years immediately after the council the Catholic Church issued various decrees which aimed at bringing current practices into line with the thinking of the council. Among such changes was a 1967 ruling of the Congregation for the Doctrine of the Faith (formerly the Holy Office) which replaced the oath against modernism with an abbreviated profession of faith. The revised profession of faith consists of the Nicene-Constantinopolitan Creed (the same as that used in the liturgy on Sundays and feast days) with a brief additional statement at the end. The details about the historical foundations of the church in the 1910 oath against modernism have been removed.

Chapter Two

The World of Jesus and the Early Church

The fourth gospel (Jn 19:19–20) tells us that the inscription of Jesus' cross was written in Hebrew (Aramaic), Latin, and Greek. The three languages represent the three worlds of which Jesus and the first generations of his followers were a part. Some knowledge of these worlds in their political, cultural, and religious dimensions is indispensable to our understanding of Jesus and the early Christians.

Judaism in the Exilic and Early Post-Exilic Period (587–333 B.C.)

The Judaism of Jesus' day can be understood only if we back up to the time of Israel's exile and Israel's restoration in the sixth century B.C. At that time the Babylonians, in retaliation for Israel's siding with the Egyptians in the struggle between Babylon and Egypt, entered Jerusalem, destroyed the temple of Solomon, and deported to Babylon many of the political and religious leaders of the city. While the defeat was a shattering blow to Israel's faith, the period of the exile was nevertheless marked by very important religious developments. It was during this period that many of Israel's religious traditions were given the basic written form in which we now know them: the Torah (the first five books of the Bible), the historical writings known as the Deuteronomic History (Joshua and 1 and 2 Kings) and the writings of many of the prophets. This is the period when the prophet, known to us as "Second Isaiah" (Is 40–55), expressed some of the greatest theological insights of the biblical tradition. Denied access to the temple during the exile, Israel experienced a shift of its religious identity to its body of written tradition, especially to the Torah. The religious practices of circumcision and sabbath observance became signs of Jewish identity. It was during this same period that the synagogue emerged as an important institution of Jewish life.

Israel's exile ended when Cyrus of Persia conquered Babylon and, in 538 B.C., allowed the exiles to return to Palestine. Under Cyrus' protection and with his support, the temple was rebuilt. The completion of the temple and its rededication in 515 B.C. marks the beginning of the second temple period in Jewish history. This was a period marked by economic and political tensions and, perhaps even more so, by differing interpretations of what was normative to Judaism. There were differing views on the significance of the temple, on devotion to the law (Torah), and on the importance of oral tradition as an adjunct to written text. These tensions would remain within Judaism throughout much of the New Testament period.

The Greek Era (333–63 B.C.)

A major question which Judaism had to face throughout this period was its relationship to the non-Jewish world—the Babylonians and the Persians—and, in a new and more intense way, the Greeks. In the second half of the fourth century B.C. the power of Persia gave way to the rising power of the Greeks under Philip of Macedon and his son, Alexander the Great. The Greek era of Jewish history began with Alexander's conquest of Syria and Palestine at the battle of Issus in 333 B.C. By the time of Alexander's death in 322 B.C., Greece had achieved political control over the eastern half of the Mediterranean and over territory as far east as the Indus River. As the protective influence of Persia (modern Iran) faded, the Jews of Palestine came gradually to experience, with the rest of the world, the pervasive power of Greece.

The influence of Alexander's conquest would affect Palestine and the ancient Mediterranean world for centuries. It was Alexander's dream to oversee a worldwide empire exhibiting a political, commercial, and cultural unity. In a general way, we can identify two principal characteristics of the Hellenistic civilization of Alexander and his successors: a universalism which led to a concerted drive for unity but also a syncretism which allowed and even favored the retention of foreign elements, especially those from the orient.

The most significant bond which held the Hellenistic world together was its common language, *koine* Greek. This was the language of law and business. A desire for social respect or the reputation for being learned required one to master the language. It has been said that "the final establishment and dissemination of the *koine* was probably the most valuable and the most permanent fruit of Alexander's expedition"

(M. Hengel). The availability of a common language throughout the area would be of inestimable importance in the growth and spread of Christianity.

Two decades of ineffective rule after Alexander's death resulted in his empire's division into four parts. The eastern half of the empire fell under the dominion of two of Alexander's generals. The territory of Egypt and with it most of Palestine came under the rule of Ptolemy. The lands of Syria and Mesopotamia, and with them the region of Galilee, fell to the Seleucid dynasty based in Antioch in Syria. With the exception of Galilee, Palestine was to remain under the control of the Ptolemies for a full hundred years, coinciding almost exactly with the third century B.C. The Ptolemies maintained the policy of the Persians and of Alexander in their tolerance for Jewish religious life and general non-interference in the internal affairs of the Jews. But it was inevitable that the impact of Greek thought and Greek culture would have a deep influence on the Jews. Greek traders, merchants and travelers became present in ever greater numbers. Non-Jewish residents of Palestine were very open to Greek manners and culture. Greek cities were founded in Palestine, and Greeks settled in existing cities and brought with them their patterns of life and culture. The Jews themselves, while maintaining their own religious identity under the leadership of the high priest and Sanhedrin (council) in Jerusalem, were exposed to the culture of the Greeks and learned their language for purposes of trade and commerce. Greek influence in the region of Galilee, under the Seleucid rule, was even more pronounced. The region earned the nickname "Galilee of the Gentiles" (Mt 4:15).

For Jews living in the diaspora the problem of maintaining their identity became even more acute. Because the greater number of Jews in Alexandria in Egypt (the center of Jewish life outside of Palestine) knew only Greek (and thereby stood to lose access to their Hebrew scriptures), in the middle of the third century B.C. a Greek translation of the Torah was undertaken. The translation was called the Septuagint (the LXX); that name came from a legend that each of seventy-two elders (the number was rounded to seventy) working independently had produced an identical translation. The importance of this translation cannot be overestimated: "That the scriptures should exist in Greek was a tremendously significant development, both opening up new avenues of communication between Jew and Gentile, and preparing the way for a heightened impact of Greek thought on the Jewish mind. Later of course it vastly facilitated the spread of Christianity" (John Bright).

The Seleucids and the Maccabean Revolt

Life for the Jews in Palestine changed around the end of the third and the beginning of the second century B.C., when the Seleucids wrested Palestine from the control of the Ptolemies. The Seleucids pursued much more vigorously than the Ptolemies the policy of Hellenization in the territories under their control. Judea itself was granted a relative autonomy in the early years of Seleucid domination, years when large groups of Jews were themselves receptive to the Hellenistic culture with which they were having increasing contact. Among those most sympathetic to the Hellenistic culture were wealthy Jews and the priestly aristocracy. Those who opposed the acceptance of Hellenism stressed Judaism's covenant relationship with God, a relationship of which the law was the supreme expression. Jews so opposed to Hellenism were called the "pious ones" or Hasidim (from the Hebrew *hesed,* meaning "covenant love"). The Seleucids (also referred to as the Syrians) became more involved in Jewish affairs when they demanded greater tax revenues to offset Syrian defeats against the increasing power of the Romans. When Antiochus IV assumed the reign in Syria in 175 B.C., he adopted an aggressive policy of Hellenization, less from a concern to eradicate Jewish distinctiveness than from the desire to use cultural unity as a means of consolidating political power.

Antiochus IV's policies were a direct affront to many devout Jews. He adopted the title "Epiphanes," meaning "Manifest," to imply that the god Zeus was manifest in him. Though this move was meant to promote political loyalty, it could only appear to devout Jews as idolatrous. Moreover, to help underwrite the expenses of his military efforts, Antiochus granted the office of Jewish high priest to the highest bidder. When Antiochus made an unsuccessful bid to annex the Egyptian holdings of the Ptolemies, some of the Jews, acting upon a rumor that Antiochus had been killed in the attempt, expelled the high priest. Antiochus angrily restored his appointee to the high priesthood and plundered the Jewish temple to punish the Jews and to replenish his depleted resources. Far more significantly, Antiochus soon determined to abolish the Jewish community's separate identity. This was a momentous decision: Jews were now being persecuted precisely because they were Jews. The intensity of Jewish reaction and subsequent loyalty to their own traditions can only be understood in the light of this persecution. Jews were forbidden under penalty of death to observe the sabbath or to circumcise their children; inspectors traveled about to supervise compliance. Pious Jews preferred to accept suffering and death rather than to abandon the law. The ultimate affront to the Jews occurred when Antiochus, returning through Palestine after a second unsuccessful Egyptian campaign, erected an altar to the Olympian Zeus in the Jewish temple (167 B.C.). For the Jews this was the "abomination of desolation" (1 Mc 1:54; Dan 11:31).

It was the Jewish people of the countryside who began a revolt against the Syrian policies. In a little Judean village not far from Lydda an elderly priest, Mattathias, killed in anger both a fellow Jew who was about to offer a sacrifice on a pagan altar and the royal official who was overseeing him do it. Mattathias and his five sons had to flee to the hills of the wilderness of Judea (1 Mc 2:15–28) but they were soon joined by other Jews ready for battle. Among those who joined forces with Mattathias were members of the Hasidim (1 Mc 2:42). The hills became a base for a guerrilla activity bent on destroying pagan temples in the countryside and punishing apostate Jews. At the death of Mattathias, leadership of the revolt passed to his son Judas (166–160 B.C.). Judas acquired the surname "Maccabeus" ("designated by God"), from which comes the name—the Maccabees—given to the party led by himself and his brothers. Jewish opposition escalated from small-scale forays to direct attacks on the Syrians. In 164 B.C. Judas' forces marched into Jerusalem, purified the temple, and restored the worship prescribed by the law. (The reconsecration of the altar is commemorated to this day in the Jewish feast of Dedication, *Hanukkah*.) From a Seleucid leadership preoccupied with Roman pressure from the west and Persian threats from the east, Judas won a treaty (162 B.C.) which recognized Jewish freedom to follow their own laws in return for a recognition of Syrian sovereignty.

Many Jews were satisfied with the treaty; nevertheless Judas continued to press against the Syrians, chiefly over the issue of the appointment of the high priest. Eventually the Syrians recognized one of the Maccabees in that post. Though the Maccabees came from a rural priestly family, they were not of the high priestly family of Zadok. For this reason the Hasidim broke their alliance with the Maccabees. Some scholars think that the high priest who preceded the Maccabean appointee may have been the "Teacher of Righteousness" who founded the Jewish community at Qumran at the northwest corner of the Dead Sea. Through Maccabean support for the winner among rival claimants for the Syrian throne, the Jews won independence from the Syrians in 142 B.C. With one brief exception this was to last almost a hundred years. In 140 B.C. an assembly of Jews proclaimed the Maccabees governors and high priests "until a true prophet should appear" (1 Mc 14:41). This proclamation amounted to a recognition that the legitimate priesthood was being set aside.

The Hasmonean Rulers

One of the sons of the Maccabee brothers, John Hyrcanus, became ruler of Judea in 134 B.C. He and his successors are known as the "Hasmonean" rulers. The name comes from Hasmon, the family name of Mattathias and his sons. After a brief period during which Judea again fell under the power of Syria, Hyrcanus undertook a military campaign which extended the sphere of Judea's power. This program of expansion did not have popular support; it was undertaken only with the help of paid mercenaries.

It was during Hyrcanus' thirty year rule (134–104 B.C.) that there emerged two of the religious groups whose existence would mark Jewish life until the destruction of Jerusalem in A.D. 70. One of these groups, the Sadducees, was composed of the aristocratic and priestly families who supported the policies of the Hasmoneans. They were heirs of those who were more open to Hellenistic influence. Though they were supporters of the Hasmonean leadership, they did not enjoy popular esteem. The second group were the Pharisees, quite likely an offshoot of the group of Hasidim who were early supporters of the Maccabees. The Pharisees became disillusioned with the Hasmoneans because of their political and military adventurism, but even more because of their support of Greek ways and culture. Though many of the Pharisees came from the middle class, they enjoyed among the Jews a religious and social prominence. The potential divisiveness of the two groups did not come into full play under the able leadership of John Hyrcanus. His successors would not be so fortunate.

Hyrcanus' successor, his son Aristobulus (104–103 B.C.), annexed Galilee to the territory under Jewish control and was the first of the Hasmoneans to assume the title of king. His Greek name and the use of the royal title increased the opposition of the Pharisees. The third of the Hasmoneans, Alexander Janneus (103–76 B.C.), assumed both the throne and the high priesthood. His military campaigns were so successful that by the time of his death the territory of the former Davidic kingdom was once more in Jewish hands. But internal opposition to the Hasmoneans grew during Alexander's reign. Many Jews thought he had entirely abandoned any religious motivation in his rule. When internal opposition became open rebellion, Alexander had some eight hundred of his Jewish opponents crucified. Alexander's successor, his wife Sa-

lome Alexandra (76–69 B.C.), made peace with the Pharisees. It was during this period that the Pharisees came to have an important role in the Sanhedrin.

Rome and Herod the Great

At the queen's death her two sons fought for succession. Neighboring peoples, annexed to Judea in the military expansions of the Maccabees and Hasmoneans, took sides in the struggle. The Pharisees, for their part, despairing of either of the brothers, encouraged abolition of the Hasmonean monarchy and the acceptance of Roman jurisdiction over Judea. It was in this context that Rome became involved in the affairs of Palestine. Both sides in the struggle recognized their need of the support of the Roman general Pompey, recently victorious over the Seleucids in Syria. In 63 B.C. Pompey moved against Jerusalem, deposed one of Salome's sons, and responded to Jewish resistance with the massacre of some twelve thousand Jews. When Pompey himself entered the inner sanctuary of the temple, pious Jews saw this as a divine punishment on a guilty people. Pompey annexed Palestine to what had just become the Roman province of Syria and appointed Salome's other son as high priest in Jerusalem.

The next decades of political life in Palestine and the Middle East generally were complicated ones, with alternating leaders and shifting allegiances. Rome became an increasingly powerful force in the eastern Mediterranean while the Idumeans to the south of Judah sought to extend their own dominion at Judea's expense.

In 49 B.C. Julius Caesar crossed the Rubicon and made his bid for power in Rome. When Pompey lost to Caesar the following year both the high priest in Jerusalem and the governor of Idumea shifted their allegiance to Caesar. Caesar rewarded Jewish support by granting the Jews in Judea and in the diaspora exemption from some of the obligations Rome imposed on occupied territories. The high priest was confirmed in his rule and named ethnarch (ruler of a racial group within a province) of Judea. The governor of Idumea was named prefect of Judea, responsible for safeguarding the interests of Rome. Two of his sons were named governors; one, of the region around Jerusalem; the other, Herod, of Galilee.

Roman leadership in the final years of the Republic passed from Caesar (assassinated in 44 B.C.) to Cassius and then to Mark Antony and Octavian. Taking advantage of Rome's weakness in Syria and Palestine, the Parthians (successors of the Persian empire taken over by Alexander) ousted Herod and restored Hasmonean rule (40–37 B.C.). Herod fled to Rome, where, with the approval of Antony and Octavian, the Roman senate named him king of the Jews. Roman forces soon expelled the Parthians from Syria and executed the Hasmonean rulers of Judea. In 37 B.C. the Idumean Herod became in fact, as in name, king of the Jews.

Herod "the Great" ruled Israel from 37 to 4 B.C. After David, he was probably the most powerful ruler Israel had known. The early years of Herod's reign were marked by efforts to consolidate his authority, and he often did so in a ruthless and bloody manner. He used his marriage with the Hasmonean princess Mariamne to secure the support of those who accepted the Hasmonean rulers. During these years Herod operated very much as a vassal of Mark Antony, who commanded, from Egypt, the eastern part of the empire. At Mark Antony's defeat by his rival Octavian, Herod hastily and successfully switched his allegiance to Octavian. The latter in turn confirmed Herod as king of the Jews and extended the territory under Herod's control. It was in 27 B.C. that the Roman senate conferred the title of Augustus ("Venerable") on Octavian in recognition of his contributions to Rome. This occasion is customarily used to date the beginning of the Roman Empire. The reign of Augustus from 27 B.C. to A.D. 14 was a period of general prosperity and peace (the *Pax Romana*) in much of the Mediterranean world. It was during the reign of Augustus, of course, that Jesus was born.

Shortly after the beginning of Augustus' reign, Herod entered a second phase of his own rule in Palestine. It was a period of peace, marked by Herod's efforts, both in Palestine and abroad, to portray himself as both a patron of Greek culture and a promoter of the Jewish cause. In his efforts to promote Greek culture in Palestine he sponsored and supported vast building programs: temples, theaters, gymnasia, baths, hippodromes, gardens, even new cities. Samaria was rebuilt and renamed Sebaste (the Greek equivalent of Augustus). The ancient Phoenician coastal city, Strato's Tower, was made into an important harbor, furnished with all the embellishments of a Greek city, and named Caesarea Maritima. Throughout the land fortresses were built or refurbished. Outside of Palestine Herod adopted the style of Hellenistic princes in being a benefactor to cities in Asia Minor and in Greece.

Herod's greatest achievements were reserved for Jerusalem. In the western quarter of what is today the "Old City," south of the present-day Gate of Jaffa, he built a magnificent palace, remnants of which are still standing. The old fortress (the Acra) at the northwest corner of the temple area was rebuilt and renamed the Antonia. And in 22 B.C. Herod began work on his most famous project of all, the enlargement of the temple area and the reconstruction of the second temple. Work on the temple itself was completed in some nine and a half years; the work on the entire temple area, one of the largest of the ancient world, was completed only in A.D. 63.

In present-day Jerusalem's Old City, the "temple area" is still preserved. The temple of Herod, built approximately on the site of the temple of Solomon, is thought to have stood in the temple area north of the present Islamic sanctuary, the Dome of the Rock. The "Western Wall" (also known as the "Wailing Wall") between the temple area and the Jewish quarter of Old Jerusalem is an ancient remnant of the wall of the temple area.

Though Herod did so much for Jerusalem, his benefactions did not cease there. He used his favorable relations with Augustus to help Jews in the cities of the diaspora. He won for them a respect for their synagogue communities and social organizations; he won for them freedom of movement within the Roman world. The dispersed Jewish colonies would serve as an important bridge in the spread of Christianity some decades later.

Herod's final years (13–4 B.C.) were once again marked by intrigue and violence. Several of his sons were killed and there were mass executions of those who opposed his policies. Matthew's gospel account (Mt 2:16) of the killing of the male infants of Judea, while impossible to prove historically, fits in well with what is known of the end of Herod's reign.

At Herod's death the kingdom of Judea was divided among three of his sons. In this Augustus honored Herod's will, though none of the sons received the title of king. The political division after Herod's death provides the immediate background to the story of Jesus and the early church. The areas of Galilee and Perea, a thin section on the eastern side of the Jordan and the area to the northeast of the Dead Sea, were entrusted to Herod Antipas (4 B.C.–A.D. 39). This is the Herod who ruled Jesus' own country and under whom John the Baptist was executed. While the gospels refer to him as "king" (Mk 6:14, Mt 14:9), he held the title of tetrarch (a prince who ruled over a fourth part of a territory). Philip was made tetrarch of the territory to the north and east of the Sea of Galilee (4 B.C.–A.D. 34). He built a new city for his residence, Caesarea Philippi, at the source of the Jordan River north of the Sea of Galilee.

The areas of Judea (with the capital city of Jerusalem), Samaria to the north, and Idumea to the south were granted to Archelaeus. While Herod wanted this son to have the title of king, Augustus gave him the rank of ethnarch, a distinction which probably meant little in the popular mind (see Mt 2:22). Archelaeus ruled so harshly and arbitrarily that Jewish emissaries made a plea to Augustus for his removal. In A.D. 6 Archelaeus was exiled to Gaul (France); the territories under his jurisdiction were turned into a Roman province ruled by a Roman governor with the designation of prefect. In this changeover, the Roman legate in Syria, P. Sulpicius Quirinus, ordered a census of the territory for purposes of assessing taxes. It is with this census that Luke 2:1–2 associates the birth of Jesus. (Luke's "all the world" is simply a popular expression for "the whole land" of the province. It is evident that in Luke and Matthew the chronologies of Jesus' birth cannot be reconciled. Each author associated Jesus' birth with a significant event at the time.)

One of the prefects (the governor's title until the time of Emperor Claudius when it was changed to procurator) was Pontius Pilate. His administration (A.D. 26–36) covered the period of Jesus' public ministry. He was appointed by Augustus' successor, Tiberius (A.D. 14–37) who was Roman emperor during Jesus' public ministry.

Judaism at the Time of Jesus and the Early Church

Further details of this historical background will be mentioned as we trace the development of early Christianity in the chapters to come. Our understanding of that story will be aided by a review of the religious situation of Palestine and the diaspora in the first century A.D. The Jewish religion of that century was very much influenced by the historical events which we have just reviewed.

The two main pillars of Jewish religious life and self-identity were the temple and the Torah. Further, in the period between its final editing (the middle of the fourth century B.C.) and the Maccabean Revolt in 167 B.C., the Torah became even more important than the temple in the life of most Jews. The Torah was seen to be the "instruction" or "teaching" given to Israel through Moses and contained in the "five books of Moses," the Pentateuch. As Jews became more numerous in the lands outside of Palestine (thus more exposed to foreign influence and culture) and as Palestine itself fell under the dominion of succeeding foreign powers (the Persians, the Greeks, and finally the Romans), the understanding and application of the Torah under changing circumstances became the basic religious concern of devout Israelites. Two of the most prominent religious movements within first century Judaism, those of the Pharisees and the Sadducees, are characterized largely by their approach to the Torah.

The Pharisees

The Pharisees of the first century were descendants of the lay "scribes" or lawyers of post-exilic Judaism and, more immediately, of the Hasidim, the "Pious Ones" who sought to protect their Jewish heritage against Greek influence after the conquests of Alexander. Though originally supporters of the Maccabees, the Hasidim distanced themselves from the Maccabees and their Hasmonean successors when the originally religious thrust of this leadership became increasingly political and secular. (It was probably Pharisee disenchantment with the later Maccabees which led to the eventual exclusion of the Books of the Maccabees from the Jewish canon of scripture.) The Pharisees emerged as a clearly identifiable movement within Judaism during the reign of John Hyrcanus (134–104 B.C.).

The name Pharisee means "separated one," a name probably given them by their opponents. The name describes their self-imposed efforts to keep separate from Gentiles, from public sinners, and from Jews who were indifferent in their observance of the law, especially as the law concerned the sabbath, ritual purity, and tithing. The Pharisees were a predominantly lay group, though some of them did belong to priestly families. They came largely from the middle class of society. The Jewish historian Josephus (ca. A.D. 37–95) stated that in Herod's day their numbers were "above six thousand." They were a powerful influence on the religious life of the people.

In the popular understanding of many Christians, the Pharisees were a very legalistic and rather hypocritical group very much opposed to Jesus and his teaching. Such a reading of the gospel fails to recognize that the picture of the Pharisees, especially in Matthew's gospel, is shaped by the struggles between the increasingly Gentile Christian community and the post-A.D. 70 Jewish community. Today the historical setting of the gospels makes us recognize the apologetic and even polemic motives in the gospels; hence our estimate of the Pharisaic movement in first century Judaism is much more positive.

The distinguishing characteristic of the Pharisees in Jesus' day and during the early decades of the church's life was their position on the Torah. Beyond the written Torah, the Pharisees accepted an oral tradition to which they assigned an equal authority. This oral Torah gave the Pharisees more than other religious movements a flexibility which allowed them to adapt more easily to new circumstances. They held beliefs which were not in the written Torah: the coming of a "messiah," the resurrection of the body, the existence and role of angels, and the ingathering of all Israelites in God's final age. The Pharisees were theologically quite tolerant of the beliefs of others; such a tolerance was a major factor in their attitude toward the first generation of Christians. Two of the most famous scribes among the Pharisees, Hillel and Shammai, both of whom lived and taught during the time of Herod the Great, continued to have an influence in Jesus' day. The piety of the Pharisees was based on a knowledge of the law and of its six hundred and thirteen prescriptions and prohibitions. This could and did lead to some formalism and externalism, but even in spite of exaggerations and one-sidedness at times, the Pharisees must be given credit for being a strong spiritual force in the Judaism of Jesus' day. They nourished the piety and devotion of many Jews and inspired a strong religious attitude toward the Torah.

Recently some scholars have compared the teaching of Jesus with the teaching of the Pharisees. Such a comparison must be done cautiously because we do not have writings of the Pharisees from the time of Jesus' ministry but must depend on rabbinic literature from a later period. Nonetheless a growing number of scholars sees the importance of the Pharisees not only in their acceptance of oral tradition but in the flexibility this gave them in applying the Torah to new situations. As important, if not more so, was the Pharisaic rejection of the claims of the Sadducees that interpretation of the Torah was the exclusive prerogative of the priestly class. Further, through the oral Torah the Pharisees in effect extended the realm of the sacred from its close association with the temple and its cult, to the ordinary lives and deeds of the people. The Pharisees' emphasis on ritual purity served to extend the purity associated with the temple to everyday meals. In the Pharisaic approach to the Torah, new emphasis was given to the rabbi (master or teacher) as a religious authority alongside the authority of the priest and to the synagogue as an institution alongside the temple. The theological underpinnings of the Pharisaic interpretation was a deeper awareness of the intimacy between God and each human person. This insight is behind the religious individualism (though always within the context of the community) which is characteristic of Pharisaic piety. If this interpretation is correct, there appear to be stronger resemblances between Jesus and the Pharisaic movement than between Jesus and either the Sadducees or the Essenes. In several distinct ways, of course, Jesus had positions of his own which differed from, or were more radical than, those of the Pharisees.

The Sadducees

The second major religious movement in the Judaism of Jesus' day was that of the Sadducees. The name itself suggests an association with the old priestly family of Zadok, the high priest under Solomon (1 Kgs

2:35). As with the Pharisees, the first references we have to the Sadducees as a distinct religious group come from the time of John Hyrcanus.
The Sadducees were predominantly from the priestly line, though the
group also included members of other influential Jewish families, rich
merchants, and government officials. As a group they resented the
Hasmoneans' taking over the high priestly office, but collaboration with
the Hasmoneans enabled the Sadducees to have an influence in the
religious and political life of the nation. Open to Hellenistic culture, the
Sadducees were opposed to the Pharisees' negative stance toward association with Gentiles. The Sadducees held strictly to the Torah, the
books of the Pentateuch, and did not accept the idea of oral tradition.
This opposition was based on theological grounds (only the written Torah came from God) but was also influenced by the desire to keep
interpretation of the Torah in the hands of the priestly families. Sadducees rejected belief in angels and in the resurrection of the dead and did
not accept developments in the interpretation of the Torah.

In Jesus' day the Sadducees controlled the temple and all that was
associated with it. Not surprisingly, they took offense at anyone who
challenged their authority. This probably explains why the Sadducees
(in the persons of the chief priest and elders) figure so largely in the
gospel accounts of the trial of Jesus (see also the mention of the high
priest in John 11:47–50). Because the Sadducees were an aristocratic
and religiously conservative group, they enjoyed little popular regard.
The Sadducees' efforts to moderate Jewish hostility to Roman rule were
ultimately a failure as we see in the Jewish revolt of A.D. 66–70.

The Scribes and the Sanhedrin

Associated with the Pharisees were those known as scribes. This group
has its background in the students of the law, many of them not priests,
who tried to preserve the understanding of the law and the knowledge of
Jewish history during the period of the exile in the sixth century B.C.
After the exile those learned in the law continued to function as instructors of the Jewish traditions amidst a people who were in increasing
contact with foreign ideas. There is some reason to believe that in Jerusalem and in other towns and villages the scribes organized weekly meetings to give instruction in the law and in so doing contributed to the
development of the synagogue services. The influence of the scribes as a
body was gradually replaced by the Sanhedrin. The instructional function of the scribes lived on through the movement of the Pharisees.
Certain prominent teachers among the Pharisees, the most famous of
whom were Hillel and Shammai, were also known as scribes. Admission

to the company of the scribes came not by birth but by education and proven ability. Scribes were given a title of respect, "rabbi"; they were allowed to wear the long robes of the scholar and were given places of honor in the synagogues. Some of the scribes were priests or members of prominent families. But there were also scribes who were merchants or craftsmen. Scribes enjoyed a great respect among the people.

Pharisees, Sadducees, and scribes were all represented among the seventy-one members of the Sanhedrin, the supreme council at Jerusalem. The word "Sanhedrin" is an Aramaic adaptation of the Greek word for council. Under the Roman prefects the Sanhedrin functioned as the dominant Jewish religious authority. This authority extended not only to the Jews of Palestine but to those of the diaspora as well. The president of the council was the high priest (Caiaphas, at the time of Jesus' public ministry). The other seventy members of the Sanhedrin—the number was taken from the injunction of Numbers 11:16—included leaders of the priestly and financial aristocracy (Sadducees generally) and members of the Pharisees, all of whom were also scribes. Because of the Pharisees' acknowledged competency in the Torah and because of their closer connections to the general populace, they had an important role in the council. In the gospel the Pharisees within the Sanhedrin are called either "the Pharisees" or "the scribes" (e.g., Mt 21:45; Lk 20:19).

The Essenes

While the Sadducees, the Pharisees, and the scribes were the most prominent religious voices in Judaism in the first century A.D., there was another group, the Essenes, whose presence and influence were also factors in Jewish life. The name Essene probably comes from the Aramaic word for "holy" or "pious" and corresponds to the Hebrew *hasid*. With the Pharisees, they too seem to be descendants of the Hasidim who emerged early in the period of Greek domination of Palestine. Many scholars believe that the history of the Essenes began at the time of the Maccabees, when one of Mattathias' sons took to himself the office of high priest. In protest to what they looked upon as an illegitimate temple authority, they established themselves in the desert, on the west bank of the Dead Sea. Though the Essenes are not mentioned in the New Testament, they became a focal point of interest with the 1947 discovery of the "Dead Sea Scrolls" in the caves at Qumran. While problems exist in identifying the Qumran community with the Essenes, most scholars today believe that the people at Qumran were Essenes or a branch of them. We know from Jewish and Roman authors of the time that the Essenes were not restricted to the community of the caves by the Dead

Sea. The basic community lived under strict discipline in the desert, but associate members with similar if not identical beliefs lived in villages and some even in cities throughout Palestine. According to Josephus they numbered about four thousand around A.D. 50.

The written Torah was at the center of the life and belief of the Essenes. The group's distinctive interpretation of the Torah came from the "Teacher of Righteousness." The Essenes were even more insistent than the Pharisees on strict observance of the law, especially the observance of the sabbath and ritual purity. They looked for a Messiah from the house of Aaron (the tribe of Levi) along with a Davidic Messiah. They saw themselves as the true and only heirs of God's covenant with Israel and believed they were living in the final days of God's plan. There are some parallels between the Essenes and the followers of Jesus.

The Zealots

Another group which in its own way would play a very important role in first century Judaism were the Zealots, a resistance movement determined to free Palestine from foreign (Roman) rule even if it were necessary to do so by armed violence. It has been suggested that as the Pharisees were the heirs of the Hasidim, the Zealots were the heirs of the Maccabees (R. H. Pfeiffer).

A militant opposition to Rome was a sporadic feature of Palestinian life after Pompey took control in 63 B.C. An incident of armed resistance, for example, occurred when Quirinus ordered the census of Syria and Palestine in 6 B.C. Another unsuccessful uprising took place between A.D. 44 and 46. The Zealots appear as a distinct movement, however, only on the eve of the revolt against Rome in A.D. 66.

The Zealots were militantly political but their inspiration and their name came from their zeal for the law. They argued that anyone who acknowledged the emperor as "lord" or paid taxes to him was violating the first commandment of the law which required people to worship God alone. Zealots were convinced that God would vindicate their efforts to free Judah from Roman control and were prepared to engage in the struggle even at the cost of their lives. The Zealots looked at the earlier victories of the Maccabees and the Hasmoneans as signs of hope that Jews would one day be victorious over the Romans.

The "People of the Land"

Focus on particular groups among the Jews must not cause us to lose sight of the fact that the majority of the Jewish people of Jesus' day did not belong to any movement. These were common people, predominantly farmers. But many were engaged in fishing and sheepherding, in craftsmaking and in commerce. In the cities, Jerusalem, Tiberias in Galilee, Caesarea, and Tyre and Sidon on the coast, there were traders, merchants, professionals, and public officials. Many of these people were religious, of course, but the fidelity to the law demanded by the Pharisees was beyond their reach. Those whose livelihood depended on contact with the Gentiles were barred from temple worship and other social and public functions. These were the people condescendingly known as the "am-ha-aretz" ("people of the land") by those who were critical of the way in which they observed the law. (In the early post-exilic period the same term was often applied with a sense of reproach to those who had not experienced the exile.) The majority, peasants, looked upon the priests, the wealthy aristocracy, and even to some extent the scribes and Pharisees as "others," outsiders to the world in which they lived. It was from the common people that Jesus and most of his followers came.

The Temple and the Synagogue

Two structures were of decisive importance in first century A.D. Judaism: the temple in Jerusalem and the synagogues in Palestine and in the diaspora. Even if in the period since the exile the primary religious emphasis within Judaism was shifting to the Torah, the temple continued to play a vital role in Jewish religious and national identity, especially in Palestine. With the exception of the Essenes (and taking account of the Pharisees' attempt to extend temple sacredness to the everyday life of the people), most Jews were united in the esteem which they accorded to the cult of the temple and the importance with which they regarded the pilgrim feasts to the holy city of Jerusalem. The temple was considered God's own dwelling place in the midst of his people. It was a symbol of God's choice of Israel as God's chosen people and of God's love for Jerusalem. Little wonder that Jews were so aroused when Antiochus Epiphanes profaned the temple and Pompey dared to enter the Holy of Holies, its innermost sanctuary. This esteem for the temple will help us understand Jewish opposition to Stephen and those Hellenist Christians who challenged the accepted religious importance of the temple.

The temple and the city of Jerusalem were focal points in the three great pilgrim feasts of the Jews: the feast of Passover, in the spring of the year; the feast of Pentecost, some weeks later; and the feast of Tabernacles, in the autumn of the year. Also in the autumn of the year was the

Day of Atonement when the high priest, on that day alone, entered the Holy of Holies. The temple's destruction in A.D. 70 would have dramatic consequences for Jewish religious life and, indirectly, for Christian self-understanding. But Judaism was able to survive the destruction of the temple and the city because the Torah had become even more important in Jewish religious life. It was the synagogue which was the primary instrument in bringing the Torah to the life of the people.

The actual beginnings of the synagogue as a Jewish religious institution are not known to us. The Greek roots of the word (*syn,* "together"; *agein,* "to lead, bring") suggests that the synagogues were seen as meeting places for prayer, for the reading of the Torah, and for instruction. The synagogue may have been born during the exile when Jews gathered together to pray and reflect on the scriptures. There is definite evidence of the existence of synagogues in the Egyptian diaspora in the third century B.C. and in Antioch in Syria a century later. Certainly the synagogue was a focal point of Jewish worship and instruction in the villages and cities of Palestine and in the cities of the diaspora in the early part of the first century A.D. Over one hundred and fifty cities of the Roman world are known to have had synagogues at the time of Jesus. Larger cities, like Jerusalem, Rome, Antioch, and Alexandria, had several. Unlike the temple which was controlled by the priests, the synagogues were controlled by lay people. In the diaspora women had a minor role in the life of the synagogue. Each congregation had a "ruler of the synagogue," sometimes a scribe, and an "attendant" who took care of the scripture-scrolls.

Prayer services were held mornings and evenings. The sabbath service had two parts, the first given to prayer and the second to readings and instruction. Prominent in the prayer service was the Jewish kergyma, "Hear, O Israel," (a statement of three passages of scripture, fixed after A.D. 70 as Deuteronomy 6:4–9 and 11:13–21 and Numbers 15:37–41) and the Eighteen Benedictions, prayers of praise and petition. The second part consisted of readings from the Torah and from the prophets. The passage of the scriptures was read in Hebrew, but because many of the common people no longer knew the language, a translation would be given in the Aramaic vernacular. (The "Hebrew" inscription on Jesus' cross was probably Aramaic; hence the parentheses in the first sentence of this chapter.) The reading was followed by a sermon given by a scribe or by any competent layman. The gospels tell us that Jesus, who was a layman (because he was not of the priestly tribe of Levi), often preached in the synagogues (see Lk 4:15, 16–28; 6:6, etc.). The synagogues were vital centers of the community life of Jews both in Palestine and in the diaspora. The synagogue structure would be an important instrument in the survival of Judaism after the events of A.D. 70. The synagogue would also figure in the spread of the Christian gospel.

Synagogue services in the diaspora also attracted those who were not Jews. These people saw in the prayers and psalms and the scriptures—read in Greek—an ancient and honorable religious tradition which was also a philosophy of life. While only a few took the step of becoming proselytes by accepting circumcision and the full observance of the law, many did accept the obligation of professing a monotheistic faith and observing the basic commandments. These latter were known as "God-fearers" (see Acts 13:50; 16:14; 17:4, 17; 18:7) who not only increased the Jewish communities of the diaspora but in some cases were among the earliest of the Christian converts. There would be tensions between Christian missionaries and the leadership of the diaspora synagogues.

Scholars have made educated guesses on the size of the Jewish population at the time of Jesus. These are only estimates, of course, but they are made on the basis of the records of the court-historian of Herod the Great, or on such data as the availability of housing in the Jerusalem area at the time of Jesus. Scholars T. W. Manson and J. Jeremias estimate that the population of Jerusalem at the time of Jesus was about twenty-five to thirty thousand; this number, of course, would include Gentiles. The Jewish population of Palestine at the time of Caesar Augustus is estimated to have been between a half and three quarters of a million people.

The number of Jews who lived in the empire is estimated at four and a half million or about seven percent of the entire population of the empire. The Jews of the diaspora outnumbered by far those who lived in the homeland. These diaspora Jews, and the "God-fearers" associated with them, would be of crucial importance in the spread of the Christian faith. Even more importantly, the Judaism of the diaspora offered an example for the later adaptation of Christianity to the Greco-Roman world (J. G. Gager).

Chapter Three

The Public Ministry of Jesus

We are ready now to examine in the light of contemporary scholarship the main lines of the movement which began with Jesus' public ministry and which became the Christian church at the end of the first century.

Three Preliminary Observations

It may be helpful to keep three items in mind as we pursue this study. First, because we use the historical-critical method we should expect the findings which emerge to differ from the conclusions that were drawn from earlier studies which used a different method, guided by other presuppositions. Since the earlier approach to the church's beginnings is still widespread, it is important that Roman Catholics who accept the conclusions of current biblical studies know the underlying rationale of the church's change in method.

Second, because of the limitations of the sources, our picture will lack the clarity of the pre-critical approach. But the price of that clarity was historical fidelity. Our picture is more accurate and true to the facts, but (precisely for that reason) grey areas remain. Although we may be confident of the main outlines of our account, the precise details of some developments—how or when—still elude us at present.

Clearly the gospels preserve traditions about Jesus' ministry and about the churches for which they were written, but they will not yield an exact and complete historical record. Nor is that to be expected. The Acts of the Apostles evidences a theological and literary editing based on the author's view of the church and on its needs and problems at the time when Acts was being written. The New Testament letters and the Book of Revelation also deal with problems and concerns of various Christian communities over a period of some several decades. They give us invaluable information concerning aspects of the development of the

Christian church in various places, but do not provide us with a comprehensive account. Yet even with these limitations, there are very good reasons to hold that the portrait of the early church that emerges from recent scholarship is far more accurate than any picture previously available to us.

Our study, finally, has another limitation. Scholars who share the same historical-critical method do not always arrive at the same conclusions in their studies. This should not surprise us. Not infrequently scholarly findings bear the limitations of hypotheses and different scholars draw different conclusions. The presentation which follows seeks to represent the basic findings of recognized biblical scholarship from the 1970s to the present. Where there are significant differences of opinion of major issues, they will be noted in the text or in the notes.

Jesus and the Kingdom of God

We begin with Jesus' own ministry. In each of the first three gospels Jesus' public ministry is concerned with the proclamation of the "kingdom of God" ("reign of God") or, in the variation in Matthew's gospel, the "kingdom of heaven" (Mk 1:15 is obviously intended as a summary statement of Jesus' preaching; see also Mt 4:23; 9:35; Lk 4:43; 8:1).

In the fourth gospel, apart from chapter 3 (which tells of Jesus' meeting with Nicodemus) and chapter 18 (which gives the dialogue between Jesus and Pilate), Jesus never speaks of the kingdom. While the synoptic gospels are surely correct in having Jesus speak about the kingdom of God, for the fourth gospel the embodiment of the kingdom is Jesus. Therefore, the symbolic language of the synoptics ("the kingdom of heaven is like") has become the "I am" language of the fourth gospel. All the gospels incorporate theological reflection, but that reflection is more patent in the language used by Jesus in the fourth gospel.

Jesus' concern with the kingdom of God was not unique to him, though there were distinctive aspects of Jesus' preaching which we do not find in contemporary Jewish writings which deal with the same theme. The notion of the kingdom of God has its root in Jewish belief in God's dominion over all creation (Psalm 98). In the Judaism of the period from the beginning of the second century B.C. to the beginning of the second century A.D. this traditional belief took on a new focus. In view of the misfortunes and defeats of Israel under one foreign power after another, belief in God's kingdom became centered on the time when God's power would become manifest not only to Israel but to all the foreign nations who oppressed Israel. Further, many Jews came to believe that the present order of history was beyond redemption, so that the day on which God's rule became finally manifest would be the final day in human history. This would be followed by a new age in which Israel would be vindicated against all forces of evil and oppression, and in which God's divine ordering of all people and of all creation would be established. Biblical scholars and theologians refer to this as the "eschatological" dimension of the kingdom of God. (The term comes from the Greek words *logos,* "word" or "concept," and *eschaton,* "end.")

We know from Jewish documents of the period—such as 1 Enoch (roughly contemporary with Jesus) and the Assumption (or Testament) of Moses (probably first written around 170 B.C. before the Maccabean revolt and revised sometime between A.D. 7 and 30)—that in the early part of the first century this teaching about God's coming kingdom was central to Jewish belief. There were, to be sure, variations within this general belief. But an appreciation of this hope for God's reign is indispensable for an understanding of Jesus' preaching and the praxis of his ministry.

The Distinctiveness of Jesus' Preaching

The distinctiveness of Jesus' preaching about the kingdom of God is found in his insistence that God's ruling presence was imminent and, even more striking, that it was in some way already present. We can be confident that at least some of the gospel parables and sayings of Jesus represent his actual preaching and teaching. Certain sayings attributed to Jesus in the synoptic tradition, sayings which have a good claim to be from Jesus himself, indicate Jesus' emphasis that the reign of God was in some way already present. The saying of Jesus in response to those who doubt the source of his power as an exorcist is one of these: "But if it is by the finger ("spirit" in Matthew) of God that I cast out demons, then the kingdom of God has come upon you" (Lk 11:20; Mat 12:28). Another such indication is found in Jesus' saying about John: "From the days of John the Baptist until now the kingdom of heaven has suffered violence, and men of violence take it by force" (Mt 11:12; see Lk 16:16). The saying is a difficult one to interpret, but it seems to mean that the kingdom of God, present since John's ministry, is in conflict with the present age. A third saying, "The kingdom of God is in the midst of you" (Lk 17:21), underscores an important point, that the kingdom is present without the signs and indicators expected in the popular mind and in the religious writings of Jesus' day. These sayings and others like them imply that the reign of God is present in and through Jesus himself.

Writings which focus on the signs that would accompany the dawn of the end-time, and which in a symbolic way attempt to describe the new age, are called "apocalyptic," from the Greek word for "revelation." Apocalyptic speculation is a particular form of eschatology. Many of the eschatological statements in Jewish literature at this time, and some such statements in the New Testament, use apocalyptic categories.

Popular speculation about the "end of the world" draws some of its imagery from the apocalyptic writings of the Bible, but very often lacks the richness of the biblical view of the end-time or new age that is expected to come with God's definitive reign over all creation.

One aspect of Jesus' teaching—that the kingdom of God was present through him—stands in tension with another aspect of his teaching—that the kingdom of God is coming in the immediate future. This second aspect has a bearing on the issue of Jesus' intent in regard to the church. There was a period in recent scholarship when scholars lined up behind either of two interpretations: the kingdom is *altogether present* or the kingdom is not-yet-present but *immediately coming*. Most scholars today hold that the teaching of Jesus was more complex; according to his teaching the kingdom was both present and coming. The second petition of the Lord's Prayer ("Thy kingdom come": Mt 6:10; Lk 11:2) points to the second aspect of Jesus' teaching. Other sayings attributed to Jesus in the synoptics also stress the immediate coming of God's kingdom. In the scene just before the story of the transfiguration, Jesus says to some of his disciples, "Truly (Amen), I say to you, there are some standing here who will not taste death before they see the kingdom of God come with power" (Mk 9:1; see also Mt 26:29; Lk 9:27). Another saying comes from what is called the eschatological discourse of Mark's Gospel (Mk 13:30; cf. Mt 24:34; Lk 21:32): "Truly (Amen), I say to you, this generation will not pass away before all these things take place." The saying seems to say that the events of the final times would be occurring in the lifetime of Jesus' listeners. These last two sayings quite likely come from Jesus himself. Because none of the events of which these sayings speak came to pass in an obvious way, it is easier to think that the texts came from Jesus and were preserved as a memory of Jesus than to account for them as a composition of the early church. These texts are important for us because they suggest that Jesus did not speak of a long interval between his own ministry and the final completion of God's plan.

Readers today may be puzzled by the obvious tension in the two assertions about the timing of the kingdom which we find in the teaching of Jesus. If we approach such a tension with the demands of a logic which seeks either one characteristic or another—that is, either a kingdom that is inaugurated with Jesus' life and ministry or a kingdom that is immediately coming but not yet fully present—we are likely to become frustrated. It may be helpful to keep in mind that we are dealing here with a Jewish way of speaking about a divine reality, God's presence and power, and with its manifestation to people in time and in history. In the biblical perspective, time is not simply a quantitative reality, measured by the sequence of hours and days. In the light of biblical faith, time is also a qualitative reality, measured by the power of God present, accepted, and acted upon.

The theme of God's kingdom is not only central to Jesus' preaching and teaching; it really pervades the whole of Jesus' ministry: it is central to understanding his exorcisms and healings, the meals he shared with his disciples, his ethical teaching and his prayer.

Critical biblical scholarship today does not so easily dismiss the tradition about Jesus' healing and exorcisms as was done by some writers not long ago. While details of the healing narratives are regarded as additions of post-resurrection oral tradition or gospel editing, there is an historical core in these stories of Jesus' healing activity which goes back to Jesus himself. It should be noted, however, that such activity was also attributed to other religious figures, both in Judaism and in the Greek religions, of that time. Further, Jesus is depicted as directing others to see his healings as signs, perceivable only in faith, of God's power, the power of the kingdom, present in and through his ministry.

Did Jesus Speak of a "Church"?

If concern for the kingdom was so central and pervasive in Jesus' ministry, did Jesus also preach about a church? Further, did Jesus make any provision for a church in the interval between the inauguration of God's kingdom in him and the full presence and manifestation of that kingdom which was soon to come?

There are only two instances in all four of the gospels where Jesus is presented as speaking of "church." Both are found in Matthew's gospel. The first occurs in the famous scene at Caesarea Philippi: "And I tell you, you are Peter, and on this rock I will build my church, and the powers of death shall not prevail against it" (Mt 16:18). The word "church" here refers to a universal church. The second use of the term is found two chapters later and here refers to a local group (Mt 18:17). The Greek word for "church" is *ekklēsia*. In ordinary usage the word had no religious connotation; it referred to a regularly summoned political body, such as a local council. However, in the Greek translation of the Jewish scriptures (the Septuagint), the word was used to describe the congregation of Israel chosen and gathered together by God's call. The use of this term by New Testament writers would imply that the group of people so called was also a congregation of God, patterned after (or replacing) the Israelite congregation of old.

There are two questions before us. The first question is: Did Jesus use the Semitic equivalent of the term "church" during his public ministry? If we presume that that equivalent was *quahal,* which the Septuagint translates as *ekklēsia,* he could have been echoing the language of the Pentateuch. The fact that Mark and Luke do not have the term where Matthew has it raises a question about Jesus' personal usage of such a term. (The parallels to the Caesarea Philippi passage in Matthew are found in Mark 8:27–33 and Luke 9:18–22. The passage in Matthew 18:17 has no parallel.) There is a second question: Did Jesus have an understanding of his followers that makes the church that developed a true continuation of the mission of Jesus and those who accompanied him? This is a more difficult question and a more theological one. We shall be considering this question in sections to come.

An Interval before the Completion of God's Plan?

Did Jesus look to an interval between the work of his own ministry and the final completion of God's plan? Two considerations prompt the question. First, there is a tension between the two types of assertions in Jesus' teaching about God's kingdom: that the kingdom was *present* in his person and ministry and that it was also coming soon and therefore *not fully present.* Do we know if Jesus envisioned anything for the interval between these two comings? Second, the idea that Jesus most likely anticipated a lengthy, possibly centuries-long, interval was one of the features of the earlier understanding of the church's beginnings.

A careful study of the gospel texts makes us very modest about specifying what Jesus may have said about any interval between his own ministry and the completion of God's plan. There are some indications, however, which do shed light on this matter. First, we have seen that there are certain sayings which seem to come from Jesus and which clearly imply that the end-time events will take place before very long (Mk 9:1; 13:30). Second, while Jesus was one with other Jews in his preaching about the kingdom of God, he differed from them by announcing that in some way it was already present and by avoiding any specific time-line in which the coming of the kingdom was to happen. In fact, the saying of Jesus in Mark 13:32, "But of that day or that hour [when the Son of Man comes in clouds with great power and glory] no one knows, not even the angels in heaven, nor the Son, but only the Father," suggests that Jesus did not know when the final events would take place. Some question whether this saying comes from Jesus because it is the only place in Mark's gospel where Jesus speaks of himself absolutely as "the Son." But because it would be difficult for the early church to attribute such ignorance to Jesus, it seems more reasonable to see the saying as coming from him. As we will see when we look at some of the early New Testament letters, there was confusion over the expectation of the end. If Jesus had spoken clearly on the topic, such confusion would be very difficult to explain. A third indication comes from the gospel accounts of the Last Supper. Jesus' saying about not drinking again of the fruit of the vine until the day when he drinks it new in the kingdom of God (Mk 14:25 and parallels) is regarded as authentic and, while presenting difficulties to the interpreter, seems to speak of a break between Jesus' close association with his disciples during his ministry and a renewed communion in the kingdom (made explicit in Matthew 26:29). Jesus very probably saw that his own apparent abandonment to be followed by some form of vindication by the Father would have to take place before the end was fully present. Further, it may be that he anticipated some mission of his disciples to Israel, their persecution, and some end-time tribulation, the last a common expectation among Jews of Jesus' day. But we have no evidence to support the view that Jesus envisioned a lengthy period with a span of centuries before the complete fulfillment of God's plan. To the contrary, the majority of scholars today support the assumption that Jesus expected the end to come soon.

John the Baptist and the First Disciples of Jesus

A very significant aspect of Jesus' ministry was his call to others to follow him. And there is evidence that some of Jesus' first disciples were originally followers of John the Baptist.

John was a very significant religious figure in Jesus' day. The Jewish historian Josephus (died ca. A.D. 95) speaks more of John than he does of Jesus. John's life in the wilderness was inspired by the same text of the scriptures (Is 40:3: "In the wilderness prepare the way of the Lord, make straight in the desert a highway for our God") which was used by the community at Qumran as a guide to their own life in the desert, though there is no evidence that John was part of the community at Qumran. John preached a call to repentance and preparation for the Coming One (God or someone acting in God's name) who would bring judgment but also mercy and salvation. Scholars are divided as to the source of John's baptism. A respected opinion (R. H. Fuller) concludes from the available evidence that John probably borrowed the idea of baptismal practice from Qumran or from baptizing sects of the period and combined it with the prophetic idea of some type of cleansing before the coming of the end-time. John's preaching and his call to repentance had a powerful impact on his contemporaries. Josephus tells us that "people . . . streamed to John the Baptist from all directions."

The fourth gospel tells us that the first followers of Jesus were disciples of John the Baptist. We see in John 1:35 and 1:40 that two disciples of the Baptist left John to follow Jesus. One of them was Andrew who in turn called his brother Simon (Peter). Some scholars believe that the unnamed disciple of John 1:40 may have been the "beloved disciple" of the fourth gospel and the leader of the community for whom the gospel was written. Another early disciple of Jesus was Philip (Jn 1:43), who came, as did Andrew and Peter, from the town of Bethsaida, in Philip the tetrarch's territory across the border from Herod's Galilee. The area of Bethsaida was heavily Gentile and may explain why Jews like Andrew and Philip have Greek names. Philip in turn (Jn 1:45) sought out Nathaniel from Cana (Jn 21:2), a disciple whose name is not listed among the Twelve. (Former attempts to identify him with the Matthew or Bartholomew of the Twelve do not receive support in current critical scholarship.)

The passage in John 1:40–45, then, has a direct bearing on our story. The fourth gospel is in many instances less historical and more theological than the synoptics, and especially so in what the disciples say about Jesus in the early scenes of the gospel. Nevertheless, this gospel may be closer to historical fact than the other gospels insofar as it reports that Jesus' first disciples were originally disciples of John the Baptist, and that they came to Jesus in the Jordan valley rather than from around the Lake of Galilee (although it is evident that some of them came from Galilee and its environs).

As Jesus transferred his ministry from the area of the Jordan to the area of Galilee he continued to call or attract others to himself. While some of the discipleship sayings preserved in the gospels reflect the influence of oral tradition and literary editing, it seems clear that the call to discipleship found in many of the sayings has a basis in the life and ministry of Jesus. Jesus' call to others to follow him stands in contrast to the rabbis of his day. Rabbis gathered disciples around them to listen and to learn from them. But we do not have examples where these disciples were looked upon as an integral part of what the master was about. We get the impression that Jesus never attempted to act alone; rather, the calling of the first disciples was integral to his conception of the proclamation of the kingdom. A closer parallel to Jesus would be the prophet Elijah and his disciple Elisha, rather than the rabbis of Jesus' day.

The wide and unaccustomed diversity of people whom Jesus called to himself or with whom he readily associated was a distinctive feature of

Jesus' ministry. Each of the major religious groups of Jesus' day, the Pharisees, the Sadducees, the Essenes, was marked by a shunning of other groups. Jesus' calling people like tax collectors to join his ranks, and his associating with known sinners, were directly contrary to the religious outlook and practice of his day.

Did Jesus' disciples have a part in his preaching and teaching mission? Critical scholarship is cautious in making a reply. Scholars agree that the definitive sending forth in mission that constitutes the apostolate came only after the resurrection. The clear sense of mission which developed in the decades after the resurrection was read back into the missionary discourses of Jesus as an encouragement and a challenge to those in the church at the time the gospels were written. (See, for example, the mission discourse of Matthew 10, esp. vv. 17–20.) Details within the missionary discourses which speak more to the situation of the late 60s and the 70s and 80s of the first century than to the time of Jesus' own ministry support this view. Nevertheless, some limited association by the disciples in Jesus' own ministry remains very plausible. We may have reflections of this in Matthew 10:5–16 and in Luke 9:1–6 and 10:1–12. A critical study of the evidence does not, however, take us beyond the plausibility of such a mission.

The Twelve

Among the disciples of Jesus a special place is given to the group known as the Twelve. There are four places in the New Testament where their names are listed: Mark 3:14–19 (early in Jesus' Galilean ministry); Matthew 10:2–3 (at the beginning of Matthew's mission discourse); Luke 6:14–16 (immediately before Jesus' "sermon on the plain"); and Acts 1:13–14 (after Jesus' ascension and before the selection of a successor to Judas). A careful reading of these lists shows that the names in the last third of each list do not coincide. Past efforts to identify the Thaddeus (Lebbaeus in some manuscripts) of Mark and Matthew with Judas (Jude) the son of James in Luke's two lists (see also John 14:22) do not hold up; probably, the names do not refer to the same person. The discrepancy may be accounted for in this way: while the notion of the Twelve was very much a part of the tradition, by the time these lists were written the names of the Twelve were becoming unclear.

There is general accord among scholars that the Matthew mentioned in the lists is not the same as the writer of the gospel.

It is only in Luke's two lists that Simon is called a "Zealot." Mark and Matthew have *Kananaios,* most likely a Greek transcription of the Aramaic word for "zealous." (The term appears in English translations as either "the Cananaean" or "of the Zealot party.") Most scholars do not think the Zealot movement existed before the 60s of the first century A.D. There was in Jesus' day, though, a use of the term "zealous" which was applied to those who were purists in their observance of the law. It is with such an understanding that the term may have been applied to Simon at the time of Jesus' ministry; Mark and Matthew may be preserving that tradition. Luke may have used the early designation of Simon in conformity with the usage at the time when his gospel and the Book of Acts were written.

Three questions arise in any effort to reconstruct the historical basis behind the tradition of the Twelve. First, were the men of these lists truly companions of Jesus? The better known figures such as Peter, James, and John are so much a part of the gospel tradition that no one suggests that they were not actual companions of Jesus. Scholarly opinion holds that probably all those mentioned were associates of Jesus, even if by the time the gospels were written the precise names were becoming hazy.

Second, were the Twelve identified as such during Jesus' public ministry? There is persuasive evidence for holding that the notion of a distinct group of twelve comes from the time of Jesus himself. The gospels, of course, attribute the calling of the Twelve to Jesus (Mk 3:13–14 and Lk 6:13). The story in Acts 1 about the election of Matthias to replace Judas implies, and for some (e.g., R. H. Fuller) proves, that the notion of a distinct Twelve was associated with Jesus' ministry. The early church community would not likely create the idea of a pre-Easter Twelve and then have to deal with the problem that one of the group was a betrayer. Further, Paul's first letter to the Corinthians (probably written in A.D. 57) cites a pre-Pauline formula which implies that the Twelve were in existence at the time of the resurrection appearances. Paul uses the formula without any suggestion that the notion of the Twelve is a novelty or an anachronism. Finally, we know that the group at Qumran had a council of twelve, and the documents from Qumran show that a group of twelve in imitation of the twelve patriarchs was very much a part of Jewish thinking about the anticipated dawning of the end-time.

The Purpose of the Twelve

The third and most important question about the Twelve concerns the purpose for such a special group among Jesus' companions. The gospels present only one statement attributed to Jesus during his ministry concerning the purpose of the Twelve: "Truly, I say to you, in the new world, when the Son of Man shall sit on his glorious throne, you who

have followed me will also sit on twelve thrones, judging the twelve
tribes of Israel" (Mt 19:28; see also Lk 22:28–30). In this saying, the
Twelve are appointed—on the model of the twelve sons of the patriarch
Jacob (Gen 35:23–26)—to judge the tribes of Israel when the new age
proclaimed by Jesus is fully present. The role assigned to the Twelve,
then, is similar to the role of the twelve at Qumran; it is an end-time
judging function. During the ministry of Jesus the Twelve were a symbol
of Israel being called to renewal and to take its place in the final unfolding of God's plan. Since the Twelve associated with Jesus had their
model in the twelve sons of Jacob, it is only to be expected that the
Twelve were all men. (The reasoning that led to a choice of males in this
instance would be misused if it were applied to other contexts having
nothing to do with the symbolic role of the Twelve.)

The Role of Peter During Jesus' Public Ministry

Did Peter have a special role among the Twelve during Jesus' public
ministry? At issue here is the historical basis of gospel texts which ascribe such a position to Peter. The two most important of these texts are:
Matthew 16:16–19, the scene of the commission given to Peter at
Caesarea Philippi; and Luke 22:32, Jesus' prayer that Peter would return from the infidelity of his denial of Jesus and strengthen his brethren
among the Twelve. (The famous text of John 21 portrays a scene after
the resurrection and will be dealt with in Chapter Seven.) The first of
these texts figured in the Pontifical Biblical Commission's decree of 1911
on the gospel according to Matthew and was an important element in the
earlier approach to understanding the church's beginnings as discussed
in Chapter One of this book. Current critical scholarship sees this text
and the other gospel texts about Peter in a different light (see the collabo-
rative effort by both Roman Catholic and Protestant scholars, *Peter in
the New Testament*, 1973).

Many of the gospel texts about Peter certainly reflect the experience
and the developments of the post-resurrection church. In the case of the
famous Matthean text just referred to, the lack of any mention of a
commission to Peter in the parallel passages in Mark and Luke is one of
the principal arguments against the exact historicity of the text (compare
Matthew with Mark 8:29–30 and Luke 9:20–21). The absence of a parallel in Luke is especially significant since Peter is so prominent a figure in
the first half of Luke's Acts. The important role which Peter came to
have after the resurrection led to the development of stories in which
Peter is singled out in a special way (e.g., the prayer for Peter in Luke
22:32; Jesus' saving Peter as he sinks while walking on the water in

Matthew 14:28–31; Jesus, Peter, and the temple tax in Matthew 17:24–27; and the call of Simon and the miraculous catch of fish in Luke 5:1–11). These stories were later woven into the gospel narratives some several decades after Jesus' lifetime and two or three decades after the death of Peter. We will see several instances of this editing in succeeding chapters.

Even allowing for this editing of the gospel texts, there is good reason to think that during Jesus' ministry Peter was the most important disciple of Jesus among the Twelve. Simon may not have been the first chosen of the disciples, but he was one of the first who was called to associate with Jesus. Simon is the most frequently mentioned disciple in the synoptics and in the fourth gospel as well. Even the Gentile converts of Paul in Galatia know of Peter. It seems clear, then, that the story of the ministry of Jesus was not told without including mention of Simon. (Jesus himself may have given him the name Peter, "Rock," but because the naming occurs in different settings in three gospels we cannot be sure.) Peter stands out uniquely in the pre-Pauline formula cited by Paul in 1 Corinthians 15:3–5. It seems clear, too, that Peter made some type of confession of Jesus, even if that confession was not an adequate one. It would be anachronistic to read as exact history the picture of Peter as we see it in the gospels; it would be equally incorrect to fail to recognize the very prominent place Simon had among the disciples of Jesus.

The Women Among Jesus' Followers

The gospels tell us that women were among the followers of Jesus and were closely associated with him. The view that Jesus' positive attitude toward women was a major departure from current Jewish attitudes is challenged in current scholarship. We do have a glimpse of a rather negative attitude toward women in some of the sayings of the Book of Sirach (9:1–9; 25:24–25; 42:12–14), written by a Jerusalem sage between 200 and 175 B.C. We know from the Dead Sea Scrolls that the members of the community at Qumran were all male, and that most of them did not marry. Marriage was generally avoided, it seems, in the desire to avoid any contact with women which might bring about ritual uncleanliness. (Some groups of Essenes in the cities did marry but solely for purposes of propagation.) But there are rabbinic sayings which give a more positive understanding of women. (These rabbinic sayings, it is true, were not put into writing until the end of the second century A.D., but scholars think it is reasonable to infer that these sayings were in circulation in the first century.) In the diaspora Jewish women did have a role in the synagogue, and possibly some participation in liturgical life;

this may be a result, in part, of cultural influences in some parts of the Greco-Roman world.

It is within this complex Jewish milieu that we must see Jesus' own attitude toward women. We have indications of Jesus' attitude in Mark 15:40–41 and Luke 8:1–3. In the Marcan text we are told that among the women who stood at a distance looking at the scene of Jesus' crucifixion were "Mary Magdalene and Mary the mother of James the younger and of Joses, and Salome, who, when he was in Galilee, followed him, and ministered to him; and also many other women who came up with him to Jerusalem." The Lucan text tells us that along with the Twelve who accompanied Jesus there were some women "who had been healed of evil spirits and infirmities: Mary, called Magdalene . . . Joanna, the wife of Chuza, Herod's steward, and Susanna, and many others, who provided for them out of their means." Some scholars argue that the Lucan portrayal of the women providing for Jesus and his disciples is a retrojection of the situation of Paul in Acts. If this were not the case, the text would suggest that some of the women disciples of Jesus enjoyed considerable status from a socio-economic and political point of view. But certainly there were women who were disciples of Jesus and who traveled with him.

Jesus' Attitude to Judaism: Torah and Temple

Jesus' ministry centered on his preaching and teaching about the reign of God. Further indications of Jesus' mission come when we examine Jesus' stance toward the Judaism of his day, and more specifically towards the Torah and the temple.

We saw in Chapter Two that in post-exilic Judaism the Torah was becoming increasingly central to Jewish self-understanding and that the Jewish religious movements in Jesus' day were characterized by distinctive attitudes toward the Torah. The gospel picture of Jesus' own attitude toward the Torah and the oral traditions associated with it is affected by the debates and struggles of the times in which the gospels were written. Nevertheless we can get behind the written gospels and the oral traditions to some understanding of Jesus' own position.

One of the distinguishing characteristics of Jesus' teaching was the authority with which Jesus spoke of the will of God, an authority that came not from his knowledge of the law but from his inner conviction. Indications of Jesus' authority are seen in the expression, "You have heard it said . . . but I say to you" (see Mt 5) and in the frequent use of "Amen" to give weight to his words. The gospels' portrayal of Jesus' use of "Amen" represents a change from what we know of contemporary usage. Even if the use of the term is not unique to Jesus (J. Jeremias), it certainly was characteristic of Jesus. In effect Jesus set himself above all the accepted religious authorities of Judaism, and even above the commandments of the Torah. We see, for example, Jesus' radical interpretation of the law (Mt 5:21–30, 43–48) or what is really his annulment of the law (Mt 5:31–42). This is not to say that Jesus rejected the Torah in its entirety; rather, he put himself forward as the definitive interpreter of the Torah and, by implication, of the Jewish religion.

Jesus was no less authoritative in his stance toward the oral traditions of the Pharisees, notably those concerning the sabbath observance, ritual purity, and the *corban* casuistry by which a person might, out of spite or anger, dedicate (*corban*) to the temple what was owed to one's parents without further obligation to them. Yet Jesus did not reject all tradition, for we are told that he regularly attended the synagogue on the sabbath (Mk 1:21; Lk 4:16; 13:10). We can assume that this was his regular practice, for when the gospels were written, the Christian church was in tension with the synagogue. The gospel evidence, though, suggests that Jesus used his visits to the synagogue as occasions to teach his distinctive message (Mk 1:21–37, 39; 3:1; 6:2; Mt 9:35; Lk 4:15–21; 13:10).

Efforts to assess Jesus' attitude toward the temple center on two gospel traditions in particular, the scene in which Jesus drives out the merchants from the temple and the saying of Jesus about the destruction of the temple. We do not know how often Jesus visited the temple. The synoptics record only one visit to Jerusalem, though Luke tells us that when Jesus was in the capital, he taught daily in the temple (Lk 19:47). The fourth gospel speaks of several visits to the temple over a span of more than two years. (It is probable that the fourth gospel is more accurate on this detail than are the synoptics.) We are certain of one visit—the occasion when Jesus opposed the merchants in the temple area (Mk 11:15–17; Mt 21:12–13; Lk 19:45–46; Jn 2:13–16); we are not so sure about the significance of Jesus' action. If Mark's account is taken as a guide, Jesus' action was a symbolic prophetic gesture of God's endtime renewal of Israel being proclaimed and inaugurated through his ministry. Some scholars have argued that Jesus' action implied a rejection of the sacrificial cult which took place at the temple. But this seems too negative, given the positive attitude toward the temple held by some of the earliest Jerusalem Christians. Certainly Jesus' action was a direct challenge to the authorities of the temple. According to the synoptics it was this action which set in motion the plot to destroy him.

Jesus' saying about the destruction of the temple has its own ambiguity. It is quite likely that the saying in some form goes back to Jesus himself: "Do you see these great buildings? There will not be left here one stone upon another, that will not be torn down" (Mk 13:2; cf. Mt 24:2; Lk 21:6; Jn 2:19). But it is difficult to know what the saying might have meant. In the accounts of the interrogation of Jesus by the San-hedrin in Mark and Matthew (Mk 14:58; Mt 26:61), the saying about the temple is associated with false witnesses. It is unlikely that either evange-list did not think that Jesus uttered some kind of saying about the tem-ple. The fourth gospel clearly attributes the temple saying to Jesus (Jn 2:19). More significantly, there were diverse understandings of Jesus' saying among the early Jerusalem believers: some Jewish Christians evidently saw the saying as a promise that the temple would be the focus of God's end-time renewal; Stephen saw it as a word of judgment on the temple (Acts 6:14). One scholar (J. D. G. Dunn) suggests that Jesus' own attitude was neither so uncritical as the first interpretation suggests, nor so hostile as the second would have it.

It is not surprising that Jesus had to confront the question about the meaning and importance of the temple. The Pharisees themselves, ac-cording to some recent studies, so extended the application of the law and cultic piety to daily life that they constituted a challenge to the position of the temple and to the authority of those associated with it. The Essenes did not attend the Jerusalem temple because they believed its priesthood illegitimate and its ritual defiled. But they considered their desert community as a type of temple and looked to the day when God would create the temple anew and establish it for all times (Temple Scroll). When the Zealots gained control of Jerusalem in A.D. 67 one of their first concerns was to gain control of the temple and appoint their own high priest. After the resurrection of Jesus his early followers took different positions with regard to the temple; and the adherents of each position thought they were being faithful to Jesus in doing so.

Jesus and Jewish Prayer and Worship

Another indication of Jesus' attitude toward Judaism can be seen in his teaching on prayer and worship. Whereas in much of the Judaism of Jesus' day God was regarded as rather remote from the daily lives of ordinary people, both the Pharisees and Jesus (though Jesus in a more radical way) stressed God's nearness to people and God's approachabil-ity. Jesus' contemporaries frequently avoided speaking directly of God and made use of expressions such as the "name of God" or the "wisdom of God." These expressions served as surrogates for the word "God" and even came to be understood as intermediaries between God and human beings. By contrast, Jesus stressed the personal intimacy of God, an attitude brought out best, perhaps, by his using, when addressing God, the intimate and familial *Abba* (the Aramaic: "Daddy") as a way of addressing God; he taught his disciples to address God in the same way.

Jesus and Judaism: Continuity and Discontinuity

We may summarize Jesus' stance vis-à-vis Judaism as one of both continuity and discontinuity. There is continuity in that Jesus evidently saw his teaching and ministry as flowing from the heart of Jewish religious understanding; on that basis he sought to inaugurate a renewal from within and to offer a definitive interpretation of God's word. Even if we are unable to ascertain that the actual expression comes from Jesus himself, we see this understanding reflected in the saying of Matthew 5:17: "Think not that I have come to abolish the law and the prophets; I have come not to abolish them, but to fulfil them."

Yet there is also discontinuity. In Jesus something new and definitive was being proclaimed. The parables in Mark 2:21–22 characterize this aspect of Jesus' mission: "No one sews a patch of unshrunk cloth on an old garment; if he does, the patch tears away from it, the new from the old, and a worse tear is made. And no one puts new wine into old wineskins; if he does, the wine will burst the skins, and the wine is lost, and so are the skins; but new wine is for fresh skins." Jesus did not set about to destroy Judaism or to replace it with a different religion; his intent was, from within, to bring about its end-time renewal. Further, and importantly, we do not correctly understand Jesus' mission unless we see his efforts in the light of other Jewish renewal efforts, such as those of the Pharisees and the Essenes.

Jesus and the Gentiles

This understanding of Jesus' attitude toward Judaism finds corroborating evidence in Jesus' stance vis-à-vis the Gentiles. Relations with Gentiles had been an issue within Judaism for centuries, especially since the time of the Persian and Greek conquests. At the time of Jesus the Sadducees associated with Gentiles, while the more popular Pharisees had a strong sense of separation from all who were not Jews. But not even all Pharisees were consistent in this matter: the followers of Shammai wanted an intensification of the norm; the followers of Hillel allowed a greater flexibility. Essene concern for ritual purity led some members to avoid all contact whatsoever with Gentiles and to live in desert seclusion. Jews of Jesus' day believed that God would offer salvation to the Gentiles, but only as part of God's final saving action.

Jesus seems to have shared this view. Jesus saw end-time salvation as primarily for the Jews; and he saw his own mission as announcing its presence as directed to Israel alone. We see a reflection of this in the instructions Jesus is said to have given to the Twelve: "Go nowhere among the Gentiles, and enter no town of the Samaritans, but go rather to the lost sheep of the house of Israel" (Mt 10:5–6; cf. 10:23). Jesus' words to the Canaanite woman reflect the same attitude: "I was sent only to the lost sheep of the house of Israel" (Mt 15:24). We reason that texts such as these have a basis in historical fact. There would be no point in composing such texts when, at the time the gospels were written, the church was very actively engaged in a Gentile mission. If anything, such texts must have been a difficulty and perhaps an embarrassment, but they would be preserved precisely because they were part of the tradition. Further, given the memory of such sayings as these, the great hesitation in accepting Gentiles which marked the earliest believers is quite plausible. It is also understandable that some Jewish Christians would expect Gentile converts to accept the demands of the Mosaic law, given the example of Jesus himself who carried out his mission within the framework of Judaism.

Yet Jesus fully expected that in the end Gentiles would share in the blessings of the kingdom: "I tell you, many will come from the east and west and sit at table with Abraham, Isaac, and Jacob in the kingdom of heaven . . . " (Mt 8:11). Jesus' words are an echo of the prophetic expectation that at the end-time all peoples would be brought into the kingdom (see Is 56:6–7). But we find no evidence that Jesus, during his ministry, provided for Gentile participation through a distinctive mission directed to them.

There are, it is true, certain texts where Jesus during his public ministry has some contact with Gentiles, as, for example, in the stories of the Syro-Phoenician woman in Mark 7:24–30, the centurion in Matthew 8:5–13, and the Gerasene demoniac in Mark 5:1–20. This last is highly embellished with folkloric details. The first two instances show a reluctance on the part of Jesus to break the barrier between Jews and non-Jews. But these stories would help the gospel readers, several decades after Jesus' ministry, to accept the Gentile mission. It was the resurrection of Jesus that enabled the early believers to make a transition to a new understanding.

Baptism

Two very distinctive features of Christian religious identity are baptism and eucharist. It may be helpful to consider where and how they fit into the critical understanding of Jesus' ministry.

Jesus's own baptism at the hands of John is part of the historical bedrock of the tradition. Yet because the baptism scene in the gospels includes a theophany, a revelation from God, and because the gospel accounts are here so clearly theologically motivated, it is difficult to get to the precise meaning of this event for John or for Jesus. We may summarize recent New Testament studies as follows. John's baptism in itself had a double significance. It was a baptism of repentance, a way of expressing one's repentance which opened one to God's forgiveness. It was also a baptism of preparation for the decisive intervention of the Coming One, God's end-time agent, who would minister a "baptism in spirit and fire." The latter is a metaphor for the period of woes and tribulation which would precede the messianic kingdom. The expectation that a period of trial would anticipate the final age was common to some of the prophets, to elements of apocalyptic literature (such as the Book of Daniel), and to one of the hymns found among the Qumran scrolls.

It is in coming to know the meaning of John's baptism for Jesus that we have the greatest difficulty. Matthew's account suggests that Jesus' accepting a baptism of repentance from John was an embarrassment to the early church (Mt 3:13–15). We cannot say exactly why Jesus chose to be baptized by John; perhaps the best that can be said is that Jesus' baptism was "an expression of resolve" (J. D. G. Dunn) to undertake his ministry as he saw it, though it may also have signified his willingness to become a disciple of John to prepare for the coming of the kingdom. In the mind of all the evangelists (Mt 3:16; Mk 1:10; Lk 3:21–22; Jn 1:32–34) the main point of the event is the Spirit's coming to Jesus as a response to Jesus' symbolizing his acceptance of his mission by his acceptance of John's baptism.

Did Jesus himself engage in a ministry of baptizing others? In John 3:22 we are told: "Jesus and his disciples went into the land of Judea; there he remained with them and baptized." This mention of Jesus' baptizing others is the only such statement in any of the gospels. It may be, we saw above, that the early chapters of the fourth gospel give us reliable information about Jesus' early ministry which is not preserved by the synoptics. This text from the fourth gospel gives the impression that when John was no longer at Bethany (Jn 3:23; cf. 1:28) Jesus—accompanied by former disciples of John—was himself in the Jordan area conducting a ministry of baptism. When Jesus left the area of Judea and began his ministry in Galilee he evidently abandoned his baptizing ministry and concentrated on preaching and teaching. It may be that because Jesus ceased baptizing, John sent his disciples to ask Jesus if indeed he was the one who was to come (Lk 7:18–23; Mt 11:2–6).

John 4:2, by contrast, "corrects" John 3:22 by adding a parenthetical note: "although Jesus himself did not baptize, but only his disciples." This latter text was almost certainly edited by the evangelist so as to avoid the charge of John's followers later in the first century that Jesus was but an imitator of John. It seems likely, then, that there was a brief period when Jesus conducted a ministry of baptism which must have been similar to that of John but not a distinctively Christian baptism.

When Jesus began to preach that the kingdom of God was already present, he quite reasonably abandoned the Johannine baptism which was merely preparatory for the coming kingdom of God. It is in John's practice of baptism, and in Jesus' own baptism at the hands of John, that we find the antecedents of Christian baptism. Only after the resurrection of Jesus did Christian baptism emerge with new and distinctive elements.

Jesus' Meals with Others

While administering baptism was not a consistent feature of Jesus' public ministry, the contrary must be said of his eating with his disciples and with social outcasts, even those who were public sinners. His eating with his disciples was not something unique to him. Groups of Pharisees came together for meals as a means of better maintaining the commandment of ritual purity (see Lk 7:36; 11:37–39). The Essenes, too, had common meals which were regarded as anticipations of the messianic banquet to take place at the end-time. In the gospels Jesus is often a guest at meals (Mk 1:29–31; 14:3; Lk 7:34; 11:37; 14:1) and there are some suggestions that he may have invited others to join him (Mk 2:15; Lk 15:1–2). Jesus' meals were so well known that he seems to have been accused, among his adversaries, of being "a glutton and a drunkard, a friend of tax collectors and sinners" (Mt 11:19). Such an expression most probably has a firm historical basis: it surely must have run against the grain of the evangelists to record such an unkind assessment, but because of its basis in the tradition, it could not easily be eliminated.

It is the significance of Jesus' meals that is most important. For the people of Jesus' culture, sharing a meal implied a bond of unity, a sharing of one's life. Even more, table-fellowship in Judaism implied fellowship before God: those who broke bread at table shared in the blessing which the head of the household pronounced over the bread.

It was foreign to the mind of the Pharisees to sit at a meal with known sinners. Jesus did so and quite likely used parables such as those of the lost sheep, of the lost coin, of the prodigal son (Lk 15) and of the laborers in the vineyard (Mt 20:1–16) to justify his action. Intimately associated with Jesus' preaching and teaching, Jesus' meals with his disciples were meant to be symbols of God's reaching out to embrace God's people in the banquet of the end-time (see Mk 2:19; 10:35–40; Mt 22:1–10; 25:10; Lk 22:30). Jesus' meal gatherings were close to the heart of his message and of his mission.

The last meal which Jesus had with his disciples has stood for centuries as the highest expression of the fellowship which was so much a part of Jesus' ministry. Because of its honored place in Christian memory Catholics have come to see the Last Supper as the occasion when Jesus instituted both the eucharist and the priesthood. Current biblical scholarship helps us to recognize the complexity of this matter.

> It is one issue whether the eucharist and priesthood are so essentially related to what Jesus did at the Last Supper that in the theological sense they can be said to have been instituted here—this is what the Council of Trent affirmed. It is another issue whether at that historical moment Jesus had thought out the whole issue of eucharist and priesthood. The Council of Trent did not affirm that and current biblical scholarship would not think in those categories. We shall come to the essential relationship issue later on in the book.

A careful reading of each of the four New Testament accounts of the Last Supper (1 Cor 11:23–25; Mk 14:22–25; Mt 26:26–29; Lk 22:15–20) shows that each one is different from the other. Scholars generally agree that each of these accounts is most likely based on the liturgical form known to Paul or the evangelists at the time they were writing. There are two narrative patterns, one found in Paul and Luke (coming, possibly, from the church at Antioch) and another in Mark and Matthew (reflecting, perhaps, the liturgy in Palestine or, more specifically, Jerusalem). Precisely because the texts as we have them reflect liturgical usage, we cannot be sure that any of them is a *strictly* historical record. It is most likely true that none of them is strictly historical, even if the basis for the narratives comes from the event itself.

The one saying in the Last Supper account whose authenticity is generally acknowledged is that which associates the Supper with the kingdom: "Truly, I say to you, I shall not drink again of the fruit of the vine until that day when I drink it new in the kingdom of God" (Mk 14:25). This saying can hardly have been a creation of the church since very early it dropped from the church's liturgical tradition. The meaning of the saying is obscure, but it seems to underline a heightened end-time awareness, suggesting that the Supper is an anticipation of the final feast of the kingdom. The saying does not look to a continued series of such meals. The saying "Do this in remembrance of me" (in 1 Corinthians 11:24–25 and in the better manuscripts of Luke 22:19) does seem to be a construction of the church since it appears in only one of the two eucharistic patterns, the Lucan-Pauline. It is far easier to accept that such a text might be added to one tradition than to account for its omission in the other. The addition of the words witnesses to the conviction of the early church that the practice of the eucharist was faithful to the mind of Jesus.

A careful reading of the texts does not indicate that at the Last Supper Jesus saw himself "ordaining" the apostles or that he regarded them as "priests" who were to preside at a sacrifice, a parallel, as it were, to the Jewish priests of the temple who did preside at sacrifices and cultic offerings. The sacrificial overtones present in Paul's account of the Last Supper and in the gospel accounts can best be explained by the church's almost immediate interpretation of the Last Supper by Jesus' death which followed so soon afterward.

An acceptance of these conclusions is consistent with the view that there were later developments in the understanding of the eucharist and of those who presided at eucharist. Our method of study helps us to avoid reading later understandings back into the actual event of the Last Supper. Jesus' meals with his disciples and others during his ministry, the meal he shared with his disciples before he died, the tradition of his feeding miracles, and, very importantly, the tradition of meals shared with the risen Lord—all have contributed elements to the understanding of the eucharist which came in later decades. Other factors that also entered into this development come in the histories of the Jewish and Christian communities after the destruction of the temple in A.D. 70. We are here considering only Jesus' public ministry.

Some Catholics are aware that the Council of Trent (1545–1563) made statements to the effect that Christ instituted the sacraments of eucharist and orders, the latter with the words "Do this in commemoration of me" (Session XXII, canon 2). It is important to remember that just as scholars and the official church have come to appreciate that we cannot understand the meaning of the scriptures without the use of historical and critical methods, so too scholars and the official church have come to appreciate that we cannot understand the statements of councils or popes—statements made over the ages—without the use of similar historical and critical methods. In our first chapter we reviewed the slow and sometimes painful process by which critical methods in dealing with the scriptures received official recognition in the Roman Catholic Church. Major steps in this recognition came, we have seen, in 1943, 1955, 1964, and 1965. Very significantly, in 1973 the Roman Catholic Church, through the "Declaration in Defense of the Catholic

Doctrine on the Church Against Certain Errors of the Present Day"
(*Mysterium ecclesiae*), issued by the Congregation for the Doctrine of
the Faith, made an analogous recognition that historical and critical
methods must be used to understand past statements of the church's
teachings. One element in such an approach involves keeping in mind
precisely what were the problems or the questions which were addressed by a conciliar or papal text.

In light of the above, a careful study of Trent shows that the council's
statements intended to affirm that later church understandings of eucharist and orders were faithful to the teaching of the New Testament and
to the intent of Christ as this was understood by the apostolic church.
The council made such an affirmation because it understood the reform-
ers to deny that there was such a fidelity in the teaching of the Roman
Catholic Church. Trent did not intend to deal with such specific
historical-critical questions as to what the historical Jesus may have
thought of such matters or whether he actually said this or that statement as we have it in the gospels. We will see more of this presently as
we continue this presentation.

The Ministry of Jesus and the Beginnings of the Church

Let us try now to conclude this examination of Jesus' ministry and its
impact on the beginnings of the church. Biblical evidence does not support the idea that Jesus in his ministry set up a new community with its
own internal structures and its own identity distinct from other Jews.
Nor can we speak of Jesus and his disciples as constituting a movement
in the same way that the Pharisees or the Essenes were distinct movements or even sects within Judaism prior to A.D. 70. The Pharisees
certainly were a movement within Judaism, a party, an elite. They had a
sense of separateness and were marked by the conviction that they had
exclusive possession of the truth concerning God's law. Some scholars
would even call the Pharisees a sect, not so exclusive, perhaps, as the
Essenes, but a sect nonetheless.

Jesus and those he invited to be with him in announcing the coming of
the kingdom were not marked by the same characteristics as the Pharisees, even if there were some similarities between Jesus and his followers and the Pharisees. Certainly Jesus did see himself as an authoritative
spokesman for God and claimed to give a definitive interpretation of
God's will for the people of Israel. But the exclusivity characteristic of
the Pharisees and even more of the Essenes was lacking among Jesus
and his disciples.

As we saw above, we have no sense that Jesus ever intended to carry
out his mission by himself; rather, he sought to involve others with him
in the proclamation of the kingdom. Our evidence also suggests that
Jesus did not require that others adhere to him personally so much as he
called them to be one with him in proclaiming God's imminent reign.
We know that some of those who accepted Jesus' proclamation of the
kingdom traveled with him, but many did not. But that there was some
type of bond between Jesus and his followers is quite evident not only
from his call to others to associate with him in his proclamation but also
from the response of his followers after the resurrection who saw themselves immediately as a community. That the term for community,
koinonia, came into use very quickly after the resurrection and had a
widespread use tells us that the Christian community had originated in
the ministry of Jesus. Yet Jesus and his followers were not a group
distinct from Israel. Jesus sought to bring Israel to what he thought it
should be. He and his followers can only be seen within the context of
the community of Israel with its law, its sacrifices, and its priesthood.

The relationship between Jesus' ministry and the beginnings of the
church is complex and our evidence is not without ambiguity. We must
respect this complexity. Some further light on this matter will come
when we take a final look at the figure of Jesus himself.

Our Understanding of Jesus

Before we leave this chapter, let us compare the understanding of Jesus,
implicit in these considerations, with the picture of Jesus which is part of
the pre-critical approach to the church's beginnings. Here in a very
pronounced way do we see the difference between the two approaches.
It is beyond the scope of this essay to discuss in detail the differences
between our understanding of Jesus during his public ministry and the
post-resurrection understanding of him which gradually became part of
the church's tradition (what is known as Christology). However, a few
reflections on the topic seem both useful and necessary.

The historical-critical picture of Jesus which emerges is that of a
Jewish rabbi, a prophet, an itinerant preacher, convinced of his in-
tensely close relationship to God and of the mission which God had
given to him. That mission was to proclaim that God's end-time presence was coming soon and, indeed, was already present through him.
That presence meant forgiveness and judgment; it was an offer of salvation, and a call for people to change their lives because of it. Jesus used
the symbol of the "reign of God" to express this divine presence, though
he spoke of the reign of God in ways that were meant to express his

distinctive understanding of what that presence meant. He asserted himself with an authority unlike any other prophet or teacher of Israel's tradition, whether of the past or of his own day. We see a Jesus who lived with the conviction that the Spirit of the final age was present and at work in him and that even if his mission involved opposition, persecution, and death, God would vindicate him and those who put their trust in him.

Critical studies of the gospels show that Jesus seldom if ever made himself the focus of his preaching or teaching, even though implicit in his teaching about God's kingdom was the awareness of his role in proclaiming the kingdom and in its coming. We find no evidence that the man Jesus during his public ministry was omniscient or that he foresaw or provided for the church as we have come to see it at the end of the first century or as it is today. Insofar as Jesus called disciples to associate with him and provided for a continued discipleship in the real and symbolic meal that was the Last Supper, we can say that Jesus during his ministry was preparing for the foundations of the church. These actions, of course, cannot be seen apart from the preaching and praxis of Jesus' entire ministry. But there is no evidence that Jesus during his public ministry provided clearly for a system of sacraments, for ordained officers, or for a body of doctrine which would constitute a new religion alongside of or opposed to the Judaism of his day. Rather, Jesus, and those who joined him in his travels or who were numbered among his supporters in the villages and in the cities, remained within the community of God's people Israel. As a religious phenomenon within Judaism, Jesus and his followers were in many ways a failure; they would find far greater acceptance in places outside of Palestine and with people who were not Jews.

This understanding of Jesus and the way he saw his mission differs from a pre-critical understanding which stresses his unlimited knowledge and his planning out the future details of the church. In this latter view Jesus explicitly taught others of his divinity during his lifetime and gave at least the outlines of the church as a new religion. Such an understanding finds support only if one presumes that the discourses of Jesus in the fourth gospel and certain pronouncements of Jesus in Matthew's gospel were historical reminiscences recorded by eyewitnesses, members of the Twelve. But current critical biblical studies bring us to understand these texts differently.

A second reason why many people believed that Jesus of Nazareth possessed a divine knowledge and therefore foresaw and provided for the church is the assumption that such knowledge is implied in the belief that Jesus is divine, is God, the Second Person of the Blessed

Trinity. A few words of explanation may rectify this perception. It is a basic tenet of Christian faith defined at the Council of Chalcedon (A.D. 451) that Jesus of Nazareth, born of Mary, was fully and completely a human being like us in all things but sin (Heb 4:15). This says something about Jesus which should not be denied or minimized. During Jesus' public ministry, some people believed that he was a good man, a holy man, one in whom God's Spirit was present and at work. There were others, though, who thought that he was in league with the devil (Mk 3:22). Embarrassed perhaps by his radical teaching and strange ways, some, apparently members of his own family, said of him: "He is beside himself" (Mk 3:21; see 3:31–35). Though in his crucifixion Jesus seemed totally abandoned by God, he was raised by God's power from the dead. As Jews believed that only God could raise one from the dead, those who believed that Jesus had been raised began to see him in new ways and with new understandings. The 1964 Instruction of the Pontifical Biblical Commission referred to in Chapter One underscored this development. After Jesus' resurrection his disciples saw with new depths and new conviction that God was present in Jesus (see 2 Cor 5:16–18). Jesus' followers began to apply to him, as God's plenary agent, functions which formerly they attributed only to God. Toward the end of the New Testament period, in some few places, Jesus was even called "God" (see Jn 1:1; 20:28; Heb 1:7–8).

Second and third century Christians struggled with the many ways the New Testament writings spoke of Jesus, and especially with the belief that Jesus of Nazareth was fully human and at the same time one with God (Jn 10:30; but see also Jn 14:28). During this post New Testament period, some groups, despairing of reconciling the two beliefs, held for one and rejected the other. Such solutions the church as a whole rejected as inadequate. In the fourth and fifth centuries, councils of the church met to formulate the church's understanding of Jesus. Those councils drew up certain guidelines for expressing Christian belief in Jesus: that, though one individual, he was, in a way that is and always will be beyond our power to comprehend, fully human and fully divine. (In some of the language of the fourth council, he was spoken of as having a human nature and a divine nature.) The humanity and divinity of Jesus were not to be compromised or separated. The Council of Chalcedon taught that the humanity and divinity of Jesus were united in a single person (in Greek: *hypostasis*). The word "person" was a philosophical concept, used to express the belief that Jesus, who was human and divine, was one individual, and not two. Human attributes, such as emotions, knowledge, the various capacities which enable one to reflect, to remember, to plan for the future, to make choices and decisions, were ascribed to Jesus because of his human nature. Divine qualities, such as being eternally one with the Father, having the power to forgive sins or to be an agent of creation, were ascribed to Jesus because of his divine nature.

After the Second Council of Constantinople (A.D. 553), the person of Jesus was seen as the one divine person, the Word, the *Logos,* the Second Person of the Blessed Trinity. It was the Person of the Word which grounded, as it were, the divine nature and the human nature in Jesus. Misunderstandings concerning Jesus' human knowledge and human self-consciousness came when knowledge and consciousness were no longer understood in terms of his human nature (as in the teaching of Chalcedon), but were seen in light of his divine person. The difficulties increased when the term person shifted from its classical *philosophical* meaning to our modern *psychological* meaning of person as center of consciousness, reflection, and will. This very important change of meaning led to the incorrect understanding that Jesus in his human knowledge knew and foresaw what God knew and foresaw. The thought that Jesus' discourses in the fourth gospel were the reminiscences of an eyewitness reinforced this tendency. In effect, Jesus' human knowledge was not taken seriously. Today biblical scholarship and sound contemporary Christology hold that Jesus' human knowledge was truly human and hence limited. Recognition of this limitation does not imply that Jesus was not divine; limitations in his human knowledge were fully a part of his being human.

Many Roman Catholics have long avoided speaking of Jesus as a "human being," probably because they thought, erroneously, that such a manner of speaking would implicitly deny Jesus' divinity. The following statement of the Theology Commission of the Roman Catholic Bishops of England and Wales (1973) is helpful. "It is essential to grasp clearly that he [Jesus] was genuinely a human being. We are understandably awed when we are taught that he was God. But this fact must never be seen as diminishing his humanity. The purpose of his coming was to be one of us, to be the new head of the human race, to sanctify all creation. Unless he were truly man this would have been only a sort of religious puppet play. Therefore the church has in the past had to insist that he was truly man against the errors of those who thought his human nature was only a kind of dummy with his divine nature pulling the strings. We do not know, we shall never know totally, to what extent his human conscious life was influenced by his divinity; but we do know that whatever influence there was did not destroy or lessen his genuine humanity. Could we have met him and come to know him when he walked this earth,

we would have said without hesitation, 'There is a man, one of us.' "
("Who Is Jesus Christ? Statement on the Doctrine of the Incarnation)

This chapter has represented what sound biblical scholarship tells us
about the historical Jesus and about those things he said and did during
his public ministry which bear on the foundations of the church. We
cannot say that Jesus during his public ministry "founded a church" in
the sense that he established a clearly structured organization or set up a
new religion distinguishable from Judaism. There is a sense—and we
have seen something of this already—in which we can and must say that
the origins of the church are to be found in Jesus' ministry. (We will see
more of this in the next chapter.) What the church is does not stand or
fall solely on what was done by the historical Jesus. Rather, the basis of
the church lies not only in what Jesus did and taught during his public
ministry, but in the whole of God's action in Jesus, in his ministry, in his
death and especially in his resurrection, and in the gift of the Spirit,
living in the disciples of Jesus. The guide and norm for the church's self-
understanding and sense of mission comes not only from what scholars
can retrieve of the historical Jesus, important as that is, but from the
Word of God and the Spirit of God that comes to us in the Scriptures
and in the life of the Church. (We will see that one of the great questions
faced by the early church, whether Gentiles could be admitted without
strict observance of the Mosaic law, could *not* be answered by an appeal
to the words of the earthly Jesus.)

Tracing the line of development that extends from Jesus and his
followers to the Christian church with its own self-identity may help us
not only to understand our beginnings but also to be more attentive to
the Lord who in his Spirit addresses us now as a people called to be his
church.

Chapter Four

The First Christian Communities

Jesus' Resurrection

Correctly, we see the beginnings of the church in the preaching of Jesus and in all the other aspects of his ministry. Jesus' resurrection and the disciples' experience of the Spirit of the risen Jesus are very important also, and perhaps even decisively so.

The gospels give no account of the actual resurrection. Their focus is rather on the experiences of those to whom the risen Jesus appeared. The Greek term for *appear* is used in the gospel narratives and in Paul's account in 1 Corinthians 15. This term *appear* suggests that the experiences were not the same as seeing an ordinary object, but that they were not purely internal either. The use of the term also implies that the experience involved a revelatory action on the part of the risen Jesus. Several elements of the New Testament accounts of the appearances of the risen Jesus bear on our story. First, the New Testament text often implies and sometimes explicitly states that it was the Jesus of the public ministry, crucified and buried, who appeared to his followers and who was proclaimed by his followers to others (see Acts 2:29–32). We may speak, then, of the *continuity* between the Jesus of the ministry and the risen Jesus who appeared to some of his followers. So powerful was the impact of their first experiences of the risen Jesus that the initial preaching of Jesus' followers was centered not on the kingdom preached by Jesus but on the decisive event concerning Jesus himself, that he who had been killed at the hands of the civil and religious leaders was raised by the power of God. We see this in the letters of Paul, our earliest records of Christian preaching and teaching (see Romans 1:1–4 and 1 Corinthians 15:1–5, both of which incorporate formulas already in use) and in the early sermons of Acts (2:32–36; 3:13–15; 4:8–10). These sermons of Acts come to us in a document written in the 80s and show clear signs of Lucan composition; many scholars believe nonetheless that in his attempt to represent early Christian preaching, Luke has retained some of the atmosphere and phrasing from that early period.

The conviction of a continuity between the historical Jesus and the Jesus who was raised up must be seen in light of a second note, that of *discontinuity*. This feature becomes apparent in the language used to describe Jesus as he was experienced after his resurrection. The notion of resurrection comes from Jewish belief that God would, at the end-time, raise the dead to life. In Jesus' day, the Pharisees held such a belief; the Sadducees did not. Resurrection is to be understood not as a resuscitation, as, for example, in the story of Lazarus, but as a *transformation,* a glorification, a person's entry into a new manner of existence, made possible by the power of God. (Thus the use of the term "appear" mentioned above.) We catch something of the struggle to conceptualize the experience of these encounters with the risen Jesus in the account by an eyewitness, Paul (1 Cor 15:35–44, 50–53). Theologians today try to express the New Testament teaching by speaking of Jesus' resurrection as an "eschatological" or end-time event, brought about by God's power. What happened to Jesus at his resurrection stands outside the limits of space and time as we experience them, even if his appearances touched the lives of people who were in our world and in a history of which we are a part. Part of the mystery of Jesus' resurrection involved this irruption of God's end-time into the midst of human history. Early preaching and teaching saw Jesus' resurrection as an anticipation of the general resurrection in which, some Jews believed, all were expected to share. Paul's speaking of the risen Jesus as "the first-born among many brethren" (Rom 8:29) and "the first-fruits of those who have fallen asleep" (1 Cor 15:20 and 23) are understood in the context of this Jewish belief. This conviction—that a new and final age, the beginning of the end-time, had become manifest in Jesus' resurrection—was basic to the faith of the earliest believers.

A third and equally important element in these appearance narratives consists in the *commission* to proclaim Jesus to others. An attentive reading of the gospel accounts (Mt 28:16–20; Jn 20:19–23) and even more, perhaps, of Paul's mention of the resurrection (1 Cor 9:1; Gal 1:1; Rom 1:3–5) shows how integral to the account of the appearance is the command to undertake a mission in Jesus' name and with power given by him.

The Risen Jesus' Commission to the Disciples

Among the various appearance stories, two groups stand out in importance. The first of these, and quite probably the first chronologically, concerns Jesus' appearance to Mary Magdalene (Mt 28:9–19; Mk 16:9; Jn 20:11–18). Associated with these stories are those in which the women from Galilee receive from the messenger at the tomb the commission to bring the message of Jesus' resurrection to the other disciples (Mk 16:1–8; Mt 28:1–8; Lk 24:1–11). It is probable that these women had an important role in nurturing faith in Jesus in the early days after the shattering event of Jesus' death and the first news of his resurrection. Mary Magdalene was the most prominent among these women disciples, since she is usually mentioned first.

A second group of stories deals with Jesus' appearance to Peter and the Eleven. The gospels do not stress that Peter was the first to witness the risen Jesus. Luke 24:34 is the only gospel passage giving a hint of that tradition. The list of the appearances in 1 Corinthians 15:5–7 puts Peter first in a list (which does not include Mary Magdalene) the first part of which most scholars regard as chronological. The appearances to Peter and to the Eleven were decisive in the gospel tradition because these appearances included the commission to give public testimony to Jesus' resurrection, the central proclamation of the post-Easter community. This is the core of the later traditional claim that the risen Jesus appeared first to Peter. Historically it may well have been to Mary Magdalene that the risen Jesus first appeared.

The most detailed account of Jesus' appearance to Peter is found in John 21:1–17. This basic narrative may be related to the simpler statements in 1 Corinthians 15:5 and Luke 24:34. The commission to Peter is explicit in John 21:15–17: "Feed my lambs. . . . Tend my sheep. . . . Feed my sheep." The memory of Jesus' appearance and commission to Peter which is present in John 21 most probably also stands behind the Matthean account of the scene at Caesarea Philippi (Mt 16:16–20; compare with Mk 8:29–30 and Lk 9:20–21).

The gospels tell us that the risen Jesus appeared to the Eleven as a group and gave a mission to them as well (Mt 28:16–20; Lk 24:36–49; Jn 20:19–24, and the Marcan Appendix, 16:14–15). While Jesus may have given some share of his mission to his disciples during his ministry, the call to mission is so bound up with the appearance of the risen Jesus that the very notion of "apostle" (meaning "delegate" or "messenger") is really a post-resurrectional concept. In fact it is more accurate to speak of twelve *disciples* during Jesus' public ministry and of the eleven *apostles* after the risen Jesus gave them a commission in his name.

A careful reading of the various appearance narratives at the end of the gospels makes one aware of the discrepancies among the several accounts. Most notable are the differences which concern the time and place of the appearances. In some narratives, the appearance takes place in Jerusalem and the text excludes any further appearance in Galilee (Luke 24, John 20, and Mark 16:9–20, a text generally thought to have been edited on the basis of Luke 24 and John 20). Other texts place the appearance in Galilee and preclude any earlier appearance in Jerusalem (Matthew, John 21, and, it seems, Mark 16:7). Past efforts to harmonize the various accounts in a sequence which provides a time and place for all of the various appearances are suspect in light of our current understanding of the way the gospels were composed. Clearly there never was one unanimously accepted tradition concerning the various appearances. The evangelists (including the author of the Marcan appendix) included at least one account of an appearance of the risen Jesus to Peter and/or to the Eleven.

This view receives support from the presence of a similar pattern in each of the various narratives: the disciples are without Jesus; Jesus appears; Jesus greets the disciples and they recognize him; and Jesus gives a word of command or mission. Some years ago it was suggested (A. Descamps) that the differences in the various appearance accounts may best be explained by positing a single appearance of Jesus to the Eleven; as the story of this appearance was passed around by word of mouth, details were added. When the evangelists wrote the gospels they chose one or more of these stories as a conclusion.

Even in the light of this understanding, one may draw up a very tentative sequence of appearances which might shed light on our story. (The biblical evidence does not permit us to determine this sequence with any assurance. If one were demanded, R. E. Brown suggests the hypothesis described in the next few paragraphs.)

Quite possibly the risen Jesus appeared first to Mary Magdalene in the area of Jerusalem. But Jesus' appearance to Peter and/or the Eleven probably did not take place in Jerusalem on Easter Sunday. If such an appearance had taken place with its accompanying mission command, it would be very difficult to explain the tradition of a subsequent return of the disciples to Galilee. It seems far more plausible that the Eleven fled Jerusalem, with what probably was a profound sense of defeat and disillusionment at the arrest and crucifixion of Jesus, and returned to their homes and occupations in Galilee (Jn 21:3). We cannot know when such a return might have taken place. Before leaving Jerusalem, they may have learned that the body of Jesus was no longer in the tomb. It may well be that only after Simon had returned to his fishing did the risen Jesus appear to him on the shores of the Sea of Galilee. Only then was a resurrection faith born in Peter and only then was the commission given to him to proclaim that faith to others. It is likely that the prayer of

Jesus in Luke 22:32, that after Peter had failed he would turn again to the Lord and then strengthen his brothers, is an allusion to this event.

Soon after, the hypothesis continues, Jesus appeared to the entire group of the Eleven, perhaps confirming the beginnings of the faith which came in part from Peter's testimony. On this same occasion the group would have received the gift of the Spirit from the risen Jesus and the general commission to proclaim that in Jesus' resurrection the final age had begun. It is very difficult to say where this basic appearance to the Eleven took place, though quite likely it occurred after Jesus appeared to Peter in Galilee. Galilee may be the more likely site, although a critical study of the gospel material does not rule out a Jerusalem location. (It may be that the risen Jesus appeared to Peter and to some of the Twelve in Galilee and that there was a subsequent appearance to the Twelve in Jerusalem. It is difficult to explain the traditions of such a Jerusalem event without a second appearance.) At any rate the Eleven, some of the women disciples from Galilee (see Lk 23:49), and, almost certainly, some others went from Galilee to Jerusalem. As Jews who believed that at the feast of Passover God's end-time had been inaugurated in Jesus' resurrection, they quite possibly wanted to be in the holy city on the occasion of Pentecost. In the fervor of their new faith they may have expected that the conclusion of the Passover season might bring yet a further unfolding of God's end-time plan.

In these key appearances to Mary Magdalene and the other women, and to Peter and the Eleven, we see the basic foundations of the resurrection faith of the early community and the inauguration of the Christian mission. Further determinations of this basic commission—most significantly that this mission was to extend to all peoples, Jew and Gentile alike—would unfold only gradually over many years. The gospel accounts, composed and edited decades later, include these further specifications in the narratives of these early appearances (see Mt 28:19; 16:19; Lk 24:47; Jn 20:22–23).

While the details of the resurrection narratives vary a great deal, several references place the appearances in the context of a meal (Lk 24:30 and 43; Jn 21:12–13; Acts 1:4, according to one possible translation; see also Acts 10:41). The appearance of the risen Jesus at a meal seems to have been an intrinsic part of early Christian memory. Along with the Last Supper and Jesus' meals with others during his ministry, this tradition stands as one of the elements of the later development of the eucharist in the early church.

Of the canonical gospels it is principally Luke (Lk 24:51; Acts 1:6–11) who tells us of Jesus' ascension, though there is something of a parallel in

the Marcan Appendix (16:19) and there are reflections of a similar tradition in non-canonical writings. A study of the latter part of Luke's gospel (see Lk 9:31 and 9:51) indicates that Luke uses an early tradition about Jesus' ascension as an important element of his theological message.

Scholars reason that originally the "ascension" must have been seen as coinciding with Jesus' resurrection, as we have it in some non-canonical writings and implicitly in John 20:17. In this perspective, Jesus' appearances occurred after his ascension. In the course of time the statement of Jesus' ascension was expanded into narrative form, drawing upon Elijah stories and apocalyptic images (cloud and angels). It is such a tradition which no doubt stands behind Luke's account and the other sources where it appears. The narrative sequence was then adjusted to become a sequence of resurrection, followed by a period in which the appearances took place, and finally the ascension. The appearance of the risen Jesus to Paul, some years later, supports this interpretation.

A critical understanding of the ascension tradition does not suggest at all that there should be a change in the liturgical commemoration of the mystery of Jesus' ascension. The liturgy rightly puts its main focus on the significance, for Jesus and for us, of this aspect of Jesus' glorification; the importance of the "chronological" sequence is, at best, quite secondary.

The Election of Matthias

Acts tells us that between Jesus' ascension and Pentecost the disciple Matthias was chosen to replace Judas (Acts 1:15–26). It is impossible to know what the exact historical basis behind this story is, though most critical scholars allow that some pre-Lucan tradition stands behind the account. Luke does not give the reason for the election, other than to replace Judas, but if it is correct that Jesus himself chose an inner circle of Twelve and gave them a symbolic end-time role, we can easily understand the concern to replace Judas after his defection. Association of the Twelve with the end-time would no doubt have been strengthened by the view that Jesus' resurrection was the dawning of the end-time and by the possible expectation that the complete revelation of the end-time might be near at hand.

We know nothing of the two men whose names were put forward; surely they must have been among the wider circle of Jesus' followers. That only men were considered can be explained by the original choice of men to represent the twelve sons of Israel. The use of lots as a means of discerning the will of God fits within the framework of Jewish tradition (1 Chr 24:5; 26:13–14), rabbinical and priestly practice (see Lk 1:9), and the custom of the Qumran community. Because the Twelve were symbols of God's end-time action, they had to be chosen by God. This is the reason for the casting of lots.

While it is likely that the election of Matthias did occur in the period in which Luke places it, it cannot be ruled out that the election took place shortly after the feast of Pentecost. In Luke's theological perspective it might have been important that the symbolic integrity of the Twelve be restored before the coming of the Spirit.

Pentecost

In Luke's account (Acts 2:1–41) the event of Pentecost is a decisive moment in the beginnings of the church. Precisely because of this theological understanding, some scholars have regarded Acts 2 as almost if not completely a product of Luke's theological creativity (a position associated most notably with the German scholar Ernst Haenchen). But this assessment is not unanimous. Today there are respected critical scholars who recognize the theological importance of the account in Luke's narrative but are confident also that there is some historical reality which is at the basis of the Acts' account. What follows is a resume of a more moderate critical hypothesis (based on the work of J. Kremer and J. D. G. Dunn).

After the risen Jesus appeared to Peter and quite possibly to some, at least, of the Eleven in Galilee, this group and others with them went to Jerusalem. As Jews they may have wanted to observe the pilgrim feast of Pentecost. But, quite likely, they may have expected that as God had raised Jesus at the time of Passover, a further manifestation of God's plan might take place on this second feast which concluded the Passover celebration. It is very likely that the group from Galilee, including Mary and some of Jesus' family members (Acts 1:14), were joined in Jerusalem by others, especially the Galilean women, who had become Jesus' followers (see Mk 15:41; Lk 8:1–3). Luke's saying that there were "about a hundred and twenty" gathered in Jerusalem (Acts 1:15) is probably fairly accurate. It is quite possible, too, that the initial mission to make Jesus' resurrection known was carried out within the confines of this same group and was then absorbed into the group's anticipation of the completion of God's inaugurating the end-time. It is understandable that these Jerusalem believers would come together in one place on the actual day of the feast.

Did the event Luke describes in Acts 2 take place on the first Pentecost after Jesus' resurrection? Some scholars have pointed out that Luke's account clearly means to associate the gift of the Spirit with the Sinai gifts of covenant and law commemorated on the feast of Pentecost.

They have asked if Luke simply associated a theological construct to a convenient and meaningfully symbolic day. Other scholars respond that, even so, the early believers would likely have gathered for the feast with the expectation that the end-time begun at Passover time might become completely manifest at the first Pentecost after Jesus' death. The two feasts, in the Jewish mind, were very closely linked. The likelihood of the Pentecost date receives some further support, though hardly conclusive proof, from the mention in Acts 20:16 and 1 Corinthians 16:8 that Paul tried to arrange his travels so as to be with one or another community at Pentecost, implying a high regard for observance of the day.

Where the gathering took place cannot be stated with certainty. The identification of the place with the room of the Last Supper has no biblical evidence to support it. Because the temple figured prominently in Jewish end-time expectation, one can easily understand why the disciples of Jesus might have gathered at the temple in the hope and prayer that another manifestation of God would take place and that they would be present for it. The actual location, however, is of little consequence.

Far more important are the events themselves which may be the basis for the account in Acts 2:1–13. Briefly put, the critical hypothesis we follow holds that on this first Pentecost after Jesus' resurrection, the group of believers collectively experienced an ecstatic spiritual presence in the excitement of anticipating some further end-time manifestation. This experience was a powerful one. They concluded that God's Spirit, a gift from the risen Jesus, was granted to them in so singular and outstanding a measure that another sign marking the dawning of the end-time had taken place, even if the final manifestation of God's coming in power had not yet occurred. This experience involved some type of communal ecstasy and the phenomenon of ecstatic speech (glossolalia or speaking in tongues). This communal ecstasy had as its basis a very powerful presence of the Spirit, one which should be understood as more intimately associated with Jesus' resurrection than the Lucan account implies. As to the "speaking in tongues," there are various scholarly interpretations. Perhaps on the pre-Lucan level the tongues were interpreted as gibberish (Acts 2:13). (We know from Paul that one could not understand another person who was speaking in tongues and that one needed the gift of revelation to understand what was spoken. See 1 Corinthians 14.) Luke may have assumed that some of those who were attracted to the group were given a revelation which led to their conversion. The note about the many foreign languages being spoken at the Pentecost event (Acts 2:9–11) may have been added through the hindsight of later missionary developments.

A key element in this hypothesis is the recognition that just as the experience of the risen Jesus included a sense of mission, so the experience of the Spirit's presence at Pentecost brought a renewed sense of mission and a new sense of community to believers. Some of the distinctive features of the earliest Jerusalem community are most intelligible in this context, that the community saw itself as belonging to the Israel of the end-time. This distinctive sense of community was joined by a fresh missionary impulse. The enthusiasm of the believers after their Pentecost experience, and the power of their message, must have been strong forces in attracting others to join their numbers (Acts 2:41). So it is that, taking into account the initial faith and missionary impulse that came from the resurrection, one can justly see the Pentecost experience as in some way the "birthday" of the church community. There were also other experiences of being filled with the presence of God's Spirit, even if they took place in less dramatic ways (see Acts 4:8, 31; 8:14–17; 9:17–18; 10:44; 13:9; 19:6).

The Earliest Jerusalem Communities

The experiences of the risen Jesus and of the power of the Spirit, then, stand behind both the believers' sense of community and their mission. Because of the nature of our sources, we can reconstruct only the broad outlines of the earliest gatherings of believers and of their earliest missionary endeavors. In our effort to study these early years, we use the gospels and the Book of Acts.

The most important characteristic of the earliest Jerusalem community was its conviction that it was nucleus of the eschatological or end-time community of Israel. This conviction gave shape to features which marked the life of the community, most notably its attitude toward Jesus, its manner of prayer, and its sharing of material goods. This understanding of the earliest community as a group keenly marked by its self-perception as God's end-time people, anticipating an early return of Jesus to bring the end-time to fulfillment, is found only indirectly in the account of Acts. When the Book of Acts was written in the 80s Luke was concerned to show that Jesus was not returning soon and that the church was being called to take its place and carry on its mission in the world of the Roman Empire. Nevertheless, some of the materials used by Luke in his account in Acts, with corroborating material from Paul's letters in the 50s, are the basis for the present understanding.

The early Christian community saw itself within the confines of Judaism—it would not have occurred to the group to see itself in any other way. One of the most important indications of the abiding Jewish self-identity of these early believers comes in the frequent references to the temple in the early chapters of Acts. Even with the increasing importance given to the Torah in that day, the temple remained for many Jews a focal point of hope in God's plan of renewal and redemption for Israel. The Acts account shows the Jerusalem believers attending daily prayer in the temple (2:46; 3:1; 5:12, 21, 42). The saying of Matthew 5:23–24, about leaving one's gift at the altar and being first reconciled to one's brother or sister, may be a recollection from the early years of the Jerusalem community when the disciples of Jesus continued to participate in the sacrificial cult of the temple. It was probably in the temple area that early preaching and teaching took place (Acts 5:12, 20–21, 25, 42), though most probably in a less dramatic way than presented in Luke's account. In the eyes of their Jewish contemporaries, the earliest believers must have been regarded as Jews who lived devout and modest lives but who held some eccentric beliefs.

The distinctiveness of these groups of early Jewish believers came in their beliefs about Jesus and in their conviction about the presence of the end-time. For this group Jesus was not just a rabbi but a prophet and more than a prophet. He was a prophet in whose life, death, and, most especially, in his resurrection, God had inaugurated the last days that were so much a part of Jewish hope. Because of Jesus' role in this plan, they saw Jesus as God's anointed one (the Messiah), even though the lowliness of his life and the scandal of his death were so at odds with many of the popular messianic hopes of the early first century. These two beliefs—that Jesus was the decisive agent in God's plan and that the end-time was made present, in him—led to another belief, that Jesus would soon come again and bring God's plan to final and complete fulfillment. Such a belief came from the realization that many of the expected blessings of the messianic age were not yet fulfilled; a second coming of Jesus might well be God's way of bringing about what was lacking. We do not see much of this expectation of a second coming (*parousia*, the Greek word for "coming") in Acts for the reason mentioned above. A hint of the early belief, however, is found in the bit of tradition woven into Peter's second speech after Pentecost. In Acts 3:19–21 we have what is probably a reminiscence of early preaching with its expectation that a second coming of Jesus would bring the awaited "times of refreshing" (v. 19) and would be "the time for establishing all that God spoke by the mouth of his holy prophets from of old" (v. 21).

Another (and perhaps more important) indication of the primitive community's expectation of Jesus' return is seen in the Aramaic expression, *Maranatha*. It is quite likely that this expression can be traced to the first months of the Jerusalem community. *Maranatha* may be either a prayer formula, *Marana tha,* "Lord, come!" or an expression of hope in the second coming, *Maran atha,* "The Lord is coming!" Paul used the Aramaic expression of what seems to be the prayer form at the conclusion of his first letter to the Corinthians, 16:22, written in the mid-50s. The Aramaic prayer was so much a part of the early tradition that Paul spelled it in Greek letters without translating it. The same Aramaic formula is found as a prayer in the early second century document called the *Didache* or *The Teaching of the Twelve Apostles* (10:6). The expectation of Jesus' return and the imminent end of the present world order was a dominant view of the first generation of Jesus' followers from the 30s through the 60s. That Jesus will come again to complete God's saving plan has been a tenet of Christian faith ever since.

Early House Worship

The earliest believers continued to see themselves as devout Jews and continued both their association with the temple and their practice of Jewish prayer. But their belief in Jesus and their experience of oneness in his Spirit led them to develop their own forms of common prayer. Hence prayer gatherings took place in the homes of the believers, most likely in the homes of the more prominent members of the community. We find indications of this in Acts 2:46 and 5:42. Acts 12:12 specifically mentions the house of Mary, the mother of John Mark.

We are able to identify certain features of the house worship of the first generation of believers. There are indications that some teaching took place, probably in the form of a recollection and discussion of Jesus' sayings (Acts 2:42; 5:42; 11:26; 13:1). Another facet of this teaching must have been reflection on the Jewish scriptures and an attempt to interpret the meaning of these scriptures in the light of the events of Jesus' life, death, and resurrection (Lk 24:25–27, 44–45; Acts 8:32; 17:2–3, 11). Prayer also had an important part in the house gatherings of the believers. The Lord's Prayer had a prominent place: traditions of that prayer are preserved in Matthew 6:9–13 and Luke 11:2–4. (Matthew's version, with the addition "for yours is the power and the glory forevermore," is found in *Didache* 8.) The manner of address which Jesus used for God, *Abba,* was also an important prayer form (see Gal 4:6 and Rom 8:15), one which, like *Maranatha,* was preserved in Aramaic. Paul's first letter to the Corinthians suggests that the Aramaic "Amen" must also have been used in early worship services: it is evidently a traditional element of prayer in the Greek-speaking community of Corinth in the 50s (1 Cor 14:16). Besides these fixed forms of prayer, there were spontaneous expressions of prayer as well (see Acts 4:24–30;

12:5; 13:3). The prayer of the early believers flowed from their sense of community in the Spirit. Overall, the form of prayer was more charismatic and enthusiastic than structured.

Baptism and the "Breaking of Bread"

New Testament evidence for the beginnings of an initiatory baptism is very meager. To the best of our knowledge baptism was a feature of both the earliest communities of believers and of the earliest missionary efforts. Because of the importance of the memory of John the Baptist, baptism no doubt involved some expression of repentance, though it also appears to have been oriented to the dawning end-time. The first baptisms were performed in the name of Jesus (Acts 2:38; 8:16; 10:48; 19:5).

> The command to baptize "in the name of the Father and of the Son and of the Spirit" in Matthew 28:19 reflects the practice used by the community for which Matthew wrote his gospel in the 80s. If the historical Jesus had given so explicit an instruction as we have it in Matthew, it would be very difficult to explain baptism in Jesus' name so often referred to in Acts and Paul.

In these early baptisms in Jesus' name, the ministers of baptism were probably seen as acting in the name of the exalted Jesus. The rite itself was viewed as an act of commitment to follow Jesus and a rite of entry into the community of Jesus' followers.

It is likely that baptism in early times was performed in a charismatic ceremony by any believer, but especially by the one who was instrumental in the conversion of the inquirer (see Acts 8:12, 38; 10:48; 16:33; 18:8). Understanding baptism as a commitment to Jesus and as a rite of entry into the community of believers may well explain why the earliest believers baptized others when Jesus did not. The followers of Jesus needed a tangible way of expressing adherence to one who was no longer visibly present; at the same time, they felt themselves more of a community than did the followers of Jesus in the pre-resurrection period.

If New Testament evidence for the development of baptism is quite thin, even thinner is the case for the beginnings of the community meals within which the eucharist would develop. Further, there is no clear consensus among critical scholars on the evaluation of such evidence. We will have to use caution as we make our way in this area.

We are told that the earliest believers participated in daily fellowship meals (Acts 2:42, 46). The term "breaking of bread" comes from the beginning of the Jewish meal in which bread was blessed, broken, and shared. The meals of Jesus' disciples (in the early Christian community) were probably seen as a continuation of Jesus' meals in his public life. Almost certainly—in the enthusiasm of what was regarded as the dawning of the end-time—they were seen as an anticipation of the end-time banquet.

It is not clear how these meals were related to the Last Supper. On the one hand, the end-time enthusiasm and the expectation of the imminent fulfillment of God's plan would have given little impetus to establish a ritual of remembrance. On the other hand, the earliest communities did preserve and transmit the words of interpretation over the bread and wine. One scholarly view (J. D. G. Dunn) concludes that in the earliest months and years there probably was not a clear distinction in the minds of the believers between the regular fellowship meals and those in which they specifically recalled the words of the Last Supper. It has been suggested (again, Dunn) that at the very beginning the Lord's Supper may have been an annual celebration, a type of Christian Passover. This thought is based on the fact that a group of Jewish Christians, the Ebionites (whose beliefs closely paralleled those of the primitive Jerusalem community but who later were regarded as a heretical sect), celebrated the Lord's Supper as an annual feast. But Paul's commentary, "As often as you eat this bread and drink the cup, you proclaim the Lord's death until he comes" (1 Cor 11:26), is a strong indication of greater frequency.

The "Community of Goods"

Another feature associated with the early Jerusalem community is the so-called "community of goods." We see indications of this in Luke's summary statements in Acts 2:44–45 and 4:32, 34–35, and in the accounts concerning Barnabas (Acts 4:36–37) and Ananias and Sapphira (Acts 5:1–10). There have been various views about the basis for these references in Acts. In the early part of this century the view was put forward (by Ernst Troeltsch) that there was a "primitive Christian love-communism" in the Jerusalem community. Its failure led to the financial crisis which inspired Paul's efforts to provide financial relief for the Jerusalem community. Such a view is generally abandoned today.

More probably some sharing of goods did take place in the early Jerusalem community under the impulse of the end-time expectation of Jesus' second coming and the consequent end of the present order of things. With this in mind we can find it understandable that some would have given little thought to needs of the future. The earliest Jerusalem community also had within it people from Galilee who had left behind such possessions as they had and had come to the holy city in anticipation of the final unfolding of God's plan.

Barnabas' sale of a field and his donation of the money to the apostles was probably more an exception than the rule. Because Barnabas was so important a figure in the early community, and quite possibly because his generosity was out of the ordinary, the story of Barnabas might have been preserved by the early believers and thus come to Luke's attention. The story of Ananias and Sapphira is probably best seen in light of the similar story of the deceit of Achan in Joshua 7:16–26. In both stories a holding back on what is due to God offends against the purity of the people of God as it enters the fulfillment of God's promise. The story in Acts probably reflects the very primitive notion of community purity in which Peter, acting as chief of the Twelve, functions as one of the judges of the last time. (Later on this judging power was institutionalized as the power to bind and loose.)

It also seems quite likely that by his treatment of the "community of goods" in conjunction with his theme of a people "of one heart and soul" (Acts 4:32), Luke intended to show his readers in the 80s that the early Christian community was a fulfillment of the Greek ideal of true friendship (friends are of one soul and have all things in common). The analysis of this section of Acts provides a good example of how we must use Acts with caution: Luke was far more interested in offering guidance for the church for which he was writing than in providing posterity with an historical record.

We may have a further indication of the outlook and the prayer of the earliest believers in Jerusalem and Judea in the four canticles found in Luke's gospel: the canticle of Mary (1:46–55); the canticle of Zachary (1:67–79); the song of the angels (2:13–14); and the canticle of Simeon (2:29–32). The canticles have close literary parallels in Jewish hymns and psalms composed in the period between 200 B.C. and A.D. 100, in the literature of the Maccabean period, and in some of the Qumran writings. Distinctive touches in the canticles support the theory that the songs were composed by a Jewish Christian community. The texts may even come from a community of Jewish Christian *anawim* (poor ones), whose piety was marked by a trust not in their own resources but in God's care and God's salvation. The canticles may have been compositions of early Jewish Christians who believed that God's promises of old had been fulfilled in Jesus.

The texts do not necessarily come from the earliest Jewish Christians. They may have come from Greek-speaking Jewish Christians and Gentile converts who preserved the Jewish mentality of the early Christians. Luke, writing in the 80s, may have seen them as an expression of the early Jewish Christian faith he described in the early chapters of Acts which, with some small editing (e.g., Luke 1:76–77), he incorporated these canticles into his gospel. There is good reason to believe that in these canticles, still prominently used in public worship in the church, we have a precious heritage that reflects the piety of the very early believers.

The early converts to the Christian community were people in the villages and cities. Many converts no doubt came from the *'am-ha'aretz*, the "people of the land." Acts 6:7 tells us that there were "many priests" who became believers. An earlier view that these were priests from the Qumran community does not have many supporters today. More likely the reference is to Jewish priests, many of whom lived in the country and were so poor that they were obliged to have a trade for the ten or eleven months when they did not have duties in the temple. Some of these priests could easily have been attracted to the communities of those who believed in Jesus. Acts 15:5 also tells us that there were "believers who belonged to the party of the Pharisees." The actual reference is made in connection with the assembly which took place in Jerusalem ca. A.D. 48 or 49, but it is probable that Pharisees were among the ranks of believers within the first couple of years after the resurrection.

"The Way"/The "Sect of the Nazarenes"

The earliest believers in Jesus were Jews who saw themselves as Jews. They were marked by the distinctive beliefs that Jesus was God's promised anointed one, and that, in Jesus, God's end-time had dawned. These beliefs would be regarded as eccentric by many Jews. But even as those who held other out-of-the-ordinary beliefs were tolerated by official Judaism in the middle decades of the first century A.D., so the beliefs of the Christians were tolerated. Many of the early Christians observed the law, were attached to the temple, and seemed to have had no concern for Gentiles or, early on, for a mission beyond the bounds of Judaism. At times, though, these Jewish believers were seen in an unfavorable light as a splinter-group, "the sect of the Nazarenes" (Acts 24:5).

With this in mind we can understand one of the self-designations of the early followers of Jesus: they called themselves "The Way" (Acts 9:2; 19:9, 23; 22:4; 24:14, 22). Acts 24:14 implies that the term was used by the followers of Jesus because of their belief that they embodied authentic Judaism. The community resisted seeing itself as a "sect" (*hairesis,* the basis for our term heresy), a term used of it by outsiders (Acts 24:5, 14) who saw believers in Jesus as another grouping within the complexity of mid-first century Judaism.

The expression "The Way" most probably has its basis in Isaiah 40:3: "A voice cries: 'In the wilderness prepare the way of the Lord.' " According to all four gospels, this was an element in the preaching of John the Baptist. The term was also used by the sectarians at Qumran because in their attempts to study the law and to live perfectly its prescriptions they saw themselves as end-time Israel preparing the way of the Lord. The followers of Jesus would have applied the term to themselves because they saw themselves as fulfilling God's plan for Judaism by reason of their belief in Jesus and their living in the end-time gift of his Spirit.

Because of the claim implicit in this self-designation, it is not surprising that the official reaction was not solely bewildered toleration, but, at times, opposition. Acts 4 and 5 are probably a synopsis in story form of this ambivalent reaction during the first decades of the early community's existence. On the one hand, the community's claims about Jesus and about itself were a threat to official Judaism. Not surprisingly these claims provoked negative reactions in those who in good faith believed they were acting in fidelity to Jewish religious principles. In his early years Paul is an example of one who acted on such an understanding. On the other hand some Jews must have wondered if perhaps the hand of God had been revealed in Jesus and was being revealed through the community of those who believed in him.

The Gamaliel scene in Acts 5:34–39 may be Luke's way of representing the wait-and-see attitude taken by some members of official Judaism. Gamaliel was one of the most highly respected Jewish teachers in the middle third of the first century A.D. Other than Luke's account in Acts, we have no evidence of Gamaliel's being involved in official Judaism's dealings with the early Jewish Christians. We know that in the 80s Luke wanted to have Roman officials adopt the same attitude with which Gamaliel is credited some fifty years earlier (see the last verse of Acts 28:31). In any event the position which Luke ascribes to the great teacher must surely have been held by some of the Jewish leadership in the 30s and 40s, even if we do not know if Gamaliel himself adopted it.

The Hellenists

A study of early Christian beginnings leads us to recognize that a marked plurality of groups, of theological views, and (once they emerged) of community structures was present even from very early times. Not surprisingly this plurality occasioned tensions and, at times, intense struggles. We see this in the Hellenists and in the story of Stephen.

On a surface reading the story of the Hellenists (Acts 6:1–6) is simple enough: there was a need for help in ministering to the widows of the Hellenists; steps were taken to provide such help. Those who have ever attended an ordination to diaconate will recognize the reading and the implication that Stephen, Philip, and the others were the first deacons. Critical scholarship is unanimous in seeing a much more complex situation behind these few verses in Acts.

Not all scholars agree on exactly what constituted a Hellenist. Most think that the Hellenists of Acts 6 were diaspora Jews living in Jerusalem. They were Greek-speaking (though some may also have spoken Aramaic) and were heavily influenced by Greek ways. These Greek-speaking Jewish believers shared with Aramaic-speaking Jews (the Hebrews of our passage) the belief that Jesus was the Messiah and that the end-time had dawned in him. But at least some of the Hellenists differed from the Hebrews in their attitude to the temple, and possibly in their greater interest in bringing the gospel to others. They were critical of the temple not, as in the case of the Essenes, because they thought the high priesthood had been compromised, but because a close association with the temple represented a narrow cultic nationalism that went against their more expansive outlook. Scholars believe that almost at the outset, and certainly within the first couple of years, the earliest Jerusalem believers embraced two fairly distinct groups, the Hellenists and the Hebrews.

The complaint recorded in Acts suggests that the two groups were even somewhat isolated from each other. The Hellenists may have lived in a separate section of the city. Jewish Christians who maintained strong ties to their Jewish heritage may well have looked down on these diaspora Jews who were more open to Greek ways. Even more, they may have been suspicious of the proselytes who associated with the Hellenists and who were more comfortable with them than with the Hebrew Christians. Tensions between the two groups broke into the open over the failure of the Hebrews to distribute to Hellenist widows a fair share of the common funds. This neglect was really a symptom of much deeper differences in outlook and understanding.

The solution to the immediate difficulty came in selecting seven administrators for the Hellenist group. The number seven parallels the number of elders in the synagogue congregation as described in the writings of Josephus. The selection in this instance probably meant that those whose leadership qualities were already known among the Hellenist believers were now to be recognized by the wider community. The Twelve are credited by Luke with summoning the assembly of the believers, the "multitude," to settle the issue. There is no scholarly consensus on the precise meaning of the gesture of the laying of hands on the designated leaders. But this is the first indication we have in the early church of administrator-leaders being set up in a local group. That the administrators are not to be regarded as deacon-assistants comes from the roles which are ascribed in Acts 6 and 7 to two of the seven, Stephen and Philip. Not only do they oversee the distribution of common goods; they are also involved in preaching and teaching roles as well.

> In light of this it is fair to say the use of Acts 6 in the rite of ordination to diaconate could be misleading if it were to be seen as an historical allusion to the first deacons. One can, however, correctly see in the text an indication of the early church's adopting new structures to meet its current needs. In this sense, the text could be used for the liturgical installation of any type of minister. We do not know if the leaders of the earliest communities had titles. The title which later would most closely describe the role of the seven would be that of presbyter or bishop.

There is good reason to believe that while Acts 6:1–6 says nothing about the leaders of the Hebrew section of the Jerusalem community, it may be that local administrators were set up for the Hebrews at the same time as they were set up for Hellenists. Acts 11:30, purporting to describe a period some years later, takes it for granted that there are presbyters (elders) who have been set in place and are in charge of the common food for the Jerusalem and Judean communities. One among such Hebrew leaders may have been James, the "brother of the Lord," who gradually came to have the dominant leadership role in the Jerusalem community.

Stephen and the Persecution of the Hellenists

The attitude of the Hellenist Christians toward the temple, and toward the Judaism of which the temple was a symbol, becomes clear to us in the story of Stephen, the first named of the Hellenist leaders. This story, in Acts 6:8 through 7:60, is not without difficulties for exegetes, but the many distinctive features of Acts 6 and 7 make these chapters stand out from the rest of Acts so much that scholarly opinion (e.g., J. D. G. Dunn) holds that there is good reason to accept the basic historicity of the account.

The views of the Hellenist believers concerning the temple and their ties to Judaism led to tensions between them and the Hebrew believers. The same views provoked open hostility and outright persecution from diaspora Jews who did not share a belief in Jesus. Stephen apparently made some attempt to evangelize these non-believing Hellenists in their own synagogues (Acts 6:9–10). Jews who left their homes in the diaspora to live in Jerusalem, the city of the temple, may well have found Stephen's position on the temple intolerably offensive. Opposition led to Stephen's arrest (Acts 6:11–13) and ultimately to his death (Acts 7:57–60). The death of Stephen was but a prelude to an open persecution of the Hellenist believers and they were driven from the city of Jerusalem to the adjacent areas of Judea and Samaria. It is most likely that Stephen's execution was the work of an angry mob rather than a legal execution. Scholars reason that Stephen's death and the ensuing persecution took place at the time of the change of prefects in A.D. 36, thus no more than two or three years at most from the end of Jesus' ministry. In A.D. 36 Pilate was replaced by the prefect Marcellus. Since one of the responsibilities of the Roman prefect was to maintain order, a change in prefects offers a plausible explanation of why such a disorder might take place.

The Jerusalem Believers and the Hellenist Mission

The persecution of the believing Hellenists had two very important results. First, when the Hellenist believers were almost wholly driven out of the city, this left Jerusalem to the Hebrew believers and explains why the city became the center of the more conservative Jewish Christian position in the debates over the Gentile mission in the years ahead. The Hebrew believers may have given little if any support to the Hellenist believers at the time of the persecution and this in turn may have driven the two groups even further apart.

The positions of the two groups were each based on differing interpretations of Jesus' teaching. The Hebrew believers thought they were being faithful to Jesus' own ministry by remaining within the framework of Judaism. This attitude would account for their escaping persecution and their being allowed to remain in the city. The Hellenists who accepted Stephen's position would have seen themselves being faithful to the particular Jesus-tradition (Mk 14:58), with Jesus' words concerning the destruction and rebuilding of the temple interpreted as a judgment on the temple. This Hebrew-Hellenist dispute is the first instance of Christians differing, and doing so very sharply, in their understanding of Jesus' teaching. While the immediate theological issue was the role of the temple and what it represented, it is not surprising that because the sacrifices of the temple were so much a part of the law, other parts of the law would soon be questioned.

A second result of the persecution of the Hellenist believers was even more important. Scholars are nearly unanimous in seeing in the dispersed Hellenists the first major effort to bring the gospel to Samaritans and to Gentiles and to advocate incorporation of these groups into the community of believers.

The Book of Acts gives several indications of the scattering of the Hellenists and of their missionary efforts to various places in Palestine and Syria. Acts 8:4–5 tells us that Philip, the second-named of the seven, went to a city of Samaria, north of Jerusalem, and later (Acts 8:26) to the area south of Jerusalem, on the way to Gaza on the Mediterranean coast. Acts 11:19–20 tells us that other Hellenists, scattered after Stephen's execution, traveled to Phoenicia (modern day Lebanon) and to Antioch in the Roman province of Syria. While Luke's account of the Christian mission in Acts 8–11 is highly schematized, there is good reason to believe that the dispersed Hellenists did in fact engage in a significant way in early missionary activity. In the Book of Acts Luke clearly wishes to highlight the roles of Peter and the apostles. Crediting the Hellenists for the origins of this missionary effort runs counter to Luke's emphasis on the Twelve. Precisely for this reason, we can see an historical basis in these accounts in Acts.

The Mission to Samaria

Clearly, one of the first areas to which the scattered Hellenists traveled was Samaria, not far to the north of Jerusalem. Stephen's speech in Acts 7:1–50 may well be based on an early tradition coming from the Hellenist mission to Samaria. Scholars who have studied the speech in detail find in it many elements which would be most appropriate within such a framework. Because of the prominence of Stephen and his leadership among the Hellenists, Luke may have put the speech on Stephen's lips and added the last few verses to explain the violence of the opposition against him. Samaria could well have been regarded as a fertile missionary ground because, as Josephus has it, there was a greater openness there to Greek ways and a clear sense of distance from the Jewish leadership and from traditions associated with the temple. Given the general antipathy between Samaritans and Jews, the Hellenists may have expected to find in Samaria a more ready hearing for their way of understanding Jesus and his message. We may roughly date the mission to Samaria in the late 30s.

We see further evidence of this (or a similar early Samaritan mission) in John 4, the story of Jesus and the woman at the well in the Samaritan town of Sychar. It should be noted that Acts portrays Jerusalem assenting post factum to the Samaritan mission (Acts 8:14–25) and the fourth gospel has Jesus tell the disciples that they will reap what they did not sow (Jn 4:38). The evidence tells us that the Samaritan mission remained in communion, *koinonia,* with Jerusalem believers.

"Christians" at Antioch

Significant as was the mission to Samaria, even more so was the Hellenist mission to the Roman province of Syria and to its capital city of Antioch. The Syrian capital was, after Rome and Alexandria, the third largest city (and one of the three or four most important cities) in the Roman empire. The Hellenist city of Antioch was founded by one of Alexander the Great's generals, Seleucus I, who, after the death of Alexander in 323 B.C., became king of Syria. The city played an important role in extending Greek influence over Syria; it was the capital of the Seleucid dynasty (see Chapter Two). Situated on the best land route between Asia Minor, Syria, and Palestine, the city grew rapidly as an important commercial, cultural, and political center. Under Roman domination in 64 B.C., Antioch became the capital and military headquarters of the new province of Syria. The city was enlarged and building projects were undertaken by Julius Caesar, Tiberius, and Herod the Great. There was a large Jewish presence in the Syrian capital in the early first century A.D. Except for the reign of Antiochus Epiphanes, the Jewish community was allowed to live according to its own customs and practices. It attracted to itself a number of Gentiles who were drawn by Jewish monotheism and ethics. Generally the populace of the city was characterized by an openness to things religious.

The New Testament writings give us two valuable sources on the beginnings of the Christian movement in Antioch. We have the first-hand testimony of Paul, in Galatians 2:11–21 (or perhaps only 2:11–14), though this testimony deals with an incident which occurred in the late 40s. Acts 11–15 is another source, though written some decades after the events it describes. Even scholars who take a skeptical view of the historicity of Acts accept that Luke's narrative in these chapters is reliable at least in its basic outline. A few non-biblical texts for background information on the Antiochene church also exist.

Acts 11:19–20 tells us that the gospel was brought to Antioch by "those who were scattered because of the persecution that arose over Stephen," a reference to the events concerning the Hellenists recorded in Acts 8:1 and 8:4. At first, Acts tells us, the Hellenist missionaries preached only to Jews. But some of them, "men from Cyprus and Cyrene," brought the Christian message to "the Greeks" as well. The term, "the Greeks," could refer to Greek-speaking Gentiles, not necessarily all of them Greeks by birth, but all of them clearly non-Jews. Some of the Gentiles were no doubt those who had been attracted to the Jewish community in the Syrian capital. Since Luke's account in Acts 6:5 states that one of the Jerusalem Seven, Nicolaus, was originally a Gentile proselyte (convert to Judaism) from Antioch, it seems natural enough that some of the scattered Hellenists should seek to convert other Gentiles when they reached Antioch. The Hellenist missionaries did so, without requiring circumcision—a major breakthrough.

Acts 11:22–23 further tells us that when the church at Jerusalem heard of the success of the Antiochene mission it sent Barnabas to Antioch to encourage and guide the missionary effort. Scholars are divided as to whether Barnabas was a Hebrew working closely with the Twelve or a Hellenist; as a consequence they hold different views about Barnabas' role in the Antiochene mission. A recent study (John P. Meier) thinks it best to follow Luke's treatment. Barnabas may well have been a Hellenist and a follower of Stephen, but one whose moderate views made him acceptable to the Twelve and enabled him to remain in Jerusalem after the persecution. A delicate middle position may have facilitated his serving as a mediator between the conservative Jerusalem community and the more out-going Hellenist mission at Antioch. In this he exercised some supervision in the name of the Jerusalem community over the Antiochene mission and so became one of the early leaders of this church.

It was at Antioch, Luke tells us (Acts 11:26), that the disciples of Jesus were first called "Christians." The community grew in size and became, with the addition of Gentile converts who were not circumcised and did not fully keep the Mosaic law, distinctive enough from the Jewish synagogue to provoke a new designation. The term "*Christianoi*," "followers or supporters of Christ," is best explained as a Latin title given by Gentiles, perhaps by the Roman authorities, who took *Christus* to be a proper name, not a title.

> The term *Christ* is based on the Greek word "to anoint" and is the translation of the Hebrew *Messiah,* the anointed one. The title Messiah was used in pre-Christian Palestinian Judaism to designate the anointed agent who would be sent by God for the welfare or salvation of God's people. After the resurrection the followers of Jesus used the title as a way of speaking about Jesus.

As used of the followers of Jesus, the term *Christian* was probably more a nickname or even a term of reproach (see Acts 26:28) than a title of honor. The use of the term highlights the great significance of the

Antiochene mission: Christians were beginning to be seen as a group distinct from Judaism. The Christians themselves would soon have to face the question of how they were related to God's plan of salvation proclaimed and revealed in Judaism.

There is one further detail which scholars believe is historically reliable and deserves our attention: the list of "prophets and teachers" at Antioch in Acts 13:1. Barnabas is put at the head of the list, another indication that he, and not either Peter or Paul, was the most prominent leader in the beginnings of the Christian missionary movement. Next listed is "Symeon who was called Niger." Symeon is a Jewish name; Niger is the Latin word for "black." Symeon must have been dark skinned or possibly black and may have been a proselyte whose family came originally from the Western (Latin) section of North Africa. Fourth on the list is Manaen (or Menahem) a companion since childhood of Herod Antipas, tetrarch of Galilee and Perea. That such a person should be a leader in the early days of the Antiochene church is an indication that Christianity did not start out as a "slave" religion but had within it members of the higher strata of society. Luke's list of the leaders at Antioch mentions no women, though clearly Paul's letters recognize the prominence of women in the early Christian missionary efforts and in the early house churches. Luke, in Acts 21:9, mentions that the daughters of Philip, one of the Seven, were known as prophets in the early church. In our next chapter we will look more closely at the role of women in the early Church.

Paul's Conversion and Early Missionary Activity

Before introducing Paul to our story it is necessary to make an important observation on the method scholars use in approaching the history of Paul. It is commonly recognized in current biblical scholarship that the historical details of Paul's life in Acts and those in Paul's own letters (more often than not given only indirectly) do not always agree. The conventional reconstruction of the chronology of Paul relied very heavily on Acts when it agreed with Paul's own statements and tended to ignore information in Acts contradicted by Paul's letters.

More recent reconstructions of the chronology of Paul accept the principle that the Pauline letters should be given priority over the information in Acts. While this principle is generally accepted, scholars do not always agree on the application of the principle. Thus various chronologies of Paul's life and missionary activity still show marked discrepancies. Scholarly works deal at length and in great detail with many of

these matters. For our purposes, it will suffice to indicate the general
lines of current Pauline scholarship.

Scholars place the conversion of Paul at about the same time as the
martyrdom of Stephen and dispersion of the Hellenists. Paul came from
the city of Tarsus, the capital city of the Roman province of Cilicia,
adjacent to the province of Syria at the Mediterranean edge of Asia
Minor. Because of its geographical location Tarsus was a flourishing
trade and commercial center; it was also renowned as a center of Greek
culture.

Paul was a diaspora Jew, one who possessed Roman citizenship.
(Paul was a Roman name; the name Saul was probably a more familiar
Jewish name used by members of his own faith.) Paul was a Pharisee of
the more strictly orthodox school of thought, i.e., one which insisted
upon circumcision and the full observance of the Mosaic law for all
proselytes who wished to join the synagogues of diaspora Judaism.
There are good grounds for believing that Paul participated in the
Pharisaic missionary movement in the diaspora though within the limits
of strict orthodoxy. Paul's persecution of the Christians before his own
conversion was directed not against all Christians generally, but against
those Hellenist Christians who called into question the place of the
temple and who did not insist on the Mosaic law of circumcision, and
who challenged a claim to salvation exclusively tied to Judaism. His
persecution was carried on within the framework of the internal penal
authority (scourging, ban, excommunication) of the orthodox Pharisaic
synagogues of the diaspora.

Paul's persecution of the Hellenist believers took him to Damascus,
in the southern part of Syria. Acts' account of Paul's presence at Stephen's death and of his functioning in Damascus under orders from the
high priest at Jerusalem (Acts 8:1; 9:1–2) are not, on several counts,
considered reliable. For one, Paul tells us in Galatians 1:22 that he was
not known by sight to the churches in Judea (and thus in Jerusalem);
also, the high priest in Jerusalem would have no jurisdiction in Damascus, a Syrian city in a Roman province far beyond the frontiers of
Judea. It was in Damascus that Paul experienced his conversion and
received his call as an apostle. According to Paul's own account in
Galatians 1, after his conversion he went to Arabia, the Gentile district
east of the Jordan River and southeast of Damascus. The image of
Paul's spending a period of monastic solitude in the desert finds no
support in his letters; it probably reflects the concerns of the traditions
of the anchorites in the early church. The district of Arabia was the
home of nomadic Bedouins but also the location of such Hellenistic

cities as Petra, the residence of the Nabatean king Aretas IV (9 B.C.–
A.D. 9), and the cities of Gerasa and Philadelphia (present-day
Amman, the capital city of the kingdom of Jordan). Given Paul's
strong sense of mission we presume that Paul spent this time preaching
the gospel, though it seems that his preaching bore little success since
we have no record of any such success in Acts or in his own letters.
Probably his lack of success and the possible opposition he stirred led
to his return to Damascus (Gal 1:17). Here Paul's preaching met opposition from Jewish groups supported by the ethnarch of the Nabatean
king. Paul had to make an unceremonious exit in a basket through a
window in the city wall (2 Cor 11:33; see Acts 9:23ff).

Only then, two to three years after his conversion, did Paul go for the
first time to Jerusalem. The purpose of his trip was to visit Peter, Paul
tells us (Gal 1:18), though he also saw James, the brother of the Lord.
After this short visit to Jerusalem Paul took his preaching to the regions
of Syria and his native Cilicia (Gal 1:21). Evidently Paul's work in these
regions succeeded, for news of his ministry reached Judea (Gal 1:22ff
and Acts 15:23, 36, 41). At one point, exactly when is unclear, Barnabas
called Paul to help him in the Antiochene mission. This association is
significant: now Paul had an increasingly important church as a base for
his missionary efforts.

Acts 13:4–14:26 describes a missionary journey undertaken by Barnabas, Paul, and John Mark to the island of Cyprus and to the cities of
south and central Asia Minor (modern day Turkey). From this mention
in Acts, Paul's journey to Cyprus and the cities of Asia Minor has been
called his first missionary journey, although actually his journey to Arabia, Syria and Cilicia was earlier. Luke gives precedence to Barnabas'
name in the first part of his account; this may suggest that Barnabas had
been the leader of the group at the start of the mission. In Luke's
account, it was this mission which brought to the surface the issue of the
relation between Gentile Christians and the earlier Jewish converts.
Probably this mission took place in the years between A.D. 46 and 49.

The dating of the mission to Cyprus and Asia Minor in Acts 13–14 has
been challenged. Brief but precise as it is in dates and places,
Galatians 1 makes no mention of this journey to Cyprus and Asia
Minor. Hence some scholars have concluded that the journey took
place following the assembly described in Acts 15. Such a position
dates the assembly in the year 48 and the journey to Cyprus and Asia
Minor later in that year and in the next. In that case the issues concerning the relation between Jewish law and Gentile believers surfaced in
the Hellenist and Pauline missions as we discussed them earlier.

Persecution at Jerusalem: The Death of James

The success of the Hellenist and Pauline missions did not take place
without problems. The first of these was another persecution in the
Jerusalem church.

Some background will help. In Chapter Two we learned that after the
death of Herod the Great in 4 B.C. the kingdom of Judea was divided
among three of Herod's sons: Galilee and Perea went to Herod Antipas
(died A.D. 39); the northern Transjordan region went to Philip (died A.D.
34); Judea, Samaria, and Idumea went to Archelaeus. Archelaeus was
removed in A.D. 6 and the territory was placed under the direction of
Roman prefects. The best known was Pontius Pilate (A.D. 26–36). In the
late 30s and early 40s, when Gaius Caligula (A.D. 37–41) and Claudius
(A.D. 41–54) were emperors, these various territories were gradually
reunited under the grandson of Herod the Great, Herod Agrippa I,
who, by leave of the emperors, was given the title king of Judea.

Herod Agrippa I gave strong support to Jewish interests in the territory under his control. As a consequence he avoided or opposed whatever seemed to support the spread of Greek culture or Greek thought.
Probably in an effort to court the support of the Pharisees Herod
Agrippa undertook the persecution of the Christians referred to in Acts
12:1–19. Generally dated around A.D. 42, this persecution took the form
of an attack on the apostles and probably was an attempt to cripple a
movement that by this time was increasingly associated with Gentiles
and those identified with Greek ways of thought. In the persecution
James, the son of Zebedee and one of the best known on the Twelve,
was executed. Peter was himself imprisoned. Though rescued, he was
forced to leave Jerusalem. James, the brother of the Lord apparently
remained acceptable to Jewish authorities in a way the others were not.
This series of events reinforced James as the leading voice in the Jerusalem Christian community.

In Galatians 1:19, Paul refers to this James as "the brother of the
Lord." This is probably the same James mentioned in Mark 6:1–3 and
Matthew 13:55–56 as a brother of Jesus. The Greek word used in the
New Testament is *adelphos*. The word may mean "blood brother" or
have one of several other meanings: "co-religionist" (Rom 9:3),
"neighbor" (Mt 22:22–24), "step-brother" (Mk 6:17–18). The New
Testament text leaves the precise significance of the Greek word in
doubt.

Scholars regard the James in question as a relative of Jesus who,
after distancing himself from Jesus (see Mk 3:19b–21, 31–35; Jn 7:5),

later became a believer and ultimately the leader of the Aramaic-speaking Jewish Christians in Jerusalem.

An earlier view that at this juncture (the time of Herod Agrippa's persecution) James replaced Peter as head of the Jerusalem church is today called into question. Such an understanding does not do justice to the different roles of Peter and James at Jerusalem. Peter was a dominant figure among the earliest believers, but, scholars believe, was probably never head of the Jerusalem church. When that church became large and complex enough to need regular administrators, as we saw in the case of the Hellenists, the Hebrew Christians were guided not by one of the Twelve but by James and the elders chosen with him.

Interestingly, after his execution, James the son of Zebedee was not replaced, as Judas had been replaced by Matthias. This is an indication that the role of the Twelve diminished as the mission of the community extended beyond Jerusalem. The symbolic end-time role of the Twelve, though, was preserved in later Christian tradition (see Rev 21:14).

After the death of Herod Agrippa I in A.D. 44, the emperor Claudius, probably fearful of encouraging Jewish nationalism, placed the territory of Palestine under Roman control. Thus began the second procuratorship which now included Galilee as well as Judea and Samaria. This political arrangement lasted until the outbreak of the Jewish War in A.D. 66.

Jewish Christians and Gentile Converts

Resulting from the preaching missions of the Hellenists and of Barnabas and Paul—from the mid 30s to the mid or late 40s—the increasing numbers of Gentile converts raised a serious and acute problem for the early church. The problem centered on the relationship between the Christian message and Jewish circumcision and Mosaic law. A review of the leading positions and personalities helps us understand the significance of this issue and prepares for the apostolic conference described in Acts 15 and Galatians 2.

Today scholars have abandoned as simplistic the notion that in the early church there were two dominant ways, a "Gentile Christian" approach associated with Paul and a "Jewish Christian" understanding associated with those who opposed Paul. A careful study of the New Testament writings shows at least four basic positions. (The analysis which follows is based on the work of R. E. Brown.)

The *first group* consisted of Jewish Christians and their Gentile converts who insisted on the full observance of the Mosaic law, including circumcision. In effect, this ultraconservative position insisted, in effect,

that Gentiles had to become Jews to receive the full salvation brought by
Jesus Christ. Jewish Christians at Jerusalem, called at times the "circumcision party" (Acts 11:2), held this position and carried on an active
mission among Gentiles, making inroads in Galatia in Asia Minor and
among Gentile converts in some of the cities of Greece (see Phil 3).

A *second group* consisted of Jewish Christians and Gentile converts
who did not insist on circumcision but who required Gentile converts to
observe some of the Jewish purity laws. This movement, too, originated
in Jerusalem and was associated with Peter and with James, the brother
of the Lord and head of the Jerusalem church. Those identified with this
position became the dominant voice at Jerusalem and Antioch, and
probably at Rome and in Pontus, Cappadocia and sections of the province of Asia. They too carried on an active mission effort among the
Gentiles.

A *third group* consisted of Jewish Christians and their Gentile converts who did not insist on circumcision as salvific for Gentile converts
and who did not require converted Gentiles to observe Jewish food laws.
This position was most closely associated with the earlier Antioch mission and has Paul as its most prominent representative. These Christians
did not demand a break with Jewish cultic practices associated with the
great Jewish feasts and with the temple, nor did they require Jewish
Christians to abandon circumcision and the law.

The *fourth group* was the most radical in its break with Judaism. This
group consisted of Jewish Christians and their Gentile converts who did
not insist on circumcision and Jewish food laws and saw no lasting significance in Jewish worship (temple and feasts). This position is associated
with the Hellenists, Stephen, Philip, and the rest of the Seven. The
movement which held this position began in Jerusalem and spread to
Samaria and eventually to Phoenicia, Cyprus and Antioch (Acts 11:19–
20). Later this type of Christianity became more radicalized and, as
such, found expression in the fourth gospel and in the epistle to the
Hebrews. In these writings the temple sacrifices and the priesthood are
considered abrogated and Jewish feasts have become alien "feasts of the
Jews." In this type of Christianity the break with Judaism is most emphasized, resulting in the perception of Judaism and Christianity as two
distinct religions. In the chapters which follow we will see in greater
detail how this came about; but having some introduction helps us to
make our way.

These positions were not hard and fast. In fact scholars find a spectrum within each group. In some ways James in group two may be closer
to the first group while Peter, also in the second group, is closer to group
three. We will also see that Paul's position in his letter to the Galatians is

quite radical, leaning to the position of group four, while his letter to the Romans is in some ways not too far from the position of group two.

The Assembly at Jerusalem

From this schematic summary we return to our story of the early church's missionary outreach and the problems which that mission brought in its wake. Three events are of special significance: the assembly at Jerusalem, the disagreement between Peter and Paul at Antioch, and the decision of James. The sources of our knowledge are twofold: Acts 15 and Galatians 2:1–10 and 11–14. Almost all exegetes agree that priority should be given to Paul's own testimony though we are aware that this is not free of polemical bias. The letter to the Galatians was written, probably in the mid-50s, in the heat of Paul's struggles with the "Judaizers" (group one) who were challenging the gospel Paul preached at Galatia some years earlier. Luke's account, written in the 80s, is influenced by his overriding interest in showing the onemindedness of the early church. These limitations must be kept in mind as we read these texts.

The first verses of Acts 15 tell us that representatives from one of the groups in Jerusalem (group one) came to Antioch and insisted that the salvation proclaimed by the Christian gospel was impossible according to the law of Moses without circumcision. Obviously such a claim contradicted the preaching at Antioch and the mission which had Antioch as its base. Paul's own account stresses his independence in trying to get the issue resolved: he says he went up to Jerusalem because of a "revelation" (Gal 2:2). In any event, Paul, Barnabas, and some others traveled to Jerusalem to settle the matter (Acts 15:2). A bit provocatively, perhaps, Paul took the uncircumcised Titus to accompany them (Gal 2:1, 3). Interestingly, for all Paul's independence, he did bring the matter to Jerusalem for resolution and admitted that if the church in Jerusalem decided against his position, he would have run in vain (Gal 2:2). This suggests that Jerusalem's influence extended far beyond Antioch.

The meeting at Jerusalem, commonly though not unanimously thought to have taken place around A.D. 48 or 49, led to a settlement of the problem. Paul mentions that he discussed the issues at stake with James, Peter and John, though discussion may have taken place in a larger meeting as well. Luke speaks of a formal assembly with the apostles and elders. (Some scholars avoid the word "council" here because the term suggests ideas about the church which came into place later on.) In Luke's account, both Peter and James speak against the need of circumcision for Gentile converts, and the entire assembly—apostles, elders and the whole church—accepts their view. (As we will see, the speech of James probably comes from another occasion.) The Antiochene mission was free to continue its evangelization of the Gentiles without demanding circumcision. The group which demanded circumcision lost at the Jerusalem meeting, though we have no record that they were ever repudiated by James.

A brief recollection of the two hundred years of Jewish history before the time of Jesus helps us understand why circumcision was such an issue for the Jewish Christians who insisted on it so strongly. The ancient rite was a mark of identity, a sign of Israel's election as God's people. Pious Jews died rather than deny its necessity. The Jewish Christians saw in the rite a sign of the physical continuity of their saving history and the legitimation of their claim to be the true Israel as distinguished from those Jews who did not accept the belief that God's Messiah had come in Jesus and that the end-time dawned in him. Later polemics within the Christian church (and between it and Judaism) ought not to blind us to what must have been the deeply held convictions of many of those who opposed the stance of Paul, Barnabas, and the Antiochene church.

It is also very important that neither side on this issue could appeal to Jesus for clear guidelines. These disciples struggled to be faithful to Jesus and to traditions regarded as coming from God, but they disagreed strongly with each other about the necessity of circumcision.

Paul Confronts Peter at Antioch

Not long after Paul returned to Antioch from the Jerusalem assembly, Peter himself went to the Syrian capital and joined Paul in meals with Gentile Christians without observing Jewish regulations concerning meals with non-Jews. Soon "some people from James" (Gal 2:12) came to Antioch and were critical of Peter for his eating with the Gentile converts. Peter accepted their criticism and separated himself from the Gentiles. Other Jewish Christians, including Barnabas, followed Peter's example. Paul protested Peter's position and "opposed him to his face, because he stood condemned" (Gal 2:11). In Paul's mind, Peter and those who followed his example "were not straightforward about the truth of the gospel." From his subsequent actions we gather that Paul lost the argument. With new co-workers and without Barnabas, Paul soon set out on a lengthy mission to Asia Minor and Greece. Paul never mentions Syrian Antioch again in his letters though Acts says he did return to Antioch for another visit (Acts 18:22). He may have set out on his new mission with a feeling of isolation from the church at Antioch.

In Acts 15:36–40, Luke explains that the separation of Barnabas from

Paul arose out of a disagreement between them about whether John Mark would be allowed to accompany them; he had left them during an earlier mission (Acts 13:13). Luke's explanation may have some foundation in fact, though Paul's account suggests that there was more to it. Luke may not have known about the clash between Paul and Barnabas as Paul describes it, or he may simply have chosen not to mention it.

The Proposal from James and the Letter from Jerusalem

The issue that led to the disagreement between Peter and Paul also stands behind the second part of Acts 15, the speech of James and the letter sent to Antioch, Syria, and Cilicia (Acts 15:13–30). Today the majority of scholars holds that Acts 15 really has two basic traditions behind it, one concerning the struggle over the issue of circumcision and the other concerning the regulations proposed by James and imposed by the apostles and elders. Further, most scholars believe that this second meeting came only later and separately from the conference on the matter of circumcision. Hypotheses attempting to reconstruct the events may never achieve consensus, but a respected position is this: After the first meeting between the Antiochene group and the Jerusalem leaders, the circumcision-free mission of the Antiochene group was permitted; Peter's agreeing with Paul was the decisive factor. After this decision Paul, and the delegation with him, returned to Antioch.

Some time later, quite possibly to settle the rift provoked by the quarrel between Peter, Paul, and James, or at least in the context of that rift, a second Jerusalem meeting took place. To settle the issue of the problems raised by common meals shared between Jewish and Gentile Christians, James and the Jerusalem leaders decreed that the Gentile Christians should follow the observances of Leviticus 17–18 concerning foreigners residing in Israel. The four regulations were prohibitions: from eating food sacrificed to idols, from the use of animal blood, from eating the flesh of an animal strangled with its blood still inside, and from sexual relations and marriages within forbidden degrees of kindred. A letter with a statement of these regulations was sent to the local churches of Antioch, Syria, and Cilicia.

These regulations came from what the Pentateuch considered binding on resident aliens, an implicit insult to Gentile Christians, but they were put forward with the hope of making common life possible for a church composed of different ethnic groups. That James should be the decision-maker at this second meeting indicates how clearly he was leader of the Jerusalem community and how far his influence extended beyond Judea.

The Church at Antioch After Paul's Departure

Even as the persecution and subsequent departure of the Hellenists from Jerusalem had an impact on the character and outlook of the church in the Judean capital, so we may expect that the departure of Paul and the increasing influence of Jerusalem had an influence on the church in the Syrian capital. Evidence about the Antiochene church in the 50s is meager, but there are clues which give some basis for scholarly conjecture. Two later writings associated with Antioch (Matthew's gospel and the letters of Ignatius) show a Christian church made up of Jews and Gentiles distinct from both the Jewish synagogue and groups of dissident Christians.

We learn of "false prophets" at Antioch from Matthew and of docetists and Judaizers from Ignatius. Docetists (from the Greek *dokeo*, "to appear") were a heretical group who taught that Jesus was not truly human but only appeared as such. But we have no evidence of rival churches set up by those who followed Jerusalem and those who followed Paul, or between Jewish Christians and Gentile Christians. While some Gentile Christians may have accepted circumcision after Paul's departure (circumcision was not required, but neither was it forbidden), it seems most likely that Gentile Christians and Jewish Christians abided by the wishes of the James party by holding separate meals (and separate eucharists as well?). From Paul's writings a few years later we may guess that such an arrangement was a very unhappy one (see Paul's teaching on the eucharist in 1 Cor 11), and his absenting himself from Antioch may have been influenced by his desire to avoid a schism. Scholars think it may well have been Peter who played a moderating role in the Antiochene church by holding the various groups together. This may be a factor in the prominent role given to Peter in Matthew's gospel, written, most scholars suggest, in the area of Antioch some thirty years after the events we are describing. It may also stand behind the later tradition that Peter was in some way a founder of the Antiochene Church.

While the Antioch church did not split, there are suggestions of various groups within the one church. The "left wing," composed of Jewish converts and predominantly Gentile Christians, wanted a totally unhindered universal mission. These people stressed baptism rather than circumcision as an initiation rite into a community where all were equally members of the one people of God and where Jesus, rather than the Mosaic law, was the touchstone of Christian conduct. A tradition such as Matthew's great commission scene (Mt 28:16–20) could well have come from this group in the Antiochene church. Assuming an historical substratum for the story of Cornelius in Acts 10, where Peter is led to receive a Gentile into the community, it is reasonable to see Peter as sympathetic to the "left-wing" view.

The "right wing" of the Antiochene church was composed of the Christians who followed the leadership of James. This group would act as a brake on the universalist mission outlook of the Hellenist Christians; no doubt it found much support in such narrow mission statements as Matthew 10:5–6 and 15:24. Along with Peter's mediating role, the regulations from James (Acts 15:20, 29) may have kept this group from separating itself from the group of "left-wing" Christians mentioned above.

Scholars also credit the Hellenist Jewish Christians, who had initially brought the gospel to the Gentiles at Antioch, with performing a mediating role as well. There is no reason to believe that all the Hellenists, some of whom were more radical than Paul (recall group four in the schema given above), left the city after the departure of Paul and Barnabas. Those who remained were very open to the concerns and outlook of the Gentile Christians and no doubt gave them strong support; yet because the Hellenists were Jewish-Christians, and because of the increasing importance of James as a leader of the Jerusalem church, doubtless they served as an influence, keeping the two wings of the Antiochene church from splitting apart.

If scholarly focus on the very strong tensions between different viewpoints in the early church surprises us, that may be an indication of how successful Luke was in portraying the singlemindedness of the early church. (We should remember, though, that it is Luke himself who tells us about the tensions between the Hellenists and the Hebrews.) A close study of the evidence shows that the story of the early church was quite complex. We will see more of the church at Antioch in Chapter Seven.

The Beginnings of the Church at Rome

Before bringing this chapter to a close we should mention another significant church, the church at Rome, which had its beginnings during the period we are discussing. While available evidence is indirect, scholars have reconstructed the outlines of Christian beginnings at Rome, as well as the outline of the Jewish community with which it was so closely associated.

Jews came to Rome only well after they were firmly settled in Alexandria and Babylon. Only when Rome became a world power and the city itself a commercial center do we have evidence of a Jewish presence there. Our first evidence of Jews in Rome comes from ca. 139 B.C., though it probably refers to Jewish visitors or merchants rather than residents. In the next century Jewish immigrants and captives from the Palestine/Syrian area formed most of the Jewish population in Rome. One of the writings of the Roman orator Cicero, in 59 B.C., suggests a considerable Jewish presence in the city at that time. Jewish support of successive Roman leaders secured legal tolerance and privileges for Jews in the Empire and in Rome itself. Estimates of Jewish numbers in Rome in the first century A.D. range from a low of twenty thousand to a high of forty to fifty thousand.

An important aspect of Roman Judaism was its close political and intellectual affiliation with Jerusalem. There were close ties between the Herodian family and the Julio-Claudian dynasty of emperors. It was with the approval of Mark Anthony and Octavian (later Augustus) that Herod the Great presided over the kingdom of Judah, while later emperors, Caligula (A.D. 37–41) and Claudius (A.D. 41–54), returned most of the lands of Palestine to Herod Agrippa I. Intellectually there were also strong ties between the Jews at Rome and the leadership in Jerusalem. While most of our evidence for the latter dates from after the fall of Jerusalem (A.D. 70), we see an indication in Acts 28:21 that, even in the early 60s, Jewish leaders in Rome looked to Jerusalem for guidance. Acts reports that the local Jewish leaders told Paul when he arrived at Rome, "We have received no letters from Judea about you."

The presence of a prominent Jewish community at Rome supports the idea that it was not long before Jewish Christians brought their message to Rome even as they brought it to Damascus and Antioch as well.

We do not know exactly when Christianity was brought to Rome; scholarly opinion places its arrival there in the early 40s. There is no evidence that it was the mission center at Antioch which brought the gospel to Rome, while there is considerable indirect support for the view that Jerusalem was the source for Roman Christianity. From writings associated with the city of Rome—Paul's letter to the Romans, 1 Peter and Hebrews, and the first letter of Clement—a strong case can be made that Roman Christianity was clearly of the type of Jewish/Gentile Christianity associated with such figures as Peter and James.

Non-biblical references shed some light on the early years of Roman Christianity. One such reference comes from the second century Roman historian Suetonius who states that the emperor Claudius (A.D. 41–54) "expelled Jews from Rome because of their constant disturbances impelled by Chrestus." Although the statement is cryptic and although we cannot be certain about what Suetonius is referring to, we do know that in the second century "Christus" (Christ) was often written with an "e" instead of an "i." This has led scholars to wonder if the Roman author might be giving us a garbled record of struggles among Jews over Christ. It might well be that Jews who accepted Jesus as the Messiah got into squabbles with Jews who rejected this claim and Claudius, known for his low tolerance for dissension, expelled from Rome those who were most vocal in the debate over Christ. We do not know when such an expulsion took place, though the early fifth century writer Orosius placed the event in A.D. 49, roughly around the time of the Jerusalem meeting over the issue of circumcision.

This reading of Suetonius receives some confirmation in Acts 18:2–3 where Luke states that the Jew Aquila and his wife Priscilla came from Rome to Corinth "because Claudius had commanded all the Jews to leave Rome." We know from Romans 16:3 that Aquila and Priscilla (Prisca) were, later on, zealous Christian missionaries. Since there is no mention of their conversion after their departure, scholars think it almost certain that they were already believers in Jesus when they were expelled. With the support it receives from Acts, the text from Suetonius leads to the plausible hypothesis that already at the end of the 40s there was in Rome a Christian mission strong enough to cause friction and to lead to the emperor's attempt to end it.

Usually dated around A.D. 58, Paul's letter to the Romans itself supposes that the Christian community had existed there for some years. Paul remarks that he had been wishing for "many years" to come to the Christians at Rome (15:23). The strong case for Christianity's arrival in the early 40s (while Peter was still in Jerusalem) discredits the idea that Peter was the original missionary to Rome and the founder of the Roman Church. Our best evidence, Paul's letter to the Romans, suggests that Peter did not have any significant association with the Roman church before A.D. 58. It may be that Peter came to Rome only in the early 60s. We will see more of this in Chapter Six.

Chapter Five

The Churches in the Letters of Paul

Our principal source for understanding the development of the church in the 50s and early 60s comes from the letters of Paul. These letters constitute an invaluable resource for modern scholarship. Yet most if not all of them were written to respond to quite specific pastoral needs and thus do not give us a complete description of the church generally for this period or of the various local churches for which the letters were written. At best we have glimpses of particular aspects of different churches. The Book of Acts provides some details as well, though these are sketchy and must be used carefully. Given the nature of these sources, we must be content to catch such scenes as we can of individual churches as they appear in Paul's letters. In a secondary way, details of the missionary activity of Paul and others are included to help us appreciate the development of the church's mission.

It is common in current biblical scholarship to distinguish between the letters written by the apostle himself and the post-Pauline or deutero-Pauline letters written by disciples of Paul after his death. The seven letters unanimously attributed to Paul are: 1 Thessalonians, 1 and 2 Corinthians, Galatians, Philippians, Philemon, and Romans. Scholars do not agree on the authenticity or dates of the remaining letters. R. E. Brown estimates that, in a very broad approximation, sixty percent of critical scholarship judges that Paul did not write Colossians, eighty percent that he did not write Ephesians, and ninety percent that he did not write the pastorals (1 and 2 Timothy and Titus). The view that Paul wrote the letter to the Hebrews is now almost universally abandoned. Scholars date the post-Pauline letters in this way: Possibly Colossians was composed within a decade of the apostle's lifetime. It is difficult to date Ephesians; the period between A.D. 80–100 is plausible. The pastorals may well have been written in the same period. Hebrews is reasonably dated in the period 65–95. The authorship of 2 Thessalonians is disputed: W. G. Kummel thinks the letter was written by Paul a few weeks after 1 Thessalonians; N. Perrin holds that the letter was written by someone a generation after Paul.

The Church at Thessalonica

The earliest of Paul's letters was that written to the church at Thessalonica (the city of Salonika in modern day Greece). The city was founded in 314 B.C. by one of the generals of Alexander the Great who brought together the inhabitants of twenty-six villages in the region. The new city had a strategic location on the Thermaic Gulf of the Aegean Sea. When the Romans annexed the territory of this region in 146 B.C. they made Thessalonica the capital of the province of Macedonia. In Paul's day it was the second largest city of Greece and the seat of a Roman proconsul.

It is only in Acts (17:1–10) that we learn of the founding of Thessalonica's church. The traditional date assigned for the arrival of Paul, Silvanus, and Timothy at Thessalonica is about A.D. 50. According to Acts, the mission at Thessalonica began at the local Jewish synagogue with its numerous Gentile "God-fearers." After three sabbaths in the synagogue with apparently little success (Acts 17:2), the Christian missioners provoked the hostility of some of the Jews and moved their activity to the home of a certain Jason. They converted "a great many of the devout Greeks and not a few of the leading women" (Acts 17:4), but opposition continued and eventually Paul, Silvanus, and Timothy were forced to leave the city. Acts implies that the missioners' stay in Thessalonica was only a few weeks (Acts 17:2); some scholars, using 1 Thessalonians 2:9 as a basis, think that Paul and his co-workers may have been there for several months, though the stay was still not long enough to complete teaching former pagans what was needed to adopt a mature Christian faith. During his stay at the Macedonian capital Paul earned his own living so as not to burden anyone.

In Luke's account of Paul's missionary activity there is a recurring pattern in the way Paul conducts his mission. He begins always by preaching in the local synagogue. Even though Paul might be given a welcome reception, opposition develops and forces him to direct his preaching to others. Luke also portrays Paul as addressing four distinct groups: (Aramaic-speaking?) Jews; Greek-speaking Jews; proselytes; and "God-fearers." Paul's letters say nothing of preaching in the synagogues. Further, his principal efforts are directed to Gentiles and, among them, especially people involved in the workplaces of the city. No doubt Luke's account is influenced by his theological motif: the gospel is first preached to the Jews, then to the Gentiles. Paul's letters surely give a more accurate record of the details of Paul's mission, though not necessarily of Paul's role; it is possible that Paul subconsciously exaggerates his own role in these missionary efforts.

After leaving Thessalonica, Paul and the others went to Beroea. According to Luke (Acts 17:10–15) a pattern of similar events followed: association with the local Jewish synagogue; conversions, this time by many of the Jews and "not a few Greek women of high standing as well as men"; opposition, now from Jews who followed from Thessalonica; and expulsion, this time of Paul alone. Paul went to Athens. Left at Beroea, Silvanus and Timothy joined Paul at Athens. Paul then continued his interrupted ministry to the young church at Thessalonica by sending Timothy back to strengthen the church in the face of continued opposition. When Timothy returned with a report, Paul (now at Corinth) wrote 1 Thessalonians, which became the first book of the church's liturgical library now called the New Testament. The letter, an authoritative statement and a liturgical document, is generally dated at A.D. 51. It was to be read and listened to in the prayerful setting of community worship.

Through the letter we catch glimpses of the church at Thessalonica. The church was composed mostly of Gentile Christians (1 Thes 1:9). Although Paul and the others stayed only a few months, the church was soon strong enough to become an influence in the neighboring districts. Paul commended the church for this in the first part of his letter (1 Thes 1:2–10). Yet the members of the church met continued opposition, as its missionary founders experienced during their stay at Thessalonica. The opposition was one of the reasons why Paul sent Timothy back to the city.

Paul's letter gives no evidence of abuses, though there was still need for instruction in the basics of the Christian life (1 Thes 3:9–5:11). Paul's teaching falls into three areas: (1) questions about the return of Jesus (some were disturbed by the delay in Christ's return and worried about the fate of those who died before it took place); (2) a plea for moral responsibility; (3) an exhortation to mutual love.

We also get a glimpse of leadership in an early church in this first of Paul's letters. First, the letter is addressed to the entire community. Paul assumes that the whole church will listen to his words and make appropriate responses. Nonetheless he recognizes the presence of leadership roles: his own, by the letter he writes; that of Timothy, sent by Paul "to establish you [the Thessalonian Christians] in your faith and to exhort you" (1 Thes 3:2); and "those who labor among you and are over you in the Lord and admonish you" (1 Thes 5:12). These last should be respected and esteemed very highly because of their work (1 Thes 5:12–13). Paul's words about the leaders are vague. We cannot say, for example, whether Paul looked upon them as a distinct group. The letter's lack of precision suggests that the authority figures have no titles. Probably, organizational structures were not yet fixed. But the letter does indicate that a special ministry was beginning to emerge in the church, even in a church still strongly influenced by the expectation of the imminent return of Jesus.

> We cannot be certain about the chronology of Paul's life or the dates of his letters. The analysis of J. A. Fitzmyer in the *Jerome Biblical Commentary* is followed in this book. A recent study on the chronology of Paul by G. Luedemann places Paul's mission to Macedonia and Achaia several years before the Jerusalem assembly. In this schema 1 Thessalonians is dated ca. A.D. 41. If accurate, such a chronology spreads out the span of Paul's missionary activity and calls for greater development in his theology.
>
> 2 Thessalonians is concerned with quite different matters. The coming of Christ is much further off. The Thessalonians themselves are facing difficulties not unlike the persecution in the Book of Revelation. For these reasons, some authors think 2 Thessalonians (apparently a deliberate imitation of 1 Thessalonians) was written in the generation after Paul's ministry. Paul is still looked upon as an important authority for the church in this changed situation.
>
> Other authors regard the letter as written by Paul, possibly shortly after 1 Thessalonians.

Failure at Athens

After Paul's stay at Thessalonica he went to Beroea and then, alone, to Athens, the capital of modern Greece. Paul makes brief mention of this visit in 1 Thessalonians 3:1. It is Luke who gives us the well-known tableau of Paul's stay at Athens which culminated in his speech on the Areopagus (Acts 17:16–34).

In the first century A.D. the city of Athens had become politically insignificant, though it retained its prestige as a center and symbol of Hellenistic learning and piety. According to current scholarship, Luke's account is more a reflection of his desire to portray the proclamation of the Christian gospel at the center of Hellenism than an historical remembrance. Very probably Paul preached at Athens. He himself refers to his preaching there. But his ministry seemed ineffective. Paul mentions no success at Athens in his letters. Luke speaks of only modest success

(Acts 17:34) and says nothing of the foundation of a church there. Had it been otherwise he would have mentioned it.

Luke lists among Paul's converts at Athens a woman named Damaris and Dionysius, a member of the court (the term "Areopagus" refers to both the rocky hill on which the court of Athens met and the court itself). To this Dionysius was attributed an important group of writings significant for its attempt to unite Christian and Neoplatonic thought. Because of their supposed authorship the writings enjoyed an immense popularity and authority in the Middle Ages. The writings are now commonly recognized as the work of an anonymous fifth century Syrian—the so-called Pseudo-Dionysius. In the ninth century Dionysius the Areopagite was mistakenly identified with St. Dionysius (St. Denys), the bishop of Paris and the patron saint of France.

The Churches at Galatia

The second of Paul's letters is the letter to the church or churches at Galatia (assuming that 2 Thessalonians was not written by Paul). Scholars are not agreed about the recipients of this letter. In the dominant view—sometimes called the "North Galatian" theory—the term "Galatia" refers to the territory in the central parts of Asia Minor which Paul visited during what Acts describes as his second missionary journey (15:40–18:22), taken after the assembly at Jerusalem. Paul preached in this area in Acts 16:6–7 and 18:23. In the minority view—known as the "South Galatian" theory—Paul's letter was meant for the Roman province of Galatia along the seacoast including such towns as Antioch in Pisidia, Iconium, Lystra, and Derbe. According to Acts 13:4–14:26 Paul and his companions evangelized this area during the missionary journey which took place before the Jerusalem assembly. The majority of scholars regard the North Galatian theory as more probable—that the letter was addressed to the churches in the territory which comprises the central portion of modern day Turkey.

Paul and his companions were the first to bring the gospel to Galatia and to a predominantly Gentile audience. Paul's own stay may have been unintended: he became ill as he was passing through (Gal 4:13–14). After his departure, other Christian missionaries came asserting that Paul's message to the Galatians was not complete. This second missionary group insisted that Gentiles observe circumcision (Gal 5:2–3 and 6:12) and possibly some other requirements of the Mosaic law. These opponents of Paul remain unknown. Quite likely they were Jewish converts to Christianity who sought to harmonize their former faith with belief in Jesus (members of group one in the schema in the last chapter). In doing so they attacked Paul's credibility as an apostle. This explains Paul's self-defense in the first part of his letter (Gal 1:11–2:14). Clearly the Galatian churches faced a crisis over the issue of the relationship between Christian faith and the Mosaic law.

Paul's response to this situation is the polemic in his letter to the Galatians (probably written around A.D. 54). Paul strongly repudiates the argument of the Jewish Christian missionaries. In what has been called "the savagery" of his attack, Paul ties together his opposition to the Jewish missionaries in Galatia and his previous opposition to Peter and James at Antioch, and includes a derogatory reference to the latter as the "so-called pillars" of the Jerusalem church (Gal 2:9). In this context Paul refers to the Jerusalem assembly and his commission to preach to the Gentiles (Gal 2:7, 9). Perhaps Paul's Galatian adversaries later carried word of Paul's attack to Jerusalem, for Luke tells of the rumor that Paul was teaching Jewish Christians "to forsake Moses, telling them not to circumcise their children or observe the [Jewish] customs" (Acts 21:21). The rumor was false, since Paul was arguing that these impositions should not be imposed on Gentiles. But the rumor may have received a hearing in Jerusalem and explains Paul's fears, later on, that his collection for the relief of the Jerusalem church might not be accepted (Rom 15:25–32).

Yet for all the forcefulness of Paul's repudiation of his Jewish Christian adversaries, he concludes his letter with words similar to a standard prayer in the Jewish synagogue liturgy. Paul's concluding prayer is: "Peace and mercy be upon all who walk by this rule, upon the Israel of God" (Gal 6:16). The "rule" to which Paul refers is the standard of belief and way of life that comes in the cross of Christ. And the "Israel of God"? This can hardly refer to the Jews. Paul's prayer reaches toward an idea that only became clear decades later, that Christianity is the true Israel. The relationship between Christianity and Judaism was still evolving. But the blessing at the end of the letter is a good illustration of "the complex pattern of extensive Jewish scriptural, theological, and liturgical influence on the early Christians even as they gradually but inevitably moved away from their Jewish roots" (C. Osiek).

The Church at Philippi

The most affectionate of Paul's letters was written to the church at Philippi in the mid-50s. As Acts describes Paul's second missionary journey (Acts 15:40–18:22), commonly dated in the early 50s, Paul and Silvanus (in Luke: Silas) made their way overland from Antioch through Syria and Cilicia, through central Asia Minor, to Troas on the Aegean

Sea. From Troas Paul and Silvanus crossed the sea, arriving soon afterward at the Roman city of Philippi.

Founded in the mid-fourth century B.C. by Philip II of Macedon, Philippi was in Paul's day a distinctively Roman city. Here Mark Antony defeated Brutus and Cassius, Caesar's assassins, in 42 B.C. Eleven years later, after Mark Antony was himself defeated at Actium, Octavian (later the emperor Augustus) established a military colony at Philippi and settled it with Roman veterans and Mark Antony's supporters evicted from Italy. The *jus Italicum,* the privileges of a Roman city, were conferred on Philippi. The city was the starting point for the famous Via Egnatia, the road to the west which became at Brindisi, on the other side of the Adriatic, the Via Appia leading to Rome.

We are almost completely dependent on Acts for references to the church's foundations at Philippi, though the first part of Acts' account (16:11–15) may derive from a record of one of Paul's traveling companions (the first of several "we" sections in Acts where the pronoun shifts from the third person singular to the first person plural). On the sabbath, Paul and Silvanus went outside the city to a place of prayer where a few women from the tiny Jewish community gathered (Luke's "pattern" again?). Among the women was Lydia, a "worshiper of God," one sympathetic to the faith of the Jews. Lydia was a business woman from Thyatira in Asia Minor; she was a dealer in luxury cloth dyed with the purple that was produced in the city of her birth. Lydia and her household became converts to Christianity and Lydia's house was opened to Paul and Sylvanus. Lydia was one of many Gentile women who associated with Jewish communities in the diaspora and who became believers. (The mission at Philippi represents the beginnings of Christianity in Europe. Christianity came to Rome in the early 40s, though we have no record of that church's foundation.)

Paul's letter to the Philippians was written from Ephesus during Paul's imprisonment. The letter, dated around A.D. 56–57, is disjointed; some scholars view it as a conflation of three letters or parts of three letters. (Some regard the letter as written from Rome in the early 60s.) From the letter(s) we learn that while the Philippian Christians were supportive of Paul, some at least were inclined to be factious and divisive. Paul underscores the importance of greater unity among members of the church.

Paul's letter to the Philippians is distinctive in its mention of bishops (*episkopoi*) and deacons (1:1). (He never mentions presbyters [elders] in any of his letters.) It is hazardous to conclude from this mention that a formally organized ministry existed in the Philippian church. In one view (R. H. Fuller), these titles may refer to unordained charismatic officers who had special tasks in the Philippian church, quite possibly a type of relief work. This is the only church, for instance, which was permitted to contribute to Paul's support. Perhaps the titles mark a stage in the development of official roles which would become more fixed in the years after Paul's death.

One section of Paul's letter to the Philippians (3:2–4:3) shows that even though the church at Philippi was composed mainly of Gentiles, Paul's efforts were followed closely by Jewish Christian missionaries who sought to introduce Jewish religious practices. As in Galatians, Paul speaks strongly of those who sought to counter his gospel: he calls them "dogs . . . evil-workers . . . those who mutilate the flesh" (Phil 3:2). But his argument here is much less elaborate, possibly because (if written at Ephesus) he was in closer personal contact with the Philippians.

Finally, Paul at Philippi came into conflict with Roman officials. The account in Luke (Acts 16:19–40) is probably highly embellished, though we read from 1 Thessalonians 2:2 that Paul did experience "suffering and shameful treatment" from the officials at Philippi. Abruptly Paul left Philippi. But the handful of Christians who gathered at the house of Lydia in Philippi soon grew into a self-sufficient church.

The Church at Corinth

Generally the church at Philippi prospered. The same was not true of the church at Corinth. We now turn to that church.

Corinth is located on the isthmus connecting the two parts of Greece. From its two harbors it had easy access to the Adriatic on the west and the Aegean on the east. Inevitably it became an important center of commerce for southern Greece. It was also an industrial and shipbuilding center, and it was famous for its architecture and its cultivation of the arts. Cicero called it "the light of all Greece."

Because the city became a center of Greek resistance to Rome it was destroyed by the Romans in 146 B.C. After a century of desolation it was refounded as a Roman colony according to a decree of Julius Caesar in 44 B.C. Augustus made it the capital of the province of Achaia (most of Greece south of Macedonia) and the seat of the proconsul. In the first century A.D. its population included Roman officials and military, merchants, and sailors from Greece, Italy, Syria, Palestine, Egypt and other parts of the empire. There was also a sizable Jewish population.

Corinth, a famous sports center, was the home of the Isthmian games celebrated every second spring. Athletes from all of Greece and from many parts of the empire came to the city to compete. Corinth also had a reputation for licentiousness in a pagan world tolerant of sexual license.

Acts 18:1–17 gives Luke's picture of the beginnings of the church. When Paul arrived in Corinth, probably in the winter of A.D. 50/51, he joined the household of Aquila and Prisca recently expelled from Rome by the edict of Claudius. Most likely the couple were Christians at Rome and were forced out because they were leaders and activists in conflicts with the Jews of Rome. Presumably they continued missionary work in Corinth, even though Luke does not mention it in his account (because of his desire to focus on Paul?). Paul joined the couple, shared their trade and lived in their house.

Before long, as Acts has it, Silvanus and Timothy arrived with a substantial financial contribution from the believers in Macedonia. Relieved from the need to provide for himself, Paul was now able to give his full attention to his mission work. At this turn of fortune, Paul moved to new quarters in the home of Titius Justus, a Gentile "God-fearer," who lived adjacent to the synagogue. Luke records the success of Paul's efforts in the conversions of Crispus, the chief of the synagogue, and Crispus' household, and also many Gentiles. (Household baptisms are best understood in the context of the solidarity of the family, a belief common to both Judaism and the Greco-Roman world.)

The success of the Corinthian mission aroused opposition from some of the Jews who brought a charge against Paul to the proconsul Gallio (Acts 18:12–17). The proconsul rejected the charge, insisting that the Jews settle the matter themselves. After some eighteen months at Corinth, Paul sailed with Prisca and Aquila to Ephesus.

Mention of the proconsul Gallio serves as one of the most important means of fixing the chronology of Paul's missionary activity and, indirectly, the chronology of the early church. An inscription found at Delphi in 1905 links the proconsulship of Gallio to events in the reign of Claudius. A careful analysis of the references on the inscription reveals that Gallio was proconsul at Achaia (either from May 1, A.D. 51 to May 1, 52 or from May 1, A.D. 52 to May 1, 53, with a stronger preference for the later date). Probably Paul's Jewish opponents took advantage of a new proconsul to place their complaint about Paul before him. If so, Paul would have left Corinth in the early summer of 53. Since, according to Acts 18:11, he stayed there eighteen months, he would have come to Corinth in the winter of 50/51. Many use these dates as a pivot for Paul's chronology. If this reconstruction is incorrect, scholars hold, it cannot be off by more than one year.

Paul's concern for the church at Corinth continued long after his departure. During a later stay in Ephesus, probably from the autumn of 54 to the spring of 57, Paul learned of difficulties at the Corinthian church: factions, doubts, scandals, opposition to Paul himself. Paul sent a series of letters, made another visit himself, and sent Timothy and Titus at different times to the Corinthian church. Scholars do not agree on the sequence of Paul's further ministry to the Corinthian church. One effort at reconstruction (drawing upon J. A. Fitzmyer and G. Bornkamm) follows.

Reports of continuing problems at Corinth came to Paul in the spring of 57. He responded in a first letter which does not survive. It was a call to avoid association with immoral Christians (1 Cor 5:9–11). Sometime later, Paul sent Timothy to Corinth. For their part, the Corinthians sent a delegation to Paul with a series of questions. To answer them and to comment on reports he was hearing about the Corinthian church, Paul wrote the letter we know as 1 Corinthians shortly before Pentecost of 57. The letter was not well received. Paul made a hasty visit to Corinth, a "painful visit," in his words (2 Cor 2:1), and apparently an unsuccessful one. Returning to Ephesus, Paul wrote a third letter "out of affliction and anguish of heart and with many tears" (2 Cor 2:4). The most important fragments of this letter are preserved in 2 Corinthians 10–13. In addition, Paul sent Titus to try to help the situation.

In Titus' absence, leaving Ephesus after a mob protest against him (Acts 19:23–20:1), Paul went to Macedonia. There he met Titus and learned that a reconciliation between himself and the Corinthians had been brought about. Then Paul wrote a fourth time, parts of which appear in 2 Corinthians. (2 Corinthians is not a single letter, but a collection of writings to the Corinthians which were later gathered together.) A few months later, Paul made a third and last visit to the Corinthian church, probably in the winter of 57. We guess the visit went well, for Paul's letter to the Romans—written during this last visit to Corinth—gives no evidence of the previous turmoil.

A careful reading of Paul's letters to the church at Corinth reveals the troubles and difficulties that beset this young church. (These letters do not give a complete picture of the Corinthian church, much less of all the churches at this time.) The difficulties were many and numerous. The church was torn by factions—at least four of them. Different groups professed allegiance to Paul, Apollos, Peter, and Christ, apparently separating themselves from one another. Some lined up behind Paul. Others stood in opposition. Apollos, who visited Corinth after Paul's departure (Acts 18:24–19:1), attracted followers not because his teaching differed from Paul's but because he spoke with greater eloquence. Another group looked to Peter as a guide. From available evidence Peter never visited Corinth. A group "belonging" to him suggests the presence of Palestinian Jewish converts who insisted that Peter was the "rock" foundation of the church (Mt 16:18). Perhaps also they insisted on the observance of certain Jewish practices. Some "belonging" to Christ suggests that some of the Corinthian church called on Christ in opposition to Paul.

The community had other problems as well: a case of incest; public lawsuits; some felt so "free" in Christ they fornicated with prostitutes. The Corinthians questioned Paul about other issues too: marriage and virginity, relations between slaves and free people, etc. The pagan environment of Corinth posed still more questions: Could Christians eat meat offered to idols, which, as a means of providing income for the pagan priests, was sold in the marketplace (a matter of concern only to wealthy Christians)? How should one regard the scruples of those Christians who found the practice objectionable?

There were, as well, liturgical matters which provoked Paul's comment, even his strong criticism. In an obscure passage (1 Cor 11:2–16) Paul argues against wearing a unisex hairstyle in the worship assembly such that the distinction between men and women was blurred. More serious was the abuse at the Lord's supper which Paul treats in 1 Corinthians 11:17–34. The Corinthians celebrated the Lord's supper in connection with a common meal. Paul's severe criticism came not because of the Christians' lack of faith in the Lord's supper, but from the lack of concern of the wealthy about the poorer Christians who came late to the common meal and had nothing with them. Such behavior constituted a profanation for Paul of the "body" of Christ, the church.

Another problem associated with the Corinthian church concerned the gifts of the Spirit (1 Cor 12–14). Paul insisted that each member of the community was endowed with diverse gifts. But in his view the gifts had one purpose: the good of the entire community.

Many of the problems present in Corinth came from the belief of some Corinthian Christians that with their new life in Christ, the human body was morally irrelevant. In effect, they considered themselves already raised with Christ. In the enthusiasm of their new faith, they supposed they were beyond the limits of time and history. In response to this basic error Paul gave one of the most important New Testament testimonies to belief in the resurrection (1 Cor 15:1–58). Christ has been raised, Paul argued, but those who believe in the risen Christ do not already share in the risen life in such a way that they need have no concern for this life.

The Corinthian church was troubled by another problem which arose after Paul wrote the letter we know as 1 Corinthians. Itinerant preachers came to Corinth and attacked Paul's teaching (2 Cor 10–13). It is not clear who these missionaries were; the best explanation is that they were

Jewish Christians from Jerusalem who appealed to their possession of God's Spirit and their ability to achieve ecstasy as authenticating their ministry, opposing the ministry of Paul. Obviously these missionaries were acceptable to some of the Corinthian church and probably had support in certain quarters in the Jerusalem church. In his defense against these preachers, Paul refers to the "super-apostles" and the "false apostles" who came to Corinth. Perhaps the "super-apostles" refer to the "pillar" apostles at Jerusalem (Gal 2:9) and are distinguished from the false apostles who most likely overstepped their mission mandate in preaching against Paul. If this understanding is correct, it indicates continuing tensions between Paul and the Jerusalem church. We only know of the situation at Corinth through this section of Paul's letter, written with a sarcasm and irony that obscures a clear picture of the actual scene. At any rate we have another indication of serious tensions within the early church.

The Church at Ephesus

Antioch was the center of Paul's earlier missionary work. Ephesus became the center of his labors in the mid 50s. In Luke's account (Acts 18:23–21:17) Paul's stay at Ephesus took place during his third missionary journey.

Ephesus was a seaport city, already a thousand years old in Paul's day, the capital of the Roman province of Asia (today the western coast of Turkey). The city was located in one of the several river valleys which descend from the mountains to the Aegean Sea. Ephesus benefited from a major harbor, though in Paul's day it was already filling with silt. But with the advantage of a network of Roman roads, Ephesus was a thriving commercial and religious center. The city's temple to Artemis (Diana, for the Romans) was considered one of the seven wonders of the world.

According to Acts the beginnings of the church in Ephesus are associated with Prisca and Aquila (Acts 18:18–19).

The frequent mention of this couple (in Paul's letters as Prisca and Aquila and in Acts as Priscilla and Aquila) indicates their importance in the early years of the church. The fact that Prisca is mentioned before her husband—once by Paul (Rom 16:3) and two out of three times by Acts (18:18 and 26; see 18:2)—may suggest that she had a higher social status than her husband (W. A. Meeks). It may also mean that she was the more important figure of the two (E. Schüssler Fiorenza). The couple were expelled from Rome by the decree of Claudius, quite probably because as Christian Jews they were involved in the disturbance over "Christ." They

were artisans, tentmakers, and their enterprise was an extensive one.
They moved from place to place and established in three cities (Corinth,
Ephesus, and Rome) sizable households serving Paul and the local Christian congregations. The two risked their lives for Paul (Rom 16:3). They
were instrumental, too, in rectifying Apollos' faulty knowledge of Christ
(Acts 18:24–26); they probably also had a part in encouraging Apollos'
own important missionary efforts (Acts 18:24–28).

Paul's letters are our primary source for this period. Although Luke
centers the second part of Acts on Paul, this should not prevent us from
recognizing that others, women and men, had important roles in the
growth and development of the early church.

Paul arrived at Ephesus some time after Prisca and Aquila. Some of
those they sought to evangelize may have been followers of John the
Baptist (Acts 19:1–8). According to Acts, Paul stayed at Ephesus for
some two years. (Acts 19:10).

Though (like Antioch) it was one of the early major urban Christian
centers, few details of the church at Ephesus remain. Luke tells us that
Christian missionary success caused an uproar instigated by those who
profited from the worship of Artemis (Acts 19:23–41). However, the
story is not regarded as a reliable source of historical information. Still, a
considerable part of the sufferings at the hands of Jews and Gentiles
which Paul enumerated in 2 Corinthians 11 must have taken place at
Ephesus or in its environs. There were clashes, too, with Roman authorities: Paul refers to his "fighting with wild beasts" at Ephesus (1 Cor
15:32) and tells us that he was in the custody of the praetorian guard for
a while (Phil 1:13).

Paul wrote many of his letters in Ephesus. The correspondence with
Corinth, Galatia, and Philippi were almost certainly written there.
These letters indicate that even in the midst of suffering and opposition
the church at Ephesus experienced growth and vitality (Phil 1:14–17).
Probably the Johannine community was located here. We will see more
of that in Chapter Seven.

A Note to Philemon

During his imprisonment at Ephesus, Paul also wrote a short note to a
well-to-do Christian, Philemon, who lived at Colossae, some miles inland from Ephesus. Writing for himself and Timothy, Paul greets Philemon as a fellow worker who had a role in preaching the gospel and
whose home was a meeting place for a Christian congregation. Paul also
sends greetings to "our sister" Apphia and to Archippus "our fellow
soldier." The military image may allude to Paul's own imprisonment,

and to the conflict with the values of this world which Christian belief sometimes involves.

The occasion of the letter is interesting. Philemon's slave, Onesimus, ran away after robbing Philemon to help finance his escape. Onesimus came into contact with Paul during the latter's imprisonment at Ephesus. Onesimus became a convert and a friend of Paul. Paul persuaded Onesimus to return to Philemon and wrote the note to Philemon asking him to accept Onesimus back "no longer as a slave but more than a slave, as a beloved brother" (v. 16).

Neither in this case nor in the one other instance (1 Cor 7:17–24) where Paul deals with the issue of slavery does Paul launch a direct attack on that institution.

The institution of slavery in the Roman Empire during this period was more benevolent than the black slavery of the American past. In Greek law slaves lacked certain basic freedoms, e.g., status as a legal person, choice of employment or residence, etc. Slavery was widespread in the Roman Empire. Perhaps a third of the population of Corinth in the mid-first century were slaves, and another third were former slaves.

Paul did not engage in direct confrontation. The perceived impossibility of a small group's making a large change in the Roman socio-economic system may have been the reason. The hope that Christ's return would spell the end of such structures may have played a role too. Nevertheless Paul's letter to Philemon presents a challenge and a dilemma. If Philemon agreed that Onesimus should be free, he takes a position out of step with the whole financial and social world of which he was a part. If Philemon disagreed, he compromised the gospel which he preached to others. We have no record of Philemon's response, but Paul's letter shows the impact of the gospel on the life of the first Christians.

The Church at Rome

The last and the most important of the seven letters unanimously attributed to Paul leads to the final two churches considered in the present chapter: the church at Rome and the church at Jerusalem. We treated the beginnings of these churches in the last chapter; now we ask what Paul's letter to the Romans tells us about Roman Christianity in the 50s.

The letter itself was written in Greece, most probably in Corinth in the winter of A.D. 57–58, as Paul prepared to journey to Jerusalem with funds he collected in the churches of Asia Minor, Macedonia, and Greece. Because the letter contains more lengthy theological exposition than Paul's other letters, Romans seems more a treatise than a letter addressing the particular needs of a local church. However, the present (more common) view sees this letter addressed to a specific situation, and hence shedding valuable light on what we can know of the early church.

The key to the letter is also a guide to what the letter tells us about the churches at Rome and at Jerusalem. That key is in Paul's request: "I appeal to you, brethren, by our Lord Jesus Christ and by the love of the Spirit, to strive together with me in your prayers to God on my behalf, that I may be delivered from the unbelievers in Judea, and that my service for Jerusalem may be acceptable to the saints . . ." (Rom 15:30–31). Paul's collection was not only to be a monetary offering to alleviate the needs of the Jerusalem church. It was also to be a symbol of the Gentile (and Pauline) churches' respect for her status in God's plan. Further, its acceptance would help to overcome the misunderstandings and lessen the deep tensions that had risen between Paul (and his churches) and the Jerusalem community. Paul's letter to the Romans is a "dress rehearsal" (R. E. Brown) for what he will say in Jerusalem. But why this dress rehearsal for his visit to Jerusalem in a letter to the Christians at Rome?

At the time of Paul's letter, the majority of Roman Christians were probably Gentile converts (see Rom 1:5–6, 13–14; 11:13; 15:16), though certainly there were a good number of Jewish Christians in Rome. (After the expulsion order of Claudius in 49 these Jewish Christians would hardly be welcome at any of the Roman synagogues.)

Based on Paul's warning that the Gentile Christians not boast over the Jews (see Rom 11:18) it was once thought that Rome's Gentile Christians looked down upon Jewish Christians and had little to do with them. If that were the case, Paul would not have enlisted their assistance on his behalf. But the opposite could also be true. Paul may, in fact, be chastising those of a more liberal bent who were appealing to Paul as they belittled the more conservative sensitivities of the Roman Christians. Paul distances himself from such boasting and appeals to Gentile Christians at Rome in the late 50s precisely because they had been shaped by the Jerusalem church associated with Peter and James and therefore had a high regard for their Jewish background.

This view gains plausibility from a careful comparison of Paul's letter to the Romans with his polemical arguments in Galatians, Philippians, and 2 Corinthians. Paul's appeal for prayer and support is indicative that Paul knew he would encounter opposition at Jerusalem and maybe even in Rome. So Paul used his letter to the Romans to set forth his understanding that salvation comes from Christ and not through the law, but he does so in a way that is far more appreciative of Judaism than in his earlier letters.

Two examples show the change. In the solemn opening at the beginning of his letter (Rom 1:1–4), Paul cites as a summary of the "gospel of God" a formula which, scholars believe, was dear to the Roman Christians, and quite surely Jewish Christian in origin. Further, unlike other authentic letters, in Romans Paul writes in his own name. He and he alone is responsible for the content. The second example comes in Romans 9–11. In Galatians Paul heightened the contrast between the previous age, marked by the powerlessness of the law to save, and the new age, marked by a salvation that comes from Christ. In Romans 9–11 Paul recognizes and actually affirms the positive role of Judaism in God's plan, a role which comes to fulfillment in Christ.

These and other indications suggest that the Christianity of the Roman church at the end of the 50s was like the Christianity of Jerusalem in its respect for Jewish law and cult, even though Roman Christians might be more inclined to regard Peter rather than James as representative of that tradition. The letter also suggests that Paul, seeing that some of his former statements had been divisive, moderates the positions of his earlier writings.

The final parts of the letter may give further insight into the church at Rome, though some of the concerns of these chapters may also reflect Paul's previous missionary experience. In chapter 12, Paul again (see 1 Cor 12) takes up the need for unity within the body of Christ and the necessary interdependence of diverse gifts shared by members of the community. This may suggest that Paul had reports of some need for a call to greater unity, though there is no evidence of the factions we see at Corinth.

In Romans 13:1–7 Paul calls for an attitude of submission to government authorities. Because Paul does not include warnings against the abuse of civil authority, can we reason that the relations between the Christians and the empire were reasonably calm? These were the early years of the reign of Nero (A.D. 54–68) and the administration of the empire was largely in the hands of the philosopher Seneca (died A.D. 65). No doubt Paul remembered the edict of Claudius, not ten years earlier, and wanted to avoid provoking Nero. The legal status of the Christian house churches was precarious, as the next chapter will show; Paul wanted to chart a way to avoid suspicion or, worse, confrontation, between the young church and the powers of the empire. Paul's advice to the Christians at Rome was probably similar to the advice Jewish leaders gave to diaspora Jews in the same period.

A final section of the letter (Rom 14:1–15:13) concerns relations among the Christians of Rome. Surely this part of the letter reflects the situation at Corinth where Paul was writing (see 1 Cor 10:23–11:1); it may also be telling us something about the situation at Rome. Paul underscores the need to respect the consciences of scrupulous Christians whose judgments were based on an insufficiently enlightened faith. Paul himself sides with those who are not scrupulous in matters of diet and fasting. But he is concerned that those who share his outlook not despise those for whom such matters are important.

The Church at Jerusalem

Our principal sources concerning the church at Jerusalem in the 50s are Paul's letter to the Romans and the Acts of the Apostles. Through the events surrounding Paul's visit with the collection from the churches of Asia Minor and Greece we get our best view of the Jerusalem church at this time.

Acts 18:22 mentions that Paul made a brief visit to Jerusalem after his second missionary journey. Probably that visit occurred in the summer of A.D. 52. Paul returned to Jerusalem again in 58 after (according to Luke) his third missionary journey. With the thought of this visit in mind and in anticipation of his visit to the imperial capital he wrote his letter to the Romans.

> Scholars regard as Lucan constructions some of the scenes Luke de-
> scribes as he tells of Paul's final trip to Jerusalem. The story of Paul's
> bringing back to life the young man who fell from the window after
> having fallen asleep during Paul's sermon at Troas (Acts 20:7–12) is
> reminiscent of stories of Elijah and Elisha (1 Kgs 17; 2 Kgs 4). (Wayne
> Meeks observes that this Eutychus of Troas will be "forever famous as
> the first recorded Christian to fall asleep during a long-winded ser-
> mon.") Paul's magnificent speech to the elders at Miletus (Acts 20:18–
> 35) is really a reflection of Luke's understanding of church leadership
> in the 80s. The same outlook is found in the post-Pauline letters 1 and
> 2 Timothy and Titus (commonly dated between A.D. 80 and 100). The
> remainder of Paul's trip to Jerusalem is largely shaped by Luke's
> artistic purposes. Most likely, though, there were early Christian
> churches at Ptolemais (modern Haifa) and Caesarea on the coast of
> Palestine (Acts 21:7–8).

Paul went to Jerusalem with an impressive group of official delegates from the churches of the Pauline mission (Acts 20:4; note that again Luke has seven names): Sopater of Beroea; Aristarchus and Secundus from Thessalonica; Gaius of Derbe and also Timothy; Tychicus and Trophimus from the province of Asia (probably more precisely identified in one manuscript as Ephesus). Since Luke does not mention the collection here, we could get the impression that these people were traveling companions. More likely they were the collection agents of the various communities where the funds were collected. Their presence shows how seriously Paul regarded this matter.

Acts' account of Paul's last visit to Jerusalem seems based on old and trustworthy traditions, though the purpose of the journey—the collection—is known only from Paul himself. When Paul and his party arrived at Jerusalem, they were greeted by James and the elders. Luke recounts how each group reported on its successes in the missions. The Jerusalem church reported that many among the Jews had come to believe and that they were "all zealous for the law" (Acts 21:20)—a fairly accurate description of the Jerusalem Christians over whom James presided. To counter Jewish-Christian lack of trust in Paul and to offset rumors about his disdain for the law (a fallout from Paul's dealing with the situation in Galatia?) James proposed that Paul take part in a temple ceremony discharging the vows of four "Nazirites." The ceremony was based on the prescriptions of the Book of Numbers by which men devote themselves to God for a stated period. The end of this time of service was marked by a sacrifice in the temple. Bearing the cost of the sacrifice for those who did not have the means was considered by the Jews a particularly good work. Paul undertook this expense and participated in the temple ceremony. Doubtless he agreed in the hope that the Jewish Christians' distrust would be abated and that non-Christian Jews would see Paul as a friend.

The plan was a failure. Before the seven-day ceremonial period was over, Paul was observed in the temple precincts by some Jews from the province of Asia. They falsely accused him of bringing one of his Gentile companions, Trophimus from Ephesus, into the temple area and charged that Paul was guilty of sacrilege. In the ensuing commotion he was taken into custody and then arrested by the Roman guard.

Did the Jerusalem church accept the collection Paul worked so hard to take up and which he wanted so much to bring to Jerusalem? It is very difficult to say. Luke says nothing about it. Some scholars (G. Bornkamm) assert that the fate of the collection is unknown. Others (J. D. G. Dunn) go further, saying that Jerusalem refused to accept the collection. But such a position does not recognize the complexity of the Jerusalem church. There is good reason to believe that within the Jerusalem church even in the late 50s two strong groups still co-existed in an uneasy relationship. The moderate conservatives of whom James was leader held to certain aspects of the law but did not insist on circumcision. The ultra-conservative wing, never repudiated by James, held to circumcision. Paul was uncomfortable with both groups, but regarded only the second group as "false brethren." Paul's own letters all antedate his trip to Jerusalem, so we have no further word from him on the matter of the collection. Letters written by Paul's disciples (the post-Pauline writings) make no mention of it. Possibly James did in fact accept the collection. Luke's silence might be explained by his desire not to rehearse the continuing tensions that still troubled the church some ten years after the assembly at Jerusalem.

We are solely dependent on Acts for the story of Paul after his arrest at Jerusalem, his imprisonment there and at Caesarea, and his trip to Rome. Luke did not have an official record or other reliable traditions. Rather, his presentation of the subsequent story is guided by his desire to represent Paul as the great missionary to the Gentiles, and to present Christianity as innocent of the charge that it was a danger to the Roman state.

The House Churches of the Greek Cities

Before continuing our historical sketch it may be helpful to examine in a more thematic way some of the important features of the churches as we know them through the writings of Paul. (It is beyond our scope to present Paul's theology of the church, though inevitably something of that enters our picture.)

An indispensable framework for understanding the life and structure of the early churches comes in the recognition that these are "house churches." The early communities came together in the (larger) homes of the more well-to-do Christians of the various cities we have been looking at. Throughout the first century Christians did not have any public meeting-places, such as the Jewish synagogue. The only facilities available to them were the homes of those who had become Christians.

From Paul's letters, and also from Acts, we can identify some of the households where the early churches met. Perhaps the most prominent examples are associated with Prisca and Aquila; their homes in Corinth, Ephesus, and Rome were gathering places for local Christian communities (Acts 18:2–3; 1 Cor 16:19; Rom 16:3–5). Philemon had a house large enough to accommodate meetings of Christians and to take in guests as well (Phlm 2, 22). The typical house church was composed of the family, servants, and a few friends who lived in the adjacent area. While it is difficult to estimate the number of Christians in any of these early communities, one estimate (J. Murphy-O'Connor) suggests that the Christian community at Corinth numbered around fifty persons.

It seems that the house of Gaius was large enough to accommodate all the Christian groups in Corinth (Rom 16:23). Perhaps Gaius' house is so singled out because such an arrangement was unusual. Generally the home of a wealthy person had a dining area which accommodated roughly nine people and a large atrium which held between thirty and forty people. Conceivably in the two areas all of the Christians of Corinth could gather on some occasions, though conditions would be crowded. Ordinarily "the church in the house of" someone (Rom 16:5; 1 Cor 16:19; Phlm 2) would mean a smaller group.

We know that a single city might have had several house churches. Paul seems to refer to three such communities in Rome (Rom 16:5, 14, 15). His letters to the church of a given city passed among the various "churches" of the area.

The household was also the basic social and political unit in the ancient world. We have several examples where the conversion of the head of a household included all those bound in the unity of the household (1 Cor 1:16; Acts 11:14; 16:15, 31–34; 18:8). The importance of the household unit in Greco-Roman society will help to explain the introduction of the "household code" in Colossians and Ephesians and in the pastoral letters. The concern for propriety and good reputation which we find in later writings, and possibly even in Paul, is best understood in this context.

Household churches also explain some of the conflicts within the community. The structures and behavior that were accepted as part of the Greco-Roman household could easily be at odds with the Christian understanding of community. Philemon's dilemma provides a dramatic example, though there were other instances where tensions arose.

Outside of Palestine, the house churches of the mid-first century were almost exclusively urban churches. Only toward the end of the century is there evidence of Christian churches in outlying villages and rural areas.

The Social Background of Pauline Christians

Homes large enough to accommodate a small congregation make us aware that some of the early Christians were people of modest wealth. Studies in the recent past promoted the idea that the Christians of the first generations were largely uneducated, generally poor, and relatively insignificant socially. Such studies cited Jesus' cry against the rich (Lk 6:24) and Paul's opening lines in his letter to the Corinthians (1 Cor

1:26–29), which speak of the gospel's coming to those not wise by worldly standards, not of noble birth, the weak ones of the world.

In the past twenty years this assessment has given way to a realization that the social position of the early Christians was considerably more complex. Our evidence, of course, is limited to Christians in the urban centers of the Greco-Roman world of the first century. But upon careful analysis the letters of Paul indicate that early Christians were people who came from various social levels. There is little evidence of people on the top levels of society (unless Erastus, mentioned in Romans 16:23 as "the city treasurer," was such a one), nor at the bottom of the social scale—menial workers, peasants, agricultural slaves. Some of society's poorest may have been among the early Christian groups, but no evidence of it remains.

The "typical" Christian was a free artisan or small trader. Some had houses, slaves, the means to travel, and other indications of wealth. There were slaves among these urban Christians, though we have no indication of their numbers. People, once slave and now free, and descendants of such people, were numbered among Christians. There were wealthy independent women among the Christians and wealthy Jews. In sum, the Pauline congregations seem to have exhibited a fair cross-section of society.

Roles of Service in the Churches

The question of ministerial roles in the Pauline churches is complicated, and much is written on the topic. We must be careful not to read back into the 50s structures that emerged only in the 80s or in the early second century. Recognizing the complexity of the material and the indirect nature of the evidence, three roles in the churches of the 50s can be identified: apostles, fellow workers, and local leaders.

In the popular view "apostle" is synonymous with the Twelve. Given his designation "apostle of the Gentiles" (based on Gal 2:7–9) Paul is also regarded as an apostle. Identification of apostles with the Twelve comes from Luke. Only in one scene in Acts (14:4, 14) does Luke recognize others besides the Twelve as apostles. In fact, the term apostle had a much less restricted use in the early church, especially among the Pauline communities. The apostle of the Pauline letters was primarily a missionary leader, in contrast to local, residential leaders. While it is commonly recognized that apostle was not an office, those who were apostles had a clearly recognized authority in the communities they helped to establish.

During this period the role of apostle appears most clearly, of course, in Paul himself. Through his letters he teaches, exhorts, and exercises judgment on those who do not live up to the standards of the community. The source of an apostle's authority came in the conviction of being called by the Lord, in a way similar to the call of the prophets. The apostle was called to preach and sometimes to lay the foundation of a new community. Paul's frequent use of such metaphors as "to lay foundations," "to build," and "to plant" underscores this latter function.

Paul recognized the existence of many apostles in the early decades of the church. A clear indication comes in Paul's statement (1 Cor 15:7) that the risen Christ "appeared to James, then to all the apostles," with the latter clearly distinguished from the Twelve. Andronicus and Junia(s) are spoken of as "notable among the apostles" (Rom 16:7; we will see more of Junia(s) in the section on the role of women in the Pauline communities). Paul also refers to his opponents at Corinth as "apostles" (2 Cor 11:13). Others who have no foundational roles also have this term applied to them. For example, those who accompany the collection to Jerusalem are called "apostles of the churches" (2 Cor 8:23), and Epaphroditus, a messenger between the churches (Phil 2:25), is also spoken of in this way. In a list of gifts given to various members of the community, Paul places apostle in the principal position (1 Cor 12:28).

The idea of engaging in missionary work became so much a part of the common understanding of apostle that the Twelve were seen in this way. In Matthew and Luke (Matt 28:16–20 and Acts 1:8) the risen Jesus gives the Eleven a missionary mandate, but we lack evidence that many of them functioned outside of Jerusalem or had a role in the foundation of new churches.

Along with the apostles we find another group associated with Paul and the other missionary leaders and, in different ways, dependent on them. Such fellow workers are Silvanus, Timothy and Sosthenes, each of whom appears at least once as a co-author of a Pauline letter. Timothy acted for Paul in the young church at Thessalonica (1 Thes 3:2). Both he and Silvanus helped Paul in establishing the church at Corinth (2 Cor 1:19). Timothy and Titus had a hand in Paul's continuing ministry to the churches at Corinth (1 Cor 4:17; 16:10; 2 Cor 7:6–16). Euodia and Syntyche and Clement were helpers at Philippi (Phil 4:2, 3). Prisca and Aquila are called co-workers (Rom 16:3) but acted with greater independence. They served as patrons and protectors of Paul and of several local house-churches. They were also evangelists and, Acts 18:26 tells us, powerful instructors of the faith. After the split between Paul and

Barnabas at Antioch, each took one or more associates with him on his evangelizing journey (Acts 15:36–40).

In Paul's letters these "fellow-workers," "fellow athletes," and "laborers" had varied responsibilities. Some exercised their ministry in a single location; others were engaged in mission work. Some, Epaphras of Colossae, for example (Col 1:7–8; 4:12), became a missionary founder of a local community. These fellow workers indicate complexity and fluidity among those who ministered to the local churches and maintained ties between various church communities.

A third group (overlapping the above) were the local leaders. While little evidence of formal office structures in the Pauline congregations exists, roles had begun to be differentiated even in Paul's earliest letter with the mention of "those who *labor* among you and *are over* you in the Lord and *admonish* you" (1 Thes 5:12). The three underscored words highlight the functions attributed to these local leaders. "Laboring" is a general term used for those who engage in missionary work and who strive to "build up" the local community. "Admonishing" suggests guidance in moral questions. The Greek word for "being over" is probably best understood in the sense of acting as patron or protector. These last two functions imply some governing authority in the community. The letters to the Corinthians indicate the presence of patrons with a similar relationship to the congregation.

In all three of the leadership types, authority is based in large part on the faith shared between the authority figure and the community. Appeals are made to past preaching, instruction, and the experience of conversion and baptism. When there is need for admonition or correction, further warrants come from one's status as an apostle or a teacher, from a claim to revelation, or from the tradition of the early church (see 1 Cor 11:23 and 15:1–11).

In three places Paul gives us lists of people who have special functions in the community (1 Cor 12:4–11, 28–30; Rom 12:4–8). In each case he describes these functions as gifts of God or of the Spirit. This attribution and the diversity in the lists show that the Pauline congregations had a considerable variety of charismatic functions within the community. The description of persons and charismatic activities emphasizes the functions themselves rather than the status of the person. The contexts of the three passages also indicate that while Paul recognized the diversity of functions within the church, he wished always to stress the unity of the congregation. Nevertheless, the ordering of apostles, prophets and teachers in 1 Corinthians 12:28 and the opening line of the letter to the Philippians may indicate that some process of formalization was already taking place.

The Dignity and Role of Women
in the Pauline Communities

Our attempt to understand the attitude toward women and their role in the early church during the period of Paul's letters might best begin with the baptismal formula cited by Paul in Galatians 3:27–28: "For as many of you as were baptized into Christ have put on Christ. There is neither Jew nor Greek, there is neither slave nor free, there is neither male nor female [or more exactly: male and female]; for you are all one in Christ Jesus." This bold statement reflects the conviction of the early church that by baptism in Christ all have equal access to God's salvation and that in the new creation in Christ belonging to one side or the other of the great divisions of the ancient world had little consequence. The third pair in the formula is likely influenced by Jewish exegesis of the two creation accounts in Genesis (see Gen 1:27 and 2:7). In the exegesis of the first account, God created human beings in the divine image, untouched by any division and by nature incorruptible. In God that original unity was to be restored. The baptismal formula used by Paul asserts that in baptism Christ restores humanity to its true image and overcomes the divisions that are characteristic of our present life.

There are sayings in Jewish rabbinic texts which also speak of the equality of man and woman before God, though these texts were not put into writing before the end of the second century. But it is not unreasonable to suppose that these sayings circulated in oral form a century or so earlier. Adverting to Jewish parallels may prevent our drawing an oversimplified contrast between Christianity and Judaism on the status of women before God.

It is also important to note that Paul does not propose the new equality brought about by Christ as a blueprint for the order of society or of the church. Certainly, Paul was arguing for the admission of Gentiles into the church. This is the thrust of the Galatians text. But the emphasis on order in the community in 1 Corinthians (we will see more of this in a moment) may suggest that Paul was reacting to the attempt by some Corinthians to do away with the *de facto* distinctions of their present life. In fact we do not find the saying about male and female in the similar text of 1 Corinthians 12:13 written approximately three years later (see also Col 3:11). But the baptismal formula in Galatians does point to Christian belief that in Christ women and men are fundamentally equal as new creatures before God.

It is more difficult to assess the role of women in the Pauline churches. Some texts which treat this matter are very difficult to interpret.

Clearly some women are very prominent in the church communities.

Prisca and her husband Aquila are mentioned several times (Rom 16:3–
4; 1 Cor 16:19; Acts 18:2, 18, 26; see also 2 Tim 4:19). In his letter to the
Philippians, Paul recognizes two women, Euodia and Synteche, who had
"labored side by side with me in the gospel" (Phil 4:2–3). Paul's letter to
the Romans (16:1–2) recognizes the help Phoebe gave to him and to
many others as well. Phoebe was deacon at Cenchreae, the eastern
seaport of Corinth, though the text does not allow us to say much more
about the nature of her position. Also associated with the church at
Corinth was Chloe (1 Cor 1:11). Again it is difficult to describe her
precise role. From members of her household Paul learned of the divisions among the believers at Corinth. Chloe, Prisca and Phoebe were
certainly prominent members of the communities at Corinth and its
vicinity.

The church at Rome had several women whose importance was recognized. Paul may have hoped that his mention of the men and women in
Romans 16 would provide an implicit recommendation to a Roman
church which may have been uneasy with what it heard about his past
missionary work. Besides Phoebe and Prisca (Rom 16:1–3), Paul mentions Mary "who has worked hard among you" (v. 6); Tryphaena and
Tryphosa, also "workers in the Lord" (v. 12); the mother of Rufus who
may have helped Paul earlier on in some city he visited (v. 13); and Julia
and the sister of Nereus (v. 15).

Paul's final words to the Christians at Rome mention another couple,
Andronicus and Junia(s). The Revised Standard Version and the New
American Bible (1970 edition) translate the Greek accusative *Iounian* as
Junias (masculine). The revised New Testament of the New American
Bible (1987) translates the word as Junia (feminine). Many authors in
the early centuries of the church regarded the name as feminine and
today some exegetes do the same. These exegetes base their position on
the understanding of this text in the early church and the complete
absence of a single Latin or Greek inscription or other reference in
ancient literature which supports the masculine reading.

Andronicus and Junia, Paul writes, were "notable among the apostles." Believers before Paul, they apparently worked together with him
and at one point were even imprisoned with him. Since they were at
Rome when Paul wrote his letter, probably they both were itinerant
missionaries, engaged in the mission to the Gentiles. If Junia was a
woman, it is significant for our understanding of women in the early
church that she is so highly regarded.

Since the role of women in the (early) church is a topic of much
current interest, we need to examine two other texts often cited in this
regard. The first is Paul's injunction in his letter to Corinth that women

who pray and prophesy in the assembly should be veiled (1 Cor 11:2–16). Paul's argument about veils and the hair of both men and women is very obscure and exegetes disagree on its meaning, in part because the specific problem Paul was addressing is unknown. Perhaps it represents some argument for a type of subordination of women to men, though, again, all exegetes do not interpret the text in the same way. (See J. Murphy-O'Connor, *1 Corinthians,* and P. Perkins, *Ministering in the Pauline Churches.*) But clearly Paul takes for granted that women pray and prophesy (1 Cor 11:5, 13) in the liturgical assembly and he finds no objection to this.

Our second passage is 1 Corinthians 14:33b–36. Here Paul tells women that they are not permitted to speak in church. Women are to be subordinate to men in speaking publicly; if there is anything they desire to know, they are to ask their husbands at home.

> Before dealing with the meaning of the text, a judgment about the text itself must be made. The verses are clearly a part of the canonical scriptures, but do they come from Paul or are they an interpolation? Some scholars argue for the latter for several reasons. The grammar of the passage and its awkward position in the context of the letter speak for an interpolation. Second, the content of the verses so apparently contradicts what is presumed in 11:5, that women do pray and prophesy in the assembly. Third, the injunction in chapter 14 is very much like directives found in the pastoral letters. Most scholars agree that the pastorals were not written by Paul but by a disciple who used the authority of the apostle's name in addressing a church where the memory of Paul was held in great esteem. Accordingly, the author of the pastorals, or someone who had them in mind, added the disputed verses to 1 Corinthians to make them share the outlook of the pastorals (see 1 Tim 2:8–15).
>
> Other scholars reason that because the verses in question are not missing in any of the best manuscripts it is better to accept them as authentic and then explain why Paul included them in the letter.

If one accepts that the verses in 1 Corinthians 14 come from Paul, their presence might be explained in this way. Clearly Paul accepts the baptismal equality of men and women before God which comes through baptism and the charismatic giftedness of women and men in the Christian community. But Paul thought that "outsiders" could confuse the gatherings of Christians with cult gatherings of the time in which the roles of women attracted suspicion and criticism. This was true of the Isis cult of which there was a major center in Corinth. Perhaps Paul's earlier directives (11:2–16) on liturgical assemblies and his injunction

(14:34b–36) that women (wives) not ask questions in the assembly flow from his concern to protect the Christian communities from being confused with secret, orgiastic oriental cults, present in Corinth and elsewhere, which were regarded as undermining public order and decency.

It is difficult to summarize the role of women in the churches in this period (and in Paul's thought). Surely the churches and Paul himself accepted the belief that in Christ women and men had a fundamental equality as children of God. There is ample evidence, too, that some women were very prominent in the churches at Corinth, Philippi, and Rome. That women performed some of the same community functions as men and shared in some of the same "gifts" (as in Romans and 1 Corinthians) are important indications of the role of women in at least some of the New Testament churches. But there were also difficulties at Corinth. Exactly what these were and how Paul (or a possibly later author) sought to respond to them are not altogether clear. We will see more on this topic as we proceed with our account.

Worship in the Pauline Communities

Christians of the 50s lacked church buildings or temples, cult statues or traditional sacrifices. They had no cultic leaders who were called "priests." Again, early Christian worship must be seen in the context of the house-churches which were the focal point of community life.

Paul's letters presuppose throughout that groups of Christians of a local area "come together" with some frequency. We can only estimate the frequency of these early community gatherings: based on the thought that these Christian groups followed the example of Jewish sabbath observance, our best guess is that they were weekly. The closest we come to any literary indication of weekly meetings is found in Paul's directive to the Corinthians concerning their participation in the collection for the Jerusalem church: "On the first day of every week, each of you is to put something aside and store it up . . . so that contributions need not be made when I come" (1 Cor 16:2). But even this is only indirect, since Paul speaks of "each of you." (There is early second century and mid-second century evidence which tells us that Christian groups met weekly and on Sunday.)

Paul's letters, especially 1 Corinthians, tell us something of these worship assemblies. "When you come together, each one has a hymn [psalm], a lesson [teaching], a revelation, a tongue, or an interpretation" (1 Cor 14:26). This became stylized in the post-Pauline letters as "psalms and hymns and spiritual songs" (Col 3:16 and Eph 5:19). Psalms from the biblical psalter were used, as well as original Christian compositions.

Examples of the latter are found in Philippians 2:6–11 and, in what many consider a post-Pauline writing, Colossians 1:15–20. These Christian hymns addressed "to the Lord" also promoted self-identity and group cohesion.

Scripture texts (the writings Christians today call the Old Testament) were read and interpreted in the light of the Christian experience. We may assume that the preaching and exhortation which we find in Paul's letters were part of the Christian gatherings.

Prayers, too, had a place. These would include more formal prayer, such as the small prayers of blessing patterned afer Jewish prayer types. An example is found in the opening verses of 2 Corinthians: "Blessed be the God and Father of our Lord Jesus Christ, the Father of mercy and God of all comfort, who comforts us in all our afflictions . . ." (2 Cor 1:3–4). The acclamations and doxologies (literally, "words of praise") which are so unobtrusively present in Paul's letters were very much a part of community prayer (see 1 Cor 15:57; Rom 7:25a; 2 Cor 2:14). Informal prayer and glossolalia (prayer in tongues) also played a role.

Finally, Paul refers four times to a "holy kiss" (1 Thes 5:26; Rom 16:16; 1 Cor 16:20; 2 Cor 13:12). This may have been a ritual marking the end of a meeting or it may have been a transition to the celebration of the Lord's supper.

Baptism: "Ritual of Initiation"

In Paul's letters there is no detailed description of the early community's ritual of baptism. Those to whom Paul wrote knew the rite. Paul is far more intent on providing interpretations as part of his effort to use the conversion experience and rite of initiation as a means of nurturing and, where needed, correcting the lives of the people to whom he was writing. Nevertheless, indirectly, we do know something of the rite itself.

The basic rite of baptism was a water bath. The symbolism that by baptism the believer was buried with Christ suggests that the rite involved complete immersion, though we may suppose that adaptations were made. Where practicable it probably took place in a river or, otherwise, in a tub. It is not likely that even Gaius (the owner of the large house in Corinth) and Erastus (the treasury official) had houses with a private bath. Allusions in Paul's letters about taking off the "old human" and putting on Christ and taking off sinful habits and putting on virtuous ones suggest that there was some type of disrobing before baptism and being clothed anew after the rite. The anointing that was so clearly a part of the later baptismal ritual is mentioned only once (2 Cor 1:22). Baptism itself was administered in the name of Jesus (1 Cor 1:13).

128 Chapter Five

Twice Paul tells us that when one received the Spirit of God one could then cry out *Abba* ("Father"). Perhaps such an exclamation was also part of the initiation rite. The rite marked one's entry into the Christian community.

In Paul's own interpretation, the rite of baptism signifies participation in Christ's death. By baptism one dies to an old self (Rom 6:6) and becomes a participant in Christ. Only in Colossians and Ephesians is baptism understood as a participation in the resurrection as well. The theological understanding of baptism developed in the course of the life of the early church.

The Lord's Supper: "Ritual of Solidarity"

The descriptions in the sub-headings for the preceding section and in this (from W. A. Meeks) highlight the pivotal roles that baptism and the Lord's supper played in the Christian communities of the 50s. The importance of the Lord's supper (1 Cor 11:20) stems not from the frequency of its mention but from what Paul says when he writes about it.

The topic of the Lord's supper appears only twice in the seven undisputed letters of Paul. Both occur in 1 Corinthians: in the first instance, Paul deals with the question of eating meat offered to idols (1 Cor 10:14–22); in the second, he addresses the disunity evident at the celebration of the Lord's supper (1 Cor 11:17–34). From these two passages something of the practice concerning the Lord's supper in the churches of the 50s becomes clear. The context of the supper was a common meal. Gathering for festive meals was a common feature of the life of the clubs, guilds, and other voluntary associations that were a part of social life in the early Roman Empire. The ritual imitated the last meal of Jesus with his disciples "on the night he was betrayed" (11:23) and focused on two specific moments. At the beginning of the meal bread was broken and distributed. As this was done there was a prayer of thanksgiving and the formulaic saying: "This is my body which is for you. Do this in remembrance of me" (11:24). After the meal a cup of wine was passed with the utterance of a parallel formula, "This cup is the new covenant in my blood. Do this, as often as you drink it, in remembrance of me" (11:25). None of Paul's letters say anything about who presided at these supper meals.

The repeated command, "Do this in remembrance of me," not found in the versions of Mark and Matthew, suggests that the Pauline and pre-Pauline tradition upon which this was based saw the celebration as a cultic commemoration of Jesus and a re-presentation of his death. The tradition Paul cites is an old one; this is evident from the technical terms "to receive" and "to deliver" (1 Cor 11:23) which show that Paul was mindful that he was citing an early tradition which he helped to introduce to the Corinthian Christians at the beginning of the 50s. The focus of the rite as a memorial of Jesus' death figures in its development whereby the eucharist ("thanksgiving"—a later term) came to be seen as a sacrifice. In the 50s the rite was an integral part of a meal, albeit one which was a commemoration or memorial of Jesus' death.

After the initiatory rite of baptism, the supper ritual was a part of the process of becoming more thoroughly one in a community of faith and love. In the one place where Paul deals at length with the Lord's supper, he is unconcerned with explaining the rite or the belief in the Lord's presence at the meal. He presupposes that. Rather, he seeks to help his audience appreciate the significance for their lives of the rite in which they take part. Building upon baptism, the rite is a means of transforming a multitude of individuals into a community with the Lord and with each other.

Chapter Six

Turning Point

The period from the early 60s to the end of the 70s was an important turning point in the development of the early church. These two decades are marked by the death of the principal leaders of the first Christian generation, the destruction of the Jewish temple and the city of Jerusalem, and significant developments in the church's life and structure. These developments in the church came as a result of the growing recognition that the expected second coming of the risen Jesus was not to occur soon. We see something of the church during this period in the letter to the Colossians (and the letter to the Ephesians), as well as in the gospel according to Mark.

The Death of James at Jerusalem

James, the brother of the Lord and the leader for many years of the Jerusalem community, was the first of the principal leaders of the early church to die. The Jewish historian Josephus (writing ca. A.D. 94) tells us that the Sadducean high priest Ananus, the son of the Annas of the passion narrative and, according to Josephus, "a man bold in his temper and very insolent," brought James and "some others" before the Sanhedrin and accused them of breaking the law. The accused were executed by stoning. Josephus tells us that Ananus carried out the execution because there was a change in procurators and the new appointee had not yet arrived in Palestine. The date of James' death was probably A.D. 62. The execution of James and the others was unpopular. Soon Ananus was denounced and, under King Agrippa II, removed from his post. Such a protest suggests that James still enjoyed considerable respect in the Jewish community. (Scholars accept that Josephus' story of James' death is basically reliable. Acts mentions nothing about James' death, probably because of its preoccupation with the story of Paul.)

The Deaths of Peter and Paul at Rome

We have no direct evidence concerning the deaths of the other two leaders who, with James, were the guiding lights of the early church. Ancient traditions tell us that both Peter and Paul died as martyrs in Rome. Current historical scholarship enables us to reconstruct with some probability the background to these traditions.

We do not know when Peter came to Rome. We saw earlier that there is no evidence that Peter was founder of the Christian community at Rome, while there are many indications that his labors were focused in places other than the imperial capital, most especially Jerusalem and Antioch. Available sources do not permit us to determine the events that led to Peter's arrival at Rome, his length of stay, what he did there, or whether he exercised any leadership role within the Roman community. Quite likely he spent little time at Rome before 58, the probable year of Paul's letter to the Romans. Were he at Rome before Paul wrote, it seems most likely that Paul would have mentioned him in his letter. Perhaps it was only in the early 60s that Peter came to the capital.

We know much more about Paul's arrival in Rome. The final chapters of Acts (chapters 21–28) record that Paul was not well received by all quarters of the Jerusalem community when he came there in 58 (with representatives of some of the churches of Greece and Asia Minor) with the collection he had worked so hard to raise. James himself welcomed Paul but recognized that others would not take kindly to his presence in the Jewish capital. James sought to win acceptance for Paul by urging him to undertake a ritual ceremony in the temple. But when Paul entered the temple area, diaspora Jews rioted against him and he was taken into protective custody by the Roman authorities. To protect Paul from continued Jewish opposition, he was sent to the procurator of Judea, Antonius Felix, residing at Caesarea Maritima. Here Paul was held in prison for two years, probably between 58 and 60. Under a new procurator, Porcius Festus, Paul requested a trial. It was at this trial that Paul made his "appeal to Caesar" (Acts 25:11). It was because of this appeal that Paul was taken to Rome in the fall and winter of 60–61. Paul probably arrived at the imperial capital in the spring of 61.

According to the account in Acts, Paul was welcomed by some of the Roman Christians. We may attribute this acceptance to the success of his letter to the Christians at Rome. As Paul approached the capital, Luke tells us (Acts 28:15), a group of Roman Christians went out to meet him, first at the Forum of Appius, some forty-three miles from Rome, and then at Three Taverns, a stopping place on the Appian Way ten miles closer to the capital. A further indication of the esteem with which Paul was regarded by the Romans comes in the letter of Clement of Rome, written some thirty-five years later. The letter states that "the good apostles" Peter and Paul were "the greatest and most holy pillars [of the church]" (1 Clement 5:2–7). But the picture in Acts 28:30–31 (the final two verses of the book)—that Paul spent two years in house arrest at Rome where, at his own expense, he engaged in a preaching ministry—is certainly incomplete. The letter of Clement notes that both Peter and Paul met opposition at Rome. Victims of "jealous zeal and envy" (1 Clement 5:1), they were denounced to the Romans. Probably it was ultraconservative Jewish Christian missionaries, insistent on circumcision, who denounced both Paul and Peter to the Roman authorities.

The two leaders were put to death in Rome sometime in the period between A.D. 64 and 67. This was during the reign of Nero (emperor from 54 to 68), in the persecution of Christians following the famous fire that leveled much of Rome. The Roman historian Tacitus, writing some fifty years after the event, tells us that to suppress the rumor that the emperor himself had set the fire because of his desire to rebuild Rome, Nero made scapegoats of the Christians. The traditions are plausible that, in these circumstances, Peter died by crucifixion in the Circus of Nero south of the Vatican Hill and was buried in the vicinity of present day St. Peter's Basilica, and that Paul was beheaded on the Ostian Way. The death at Rome of the two greatest apostles of the early church played an important part in making Rome the most prominent church in the centuries to come. The death of James, Peter, and Paul and the other leaders of first generation Christianity had an important bearing on the church's efforts to maintain its contact with Jesus the risen Lord.

The Revolt Against Rome and Siege of Jerusalem (A.D. 66–70)

The same decade which marked the deaths of the great apostles also witnessed a chain of events which were to have profound and far-reaching effects on Judaism and, indirectly, on the development of Christianity as well. Some background will situate the unfolding of the Jewish revolt against Rome and the destruction of the city and temple of Jerusalem.

In A.D. 44, following the death of Herod Agrippa I (during whose reign James the son of Zebedee was killed), the emperor Claudius placed Palestine under the control of Roman procurators for a second time. This imperial action begins the period known as the Second Procuratorship, from A.D. 44 to 66. (The First Procuratorship began in A.D. 6, when Judea,

Samaria, and Idumea were taken from the exiled Archelaus, one of the heirs of Herod the Great, and made into a Roman province. This arrangement extended until the beginning of the reign of Herod Agrippa in A.D. 41.) The seven procurators during this second period witnessed a steady worsening of relations between the Jews and their Roman overlords. These procurators made little effort to understand the Jewish people or show sympathy for distinctive Jewish ways. During this period the Zealots clearly emerged as a force within Jewish society.

Under the procurator M. Antonius Felix (ca. 52–60) Jewish hostility against Rome flared into the open. Felix responded by crucifying great numbers of those who opposed Roman rule (Josephus, *Wars of the Jews*, II.13.2). During Felix' final two years as procurator Paul was in prison at Caesaria Maritima.

Felix was succeeded by Porcius Festus (ca. 60–62), whose sincere efforts to improve the relationship between the Jews and Rome were unsuccessful. Under Festus Paul was sent to Rome, in the late fall of A.D. 60. Things became worse during the term of Festus' successor, L. Albinus (A.D. 62–64), whose tenure was marked by blatant corruption. In the change of command between Festus and Albinus, James the brother of the Lord was executed.

The last of the procurators, Gessius Florus (A.D. 64–66), robbed and plundered at will. An ultimate affront to the Jews came in his taking a small sum of money from the temple treasury. The Jews responded with a mock collection taken for the "destitute" Florus. The procurator took revenge by plundering part of the city. The Jews sought to avoid further confrontation and offered no resistance. But the lack of resistance was interpreted as a show of contempt and a slaughter followed. The Jews withdrew to the temple precincts and barricaded the portico passageway between the temple and the Fortress Antonia, the Jerusalem residence of the procurators and a garrison for a Roman cohort (between five and six hundred men). The Jewish action was interpreted as an act of formal revolt against the authority of Rome.

In the early struggles against Rome, organized resistance in Jerusalem and in Galilee led to Jewish victories against both Florus and Gallus, the Roman legate of Syria. In face of setbacks for the Romans, Nero sent the field commander Vespasian to direct the imperial forces. By the winter of 67–68 all of the Galilean outposts fell to the Roman advance.

The Galilean resistance leader, Joseph ben Mattathias, surrendered to the Romans and, as their captive, predicted that Vespasian would soon become emperor. Joseph was spared; when his prediction came true, he was given his freedom. He adopted the family name of the emperor and became Flavius Josephus. His writings are the principal source of the history of the Jews from the Hasmoneans to the fall of Masada in A.D. 73.

In face of mounting Roman pressure, the Jews sought aid from the Idumeans to the south. After some initial support, the Idumeans withdrew before what seemed to be an increasingly hopeless situation. Apparently at this juncture the Jerusalem Christians fled the city. Most went to the city of Pella in Perea, east of the Jordan River; others went to different places in that region and to Egypt as well.

Vespasian's march toward Jerusalem in the spring of 68 was interrupted by the death of the emperor Nero in early June of that year. In the lull, various factions among the Jews in Jerusalem took to fighting among themselves. In their own civil war one group took control of the temple, while another faction ruled the city itself.

Rome at the time was absorbed in troubles closer at hand. From the spring of 68 to the beginning of summer in the following year, civil strife led to a succession of three emperors. On July 1 of 69, Roman troops in Alexandria proclaimed Vespasian emperor. For the remainder of the year, Vespasian consolidated his support and eventually returned to Rome. The new emperor sent his son Titus to complete the Roman conquest of Jerusalem.

After extensive preparations the siege of the Judean capital began in the spring of 70. In the face of overwhelming Roman forces, the Jews reconciled their differences, though to little avail. The Romans surrounded the city and in July of 70 entered and razed the Fortress Antonia. Titus intended to spare the temple of Herod, only recently completed, but in the melee it was destroyed. In two months the entire city was taken. The leaders of the Jews were taken captive and, with the great seven-branched candlestick from the temple, became part of Titus' triumphal procession at Rome in the following year. The last Jewish stronghold, the famed fortress at Masada, fell to the Romans in A.D. 73. In A.D. 81 the Arch of Titus, a commemoration of Rome's conquest of Jerusalem, was erected in the Roman Forum. The ruins of that monument, with its engraving of the temple candlestick, still stand.

After the destruction of Jerusalem, Vespasian claimed all of Judea as his private property. Roman presence in the area was strengthened by settlements of veterans and colonists. Yet even in the face of total defeat, Jewish memories of the restoration that followed the Babylonian destruction of Jerusalem in the sixth century B.C. fed hopes that there might be yet another reversal. Toward the end of the reign of Trajan (A.D. 97–117), when Rome's dominion in the east was challenged by the Parthians (living in the territory of modern day Iran), Jews revolted in various parts of the empire. When the emperor Hadrian (A.D. 127–138) decided in A.D. 132 to build a temple to the Roman god Jupiter on the temple mount in Jerusalem, the Jews undertook what is called the Second Revolt (A.D. 132–135). The Jews were led now by Rabbi Aqiba, the priest Eleazar, and the military leader Simon ben Kosibah (known through Christian documents as Bar Cochba, "Son of the Star"). Jews regained control of all Judea. But Judea was captured anew by the Romans, and Jerusalem was razed. A Roman city, Aelia Capitolina, was built in its place.

The defeat of the Jews in the Second Revolt determined the Jewish political situation until modern times. In 1947 the modern state of Israel was formed. Only after the "War of 1967" did the city of Jerusalem and the temple area come again into Jewish hands. We will see more of the religious character of Judaism after A.D. 70 in the next chapter.

The Delay in Jesus' Second Coming

One of the distinguishing features of the earliest Christian belief was the conviction that in Jesus' resurrection and in the sending of the Spirit, God's end-time had dawned and that the coming of the end-time would be completed when Jesus came again in the fullness of God's glory. When that took place, God's plan of salvation would be completed. The *Maranatha* exclamation and the Lord's Prayer witness to this belief.

But even toward the end of the first Christian generation (roughly A.D. 40–70), hope of the parousia was fading. For example, when Paul reassured the Christians at Thessalonica that those who died before the parousia occurred would share nonetheless in the glory of the coming age, he assumed that he himself would be alive when "the day of Christ" came (1 Thes 4:15–17; see also 1 Cor 7:26–31). Such was not the case when Paul wrote to the Philippians, probably in either A.D. 56 or 57.

Yet external events caused the expectation of the parousia to become very lively ten years later in the community for which Mark's gospel was written. We shall see more of this at the end of this chapter.

Guidance of the Church in the Sub-Apostolic Era

The growing awareness that the parousia might be delayed, in addition to the deaths of the principal leaders of that first generation, brought to the fore a new question: How would the church be guided and directed in this lengthening period before the parousia when the early leaders were gone from the scene? How would the church maintain its contact with the Lord?

In the past Roman Catholics devoted little attention to this question because it was assumed that before they died, the apostles chose successors who would carry on their work of leading and guiding the church. There was a succession which extended from Jesus to the apostles (the Twelve) and from them to their successors. The earliest expression of this view is found in the First Letter of Clement (ca. A.D. 96), the work of a third generation Christian author. This understanding of the early succession of authority was called into question at the time of the Reformation. Today it is regarded by both Roman Catholic and Protestant scholars as too simple a picture. Such a view does not accurately represent the role of the apostles historically and hence does not allow for the actual complexity and variety involved in the exercise and succession of leadership in the early church.

In this and the next two chapters we will review various attempts to deal with the issue of leadership after the first generation of leaders passed from the scene.

Christian and Jewish Estrangement

Another development which accelerated after the fall of Jerusalem was the growing estrangement between Jews and Christians. This development had, of course, been going on for some time, especially as Gentiles became more and more numerous in the Christian community. But the events of 66 to 70 hastened the process. Several factors were involved.

It appears that the Jerusalem Christians fled Jerusalem on the eve of the Roman takeover of the city. In the view of some historians, almost all Jews at the time of the revolt, with the exception of the Sadducees, held some form of hope that in a war with Rome God would intervene and bring a final victory for the Jews. Christian flight may thus have aggravated relations between themselves and those Judean Jews who survived the conquest. The importance of the Christian departure from the capital, however, should not be exaggerated. After the fall official Judaism distanced itself from the revolutionaries. The leadership of Judaism after 70 probably had little sympathy for the revolt.

Much more significantly, in the reorganization which took place after 70, Judaism tended understandably to be less open to Jewish Christianity than before. We will see more of this in the next chapter.

For their part Christians had a precedent for seeing the destruction of the city and of the temple as a punishment from God. Pompey's inspection of the Holy of Holies in the temple in 63 B.C. was regarded in some Jewish circles as a judgment on a guilty people. One of the Psalms of Solomon, current in Jesus' day, gave clear reference to Pompey's conquest of Jerusalem and ended with the prayer: "Let it suffice, Lord, that thy hand falls upon Jerusalem in the onrush of the Gentiles" (Ps Sol 2:1–3, 22).

In the various New Testament writings of the later years of the first century, different positions were taken on the relation between Christianity and Judaism. There is no single way of expressing this relationship common to all New Testament texts. These general remarks highlight the developments which we will presently be looking at in more detail.

The Church at Colossae

Three writings illustrate the life and growth of the church during the 60s and 70s: the letter to the Colossians, the letter to the Ephesians, and the gospel according to Mark. (This selection is not absolute, since we cannot be sure of the exact dates of the writings we are considering.) Something of the theological views of the authors will inevitably be included, though that will not be our primary concern.

Scholars are divided on Pauline authorship of the letter to the Colossians. Among other factors, the vocabulary and literary style are significantly different from the letters unanimously attributed to Paul. Some scholars account for these differences by suggesting that the letter may have been written by a secretary (see 4:18); slightly more than half of contemporary scholars hold that the letter was written by someone other than Paul. The letter was written closer in time to Paul's life than any of the other deutero-Pauline letters, possibly within a decade of his death. Possibly we have the first example here of a disciple's writing in the name (and with the authority) of a major figure to offer guidance to a community after that figure has gone.

In the mid-first century, Colossae was a small city in Phrygia, a region in the Roman province of Asia Minor (currently the southwestern section of Turkey). The city was set on the banks of the Lycus River in the narrow valley which served as the main east-west route from the Aegean coast through the Phrygian mountains.

The letter to the Colossians indicates that Paul himself did not evangelize the church at Colossae. This may have been undertaken by Epaphras (1:7), a highly respected co-worker of Paul, probably during Paul's stay at Ephesus some sixty miles to the east. Drawing upon internal evidence such as the personal references in 4:7–17 and the listing of various types of people in 3:11 and 3:18–4:1, P. V. Rogers suggests that the church at Colossae was a close-knit group of a few dozen people which nonetheless included a wide cross-section in terms of age and status.

We know about the church at Colossae only indirectly, through the author's reaction to another's report. The community is commended for its faith and sense of community. But the congregation was being troubled by the "beguiling speech" (2:4) of false teachers whose "philosophy and empty deceit" (2:8) threatened to lead them from the gospel which they had originally heard. Further, there were difficulties arising from ascetical practices and certain religious observances, both of which were objectionable to the author of the letter.

We are not able to say precisely who these teachers at Colossae were. Perhaps they were representatives of a type of Jewish and Greek religious syncretism (or of a form of Jewish gnosticism) whose presence on a trade route between East and West is wholly plausible. The situation was a serious one: in the author's view nothing less was at stake than the correct interpretation of the gospel. In response the author insists on the complete sufficiency of Christ's redemptive work and on the total inappropriateness of any appeal to angels or other celestial powers for mediation (2:8, 15). Even if known only indirectly, the situation at Colossae points to what will be a major concern of the developing church: maintaining the integrity of the faith in the midst of new challenges.

Communion with Other Churches

In the letter to the Colossians the author sends greetings to the church at Laodicea, ten miles to the west: "Give my greetings to the brethren at Laodicea and to Nympha and the church in her house. And when this letter has been read among you, have it read also in the church of the Laodiceans; and see that you read also the letter from Laodicea" (4:15–16). The comment indicates that already at this time letters to the various churches were being passed around and collected, though we have no trace of the letter to the Laodiceans. More importantly, the comment testifies to the sense of communion that was presumed to exist among the local church groups.

The Christians at Laodicea, we are told, gathered at the house of Nympha. The Greek word in the text could refer to a man (Nymphas) or to a woman (Nympha). The pronoun in "her house" in some manuscripts is feminine and indicates that the name was that of a woman. Other manuscripts have a masculine pronoun. It may be that because naming a woman would be somewhat sensational at the time the manuscripts were transcribed, the "her" was changed to a "his" in some texts (E. Lohse). Since it is easier to explain why the pronoun just mentioned would be changed from feminine to masculine than the other way around, quite possibly we have here another indication of the prominence of women in the early communities. The reference is also another reminder that the size of these communities was quite small and so could be gathered in the house of a prominent member.

The Issue of Leadership

The author of the letter to the Colossians adds a final note concerning the leader of the community, though whether the leader is at Colossae or at near-by Laodicea is not entirely clear. The author's comments may refer to the quality of leadership in the face of the false teachers described earlier in the letter. "And say to Archippus, 'See that you fulfill the ministry which you have received in the Lord' " (4:17). This call to the community to encourage its leader seems to be both an implicit rebuke to Archippus for having been lax in defending the gospel in the face of heretical trends and an indirect attempt to strengthen his authority for the future. Clearly the author of the letter recognizes the need for effective leadership in the community.

The Understanding of Church in the Letter to the Ephesians

Today the great majority of scholars believe that the letter to the Ephesians was not written by Paul. There are marked differences in language and style between this letter and the unquestionably Pauline letters. Over a third of the letter to the Ephesians parallels the letter to the Colossians; in fact, parallels to Colossians and the other Pauline letters comprise at least eighty-five percent of the verses of the letter to the Ephesians. For these and other reasons most scholars regard the letter to the Ephesians as written by a disciple of Paul.

The letter is quite impersonal in style, itself a marked difference from the letters of Paul. Perhaps the letter was written to accompany an early collection of Pauline letters. The letter was probably written between A.D. 80 and 100. The author knows the Pauline letters, making a date earlier than A.D. 80 improbable; the later date comes from the fact that the letter was known by Ignatius of Antioch who wrote at the end of the century. We treat this letter in this chapter because of its close connection with the letter to the Colossians.

The letter to the Ephesians does not tell us about a particular local church, but it is important for our story because it evidences certain developments which were taking place in the last quarter of the first century. The first is a shift in the way one regards the church. In the Pauline letters of the 50s and early 60s the dominant focus is on the local church. In Colossians, and even more so in Ephesians, the church is something beyond and greater than the local gatherings of believers (Col 1:18; Eph 1:23). The positive view of the church's role in God's plan, present in Colossians, is heightened in Ephesians. In Ephesians, the church is at the center of God's saving design (Eph 3:9–10). For Paul, Christ is at the center of God's intention. In Ephesians, Christ "loved the church and gave himself up for her" (Eph 5:25). In 2 Corinthians 5:14 and Romans 5:8 Christ is said to have given himself up for the unrighteous and for sinners. Even the angelic and superhuman powers who acknowledge Christ are seen to be part of the church (Col 1:20; Eph 1:10). The church is "the fullness of him [Christ] who fills all in all" (Eph 1:23).

The idealized view of church in Ephesians includes the church's relations with Judaism. As with Paul in his letter to the Romans, so the author of Ephesians thinks of the Christian community only in its connection to Israel. Even more, the dream of Paul in Romans 9–11, that Jews and Gentiles will both one day be united in a common salvation, seems to be fulfilled in Ephesians' description of the oneness and reconciliation of Jews and Gentiles (2:11–18). No doubt the text was written as an encouragement to unity within mixed communities. Ephesians' positive outlook vis-à-vis the Jews stands in contrast to roughly contemporary views in Acts and in the fourth gospel.

Order in the Greco-Roman World and in the Christian Communities

Another significant development in Colossians/Ephesians is the inclusion of a so-called "household code" in the parts of these letters given to moral exhortation.

Here some background is needed. The Greco-Roman world of the first century was characterized by a strong sense of order and social stratification in all aspects of life: civil society, the military, the labor force, and the family. Social status depended far less on economic wealth than it does today. Family status and legal status were far more significant.

At the top of the Roman social order were two groups (*ordines*) of aristocrats: members of the senatorial *ordo* who occupied the highest civil and religious posts, and the lesser aristocratic *ordo* of equestrians or knights who frequently served as the second-level administrators of the Empire. Many of the prefects of Judea, Pontius Pilate, Felix and Festus, for example, were probably equestrians under senatorial rank governors in Syria.

Next in the social rank were the freeborn lower classes, the mainstream of the labor force. At the bottom were the slaves and freedmen/women. This group was either born into slavery or became slaves as captives of war, as kidnap victims, or as convicted criminals. The lot of slaves in the mines and agricultural estates was the hardest. Many urban slaves, however, had responsibility, independence, some education, and, at times, some fair amount of acquired wealth. It was possible for descendants of the slave class and freedmen/women class to reach in two or three generations a higher status; for some, eventual access to the equestrian *ordo* and even to the senatorial *ordo* was a possibility.

Within the social setting of imperial Rome the household had a very important place. The quality of harmony in the state and civil society was seen to be intimately tied to the quality of harmony within the household. Good order in the household was seen as contributing to maintenance of order in the state; disruption in the smaller unit meant disruption in the larger. Two of the oldest themes of philosophical reflection, traceable back to Plato (d. 347 B.C.) and Aristotle (d. 322 B.C.) though probably going back much beyond them, were household management and the constitution of the state. The topics were interrelated and they appear in philosophical treatises and ethical manuals in the Hellenistic period and in Roman times.

Roman society was also a basically patriarchal society. Dominance over slaves and children was extended to include women; a corresponding submission was expected from them. The legal treatment of women varied in different regions and in different periods of the Empire, to be sure; certainly the status of women was better in the Empire than it was in the early republic. Under Roman imperial law women enjoyed fairly widespread independence to conduct their own business, take part in trade guilds, and carry on legal or social transactions. But women did not enjoy full legal status. We have no examples of women who held major political or administrative appointments. The ideal, proposed by male authors throughout this period, was that the public domain belonged properly to men and the domestic to women.

Against this background we must situate the "household code," a particular literary form which spells out mutually reciprocal duties among the various categories of people in the extended patriarchal household: usually husbands and wives, masters and slaves, parents and children. The three most prominent examples of household codes woven into the New Testament writings are found in Colossians 3:18–4:1, Ephesians 5:21–6:9, and 1 Peter 2:13–3:8, though the three pairs just mentioned are not found in each of these texts. Other examples are found in 1 Timothy 2:8–15 and 6:1–2 and Titus 2:1–10.

As we have them in the New Testament the codes were rather standard examples of general ethical norms able to be appropriated for Christian use (and not examples of distinctively Christian moral teaching). Some changes were made, and they are important. One good example: that wives are to be submissive to their husbands (Eph 5:22) was standard teaching; that *mutual* submission is proposed is a distinctively Christian addition (5:21).

Why these codes were incorporated into Christian moral guidance in the latter decades of the first century has emerged as a topic of lively discussion among those who seek to understand the early church in the context of its social environment. There are two responses. We will look at one now; we will examine the other when we deal with 1 Peter in the next chapter.

According to the first view (D. Balch) the codes were used as an apologetic response to the charge that Christian communities promoted misconduct and disorder. The Roman world placed a high value on order and structure in society, and the household was a key element of that social structure. Especially as we know them through the Pauline letters, Christian communities functioned in ways that easily must have caused wonder and suspicion. Christians had a new and exclusive form of worship; they were a community where authority was claimed by apostles, prophets, and teachers (1 Cor 12:28), and they proclaimed a basic equality before God which overrode some of the most fundamental divisions in society (Gal 3:28). Each of these elements stood in contrast to the social mores of the time.

Not wanting to be the object of the accusations leveled at some of the pagan mystery religions, some Christians tried to show that they were not subversive of public order and that they respected traditions important in the Greco-Roman society of the day. We have seen already that sensitivity to public reaction may have influenced Paul in his directives for the worship of the community (1 Cor 11:2–16 and 14:34b–36). According to this first view, avoidance of the suspicion of disorder and subversion, and the desire for social acceptance, explain the inclusion of the household codes in the writings of the early church. Other instances of this basic desire for public acceptance are found in the pastoral letters.

The Gospel According to Mark

This chapter concludes with a look at the gospel of Mark and the community for which it was written. A few words on the authorship, the date, and the place of origin set the gospel in context.

The name Mark was very common in imperial Rome, and a person named Mark appears several times in the New Testament writings. There is the John Mark of Jerusalem who went with Barnabas and Paul to Antioch and who later accompanied the same two on their missionary journey to Cyprus and Asia Minor. A falling-out between John Mark and Paul led to John Mark's returning to Jerusalem and his accompanying Barnabas (but not Paul) on subsequent missions. There is a Mark who is with Paul in the late 50s and early 60s; we hear of him in Paul's letter to Philemon. A Mark is also named in the letter to the Colossians (4:10) and in 2 Timothy (4:11). And, finally, a Mark joins the author of 1 Peter in sending greetings to the Gentile Christians in Asia Minor (5:13). A recent study (R. E. Brown) argues for the plausibility that this is one person throughout, the John Mark of Jerusalem. If this is so, the falling out between Mark and Paul in the late 40s had been overcome by the late 50s and early 60s.

There was in the early church an unchallenged assumption that this John Mark was the author of the gospel. The fact that John Mark was not one of the great leaders of the early church and that he had a somewhat checkered history supports the credibility of this tradition. But not all scholars accept this view: some hold that while a person named "Mark" may have written the gospel, little else about him is known.

Much has been written about the place of origin of Mark's gospel. Two locations have been proposed; neither has won universal acceptance. Some think that the gospel originated in the province of Syria, the upheavals and persecutions referring to events surrounding the Jewish War of A.D. 66–70. Others—the stronger view—hold to a Roman location and identify the persecution in the background of the gospel with that of Nero. This second view also holds that the gospel was intended for the community at Rome.

What we can say about the Marcan community is somewhat tentative. In the view of the vast majority of critical scholars, Mark is our first written gospel. So we lack parallels to other gospels which (as in the case of Matthew and Luke) are very helpful in noting distinctive features of the community or (of less immediate interest to us) the theology of the author. But even accepting a wide range of views about Mark's gospel, there are several hints which shed further light on our understanding of the developments of the early church.

Challenges from Without

The Marcan community was evidently experiencing grave challenges, the most prominent of which was a persecution which severely tried the

faith of its members. Perhaps one of the most significant indications of
the situation of the community comes in Mark 13, especially in vv. 9–13:

> But take heed to yourselves;
> for they will deliver you up to councils;
> and you will be beaten in synagogues;
> and you will stand before governors and kings
> for my sake, to bear testimony before them.
> And the gospel must first be preached to all nations.
> And when they bring you to trial and deliver you up,
> do not be anxious beforehand what you are to say;
> but say whatever is given you in that hour,
> for it is not you who speak, but the Holy Spirit.
> And brother will deliver up brother to death,
> and the father his child,
> and children will rise against parents
> and have them put to death;
> and you will be hated by all for my name's sake.
> But he who endures to the end will be saved.

The situation of the community to which this passage was addressed can
be explained by the turbulent events at Rome in the mid and later 60s.
In A.D. 64 Nero cruelly persecuted the Christians at Rome. Two years
later the Jewish War began in Palestine. In the next two years there were
reports of famine and unrest in Rome and, in 68 (the year of Nero's
suicide), earthquakes in Italy. In the bloody civil war which broke out
the following year three emperors lost their lives. The Jewish War continued and rebellions broke out among the peoples in Germany and Gaul.
In this context it is easily understood that Christians in Rome would
view these events as signs of the end-time.

Chapter thirteen of Mark's gospel was written to guide the Christian
community who, recalling persecutions not long past, feared further
opposition in the aftermath of the present turmoil. Mark anticipates that
the situation may deteriorate even further. He expects the appearance
of the anti-Christ in Jerusalem (Mk 13:14, "the desecrating sacrilege").
(M. Hengel argues that the anti-Christ was understood to be Nero come
back to life.) The evangelist sees that the Jerusalem temple itself may be
destroyed, though there is nothing in the text suggesting that this has
already occurred. Should even these events come to pass, Mark warns
that this does not mean the end has come. Further persecution and
turmoil are but a prelude to the further spread of the gospel (13:10).
Mark may be indicating the paradigmatic outcome of the present persecution in the centurion at the foot of the cross. In the centurion's cry,

"Truly this man was the Son of God" (Mk 15:39) the commander of those who executed Jesus becomes a "confessor."

Mark regards the experience of the current turmoil as a reminder that suffering and persecution are an important part of discipleship, even if the disciples and Peter himself did not always understand that lesson (Mk 8:31–35; 9:31–32; 10:32–45). Indirectly Mark may be inviting his readers to see in Peter's martyrdom at Rome the fulfillment of Peter's apostolic witness.

Another dimension of the life of the community was its growing estrangement from the synagogue. We know this only indirectly, but indications are quite numerous. The Jesus portrayed as a guide for the community clearly points to a continuity between himself (and, by extension, the Marcan community) and the promises God made to Israel. But in many ways a note of discontinuity is also underscored. Jesus' sayings about new cloth and new wine (2:21–22) function in this way. So does the author's parenthetical expression (7:19) that, by Jesus' teaching, all foods were declared clean, that is, Jewish dietary laws were abrogated in their entirety. Jesus' teaching on Jewish practices of fasting (2:18–20) and the observance of the sabbath (2:23–3:6), his negative views on the temple (11:16; 12:33; 13:2), and the citing of Jesus' controversies with Jewish officials legitimate, and indeed encourage, the community's separation from the synagogue.

We learned earlier that relations between the pre-resurrection Jesus and official Judaism were ambiguous; memory of them could reasonably support either the position of the first Jewish Christians of Jerusalem or the position of the radical Hellenists who followed Stephen. Had the pre-resurrection Jesus been as critical of Judaism as Mark describes him, we would be hard pressed to explain the strong ties to Judaism of many early believers. Where Mark points to continuity with Judaism, as is done very forcefully in the Last Supper scene (14:24: "This is my blood of the covenant"; many manuscripts read "new" covenant), he means to show that Jesus' followers are the new and authentic covenant community.

The effort to clarify the Christian relation to Judaism was a characteristic of many communities in the final third of the first century. Perhaps Mark's group could best be described as a community with a sense of continuity with God's plans and a sense of discontinuity with the Israel which did not accept that plan as revealed in Jesus (J. Neyrey). Mark's critical attitude toward Judaism may also be part of an apologetic intended for the fellow citizens of the Christians at Rome. By pointing out that the Jewish forces in revolt against Rome were once hostile to Jesus, Mark may be trying to exclude Christians from Roman anger toward the Jews.

The Internal Life of the Community

A careful reading of Mark's gospel allows us to see several issues that affected the internal life of the community. Apparently some members of the group were tempted to attach too much importance to riches and the "cares of the world" (4:19). Scandal seems to have emerged as a problem for the community (9:42–48). Some, too, may have been seeking a more important status within the community (9:35; 10:35–44). The attention this last issue receives in the midsection of the gospel (8:31–10:45), and the clear teaching Jesus gives on the issue of leadership (9:33–37; 10:42–45), may indicate a serious problem. The author is not denying that there are leaders in the community; he is at great pains to show that the leaders of the community must be given to service in the community.

Some, "false Christs and false prophets," were leading people astray (13:6, 22). We cannot identify these teachers or their precise teaching; it may be that they were part of the agitation affecting Roman Christians in the late 60s. Finally, the Marcan community had to face the question of what attitude to take toward exorcists who invoked the name of Jesus but who were not part of the community (9:38–41). Mark urges that they not be rejected.

It would be a mistake to think that the community of Mark's gospel was absorbed by struggles from without and problems from within. Mark seeks to foster a Christian sense of identity as a new community, open to welcoming new members (probably mostly Gentiles), willing to break family ties and religious associations, becoming members of a new family founded on their common discipleship. While Mark proposes such an understanding, such an association was perhaps already part of the group's self-image. Nonetheless the community was undergoing a strong test of its faith. Their struggles led Mark to write for the Christian community our first gospel.

Chapter Seven

Transition and Consolidation

The last two decades of the first century were a very important period for the developing church. These years were characterized by the church's efforts to find its place in the Roman world and to understand its relationship to Judaism after the fall of Jerusalem and the loss of the temple. During these decades Christians were called to absorb increasing numbers of adherents and to adjust to new situations. This was also a time of intense literary activity. Besides Paul's letters, a few of the post-Pauline letters, and the gospel according to Mark, most of the New Testament writings come from these two decades.

The nature of the New Testament texts from this period is a controlling factor in our account. The texts do not tell us of a single church but of different churches in quite different situations. Respecting our sources, then, we will look at the church during this period as we see it in diverse geographical areas of the Roman Mediterranean world.

Because the church's relationship to Judaism was so much an issue at this time, we need to look first at developments within Judaism in the period after the Jewish War.

Jamnia and the Development of Rabbinic Judaism

With the Roman occupation of the city of Jerusalem and the loss of the temple as one of the identifying symbols of Jewish life, Judaism was forced to rethink its position and redirect its energies if it was to survive as a religious entity. With the loss of the temple the principal focal point of Jewish sectarianism disappeared. In this new situation the Sadducees obviously lost any chance at leadership in the Judaism after the revolt. The Zealots, of course, were destroyed by the invading Romans as, apparently, were many of the Essenes. Most of those who guided Judaism through the catastrophe of the Jewish defeat were Pharisees, though in the desire to cast off the memory of their sectarian origins, they referred to themselves as "rabbis" or "sages."

While there is some evidence of a continued Jewish religious presence in Jerusalem after 70, it was the city of Jamnia (Yavneh) near the Mediterranean coast that became the center of Jewish religious reorganization. Under the leadership of the Jerusalem sage Johanan ben Zakkai and his associates, the study of the Torah became the exclusive center of Jewish life and piety. Gradually the rabbis at Jamnia assumed the prerogatives of the former Sanhedrin at Jerusalem. The group at Jamnia transferred to the synagogue part of the temple ritual and assumed the right to regulate the role of the priests at worship. The rabbinate was constituted as the authoritative interpreter of the law and efforts began to settle a canon of Scripture. The synagogue now became the undisputed center of Jewish life.

Efforts were made to overcome the rivalry characteristic of Judaism at the time of Jesus and of the early decades of the church. Judaism after 70 was marked by the desire to create a society which, while tolerating disputes about the interpretation of the law, sought to avoid the sectarian attitudes and divisions of the earlier period. As part of this effort, those who insisted upon a sectarian self-identification were gradually excluded from Judaism. Becoming more distinctive in their self-awareness and more dominantly Gentile, Christians were naturally regarded outside the pale of Judaism. Although we lack evidence of a universal policy, it appears that individual synagogues gradually adopted a practice of deliberately excluding Christians. Such practices forced Christian groups, even those most attached to their Jewish background, to reconsider their own stance vis-à-vis Judaism. This development represents a background to some of the churches we will be looking at in this chapter.

Eventually (perhaps ca. A.D. 130), as a distillation of the process of excluding Christians from the synagogue, a prayer was added to the synagogue liturgy which included Christians among those who— regarded as sects—were considered outside Judaism and hence to be "blotted out of the book of the living." This prayer, added to the Eighteen Benedictions, the *Shemoneh Esreh,* was an important part of the morning service of the synagogue.

The transition at Jamnia was not an easy one for the Jews. Traditions tell of tensions in the efforts to achieve a viable coalition. While our knowledge of this period is limited, we know that this was a very important moment in Jewish life. The Judaism of "the Jamnia period" is the connecting link between the Judaism before the revolt and the Jewish faith of the present day.

The Church in Judea and Galilee After the Jewish War

We know very little about the Christian church in Judea after 70. Christians did return to Jerusalem after the Roman conquest of the city; they were headed by Simeon, the son of Clopas, until Simeon's martyrdom in 107. Some have identified this Simeon with Simon, another "brother" of Jesus (Mk 6:3; Mt 13:55). If this is so, perhaps a succession of Jesus' relatives presided over the Jerusalem community, somewhat in the manner of a caliphate. A source from the later half of the fourth century, *The Apostolic Constitutions,* identifies Judas or Jude, another "brother" of Jesus (Mk 6:3; Mt 13:55), as the third leader of the Jerusalem community, though scholars today are cautious about accepting this testimony as it stands. The church historian Eusebius (died ca. A.D. 340) tells us that by the time of Simeon's death "many thousands of the circumcision came to believe in Christ," an implication that the church in Judea carried on an active missionary program in the area. Eusebius also lists thirteen Jewish Christian leaders who followed Simeon (to the time of Hadrian, ca. A.D. 132). Scholars debate the reliability of Eusebius and of his source, Hegesippus (a second century historian whose writings survive only in fragments quoted by Eusebius); to the extent these testimonies are reliable, we have evidence of a continuing Jewish Christian presence in the early church.

Recent work by the Franciscans has unearthed at Nazareth archeological evidence for a church-synagogue which indicates the presence of a Jewish Christian community honoring the memory of Mary. Excavations under a fifth century church in Capernaum show signs of several centuries of buildings honoring Peter, going back to what is thought to be a Jewish-Christian place of cult. These discoveries give evidence that there was a form of Jewish Christianity in Galilee which lasted for several centuries.

But the church as a whole was by the later part of the first century predominantly Gentile and the leadership of the church passed from Jerusalem to other important cities in the Empire, notably Antioch, Alexandria, and Rome.

The Church at Antioch at the Beginning of the Second Generation

We have already seen that the church in Antioch had its beginnings in the Hellenist mission which got underway quite probably within a couple of years after Jesus' resurrection. Very quickly the community at Antioch became a missionary center for Syria and Asia Minor. The church at Antioch contained representatives of each of the various groups in the early church. Different groups looked for leadership to James and Peter, or to Paul, or to the Hellenists. This pluralism did not exist without struggles and tensions.

A careful study of Matthew's gospel suggests that such tensions were exacerbated by several events in the 60s and 70s which had a deep impact on the Antiochene church. The death of James was one such event. After the clash at Antioch between Peter and Paul, the group under the influence of James was dominant among the Christians in the Syrian capital. But views more in line with the outlook of Paul or of the Hellenists continued to be represented. The death of James in the early 60s must have upset the balance. With James' death and the subsequent flight of the Christians from Jerusalem, the ties between Antioch and the Jerusalem community were severed. Those at Antioch, even more conservative than James, were cut off without support. Here we may have the beginnings of the Jewish Christian group (the Ebionites) which ultimately broke away from the Christian church. On the other hand the groups more attracted to Paul or to the Hellenists must have felt greater freedom to advance their understanding of the Christian message. This shift of influence had increasing significance as it became more and more evident that the mission to the Jews was a failure, while at the same time the mission to the Gentiles was drawing ever greater numbers of adherents to the church.

The Jewish War and the destruction of Jerusalem also had an impact on the Christians at Antioch. Christians at Antioch evidently felt excluded from the synagogue in the years after the Jewish War. At the instigation of an apostate from their number, Jews at Antioch were persecuted and even killed by Gentiles during the Jewish War. Therefore Jews at Antioch were probably very suspicious of Jewish Christians who were associated with Gentile Christians.

As Christians became increasingly separated from official Judaism another factor emerged. The Jewish religion had, almost since the beginnings of Roman domination in the eastern Mediterranean, enjoyed the status of a legal religion (*religio licita*). This was so because of Jewish support for those who eventually emerged as the dominant Roman leaders. While the Jewish situation in Judea changed after the first Jewish War, Jews in the diaspora continued to enjoy many of the legal privileges granted to their forebears. As Christians took on a distinct identity and became distanced from the synagogue, they could no longer count on the protection afforded them by the legal umbrella granted to Jews. This can only have heightened the tensions between Jews and Christians at Antioch, though opposition from civil authorities may also have helped draw Jewish Christians and Gentile Christians more closely together.

The interior life of the church at Antioch was also continuing to undergo important changes. The Antioch community had begun, we recall, with an acceptance of a circumcision-free mission. Objections to that mission (Acts 15:1, 5) were overcome (Acts 15:6–12; Gal 2:1–10), even if this was followed by friction over table fellowship (Gal 2:11–14) and the resultant compromise (Acts 15:20, 29). But coming after Paul's departure from Antioch, the compromise did serve an important purpose: it enabled Jewish and Gentile Christians to return to the full fellowship which they had at the beginning. It is understandable that the various wings of the Antiochene church would have preserved their different outlooks, but would nonetheless have had a mutual influence on each other.

In the 80s there were probably three principal groups in the Antiochene church: the ever increasing Gentile Christians, the liberal Jewish Christians who shared the outlook of Paul and the Hellenists, and the conservative Jewish Christians. (We might add a fourth group, the very conservative Jewish Christians who wanted the full observance of the law and who probably at this time began to separate themselves from the main body of Christians.) Within the Antiochene church itself it was the conservative Jewish Christians who were in the most difficult situation. At one time they were the dominant group at Antioch; now they were a minority. Even though rejected by the synagogue they refused to follow those Jewish Christians who ultimately separated themselves from Christian communion. They were willing to accept the compromise of the "apostolic decree" (Acts 15:19–20) but were not willing to jettison their heritage altogether, even in the face of separation both from the synagogue and the Christian community at Jerusalem. This group must have felt a keen desire to keep the Jewish moral ideals so attractive to Gentiles years earlier as increasing numbers of pagans converted to Christianity. Our knowledge of the situation at Corinth shows us that such a concern was not without cause. The years of the 70s posed new challenges to the Antiochene community. It was Matthew's gospel that sought to address them.

Of the four gospels there is probably more agreement that the gospel of Matthew comes from Syria or specifically from Antioch than there is agreement on the location of the other gospels. The time of the gospel's composition is commonly assigned to the decade between 80 and 90.

Widespread agreement on these points gives us a strong confidence in Matthew's gospel as a valuable source of information on the Antiochene church.

Different Voices in Church at Antioch

A reconstruction of the Antiochene community is based in large measure on the traditions which expressed the interests of the different groups. Current biblical studies try to identify these various traditions and how they relate to different segments of the community. Later, the evangelist used such traditions in an effort to bring the community closer together.

Mark's gospel served as a primary resource and authority for the Antiochene community. If Mark's gospel had its origin in Rome the gospel's prominence in Syria could be explained by the excellent communication between the two capital cities and by the increasing importance of the church of Rome after the destruction of Jerusalem. Peter was also an important figure to the Antiochene church. If the tradition associating Mark's gospel with Peter had its beginnings in the first century, this gives added importance to Mark's gospel at Antioch. The gospel's support of Gentiles and its critique of the Mosaic law would have made it very attractive to Gentile Christians and to Hellenists. In the course of the 70s Mark's gospel may have been used in the liturgy and catechesis of the Antiochene church. But the use of many other traditions and the editing of the first gospel indicate that Mark's gospel by itself was not adequate to meet the needs of the Antiochene community.

Among the other traditions which also played a role in the life of the Matthean community, the collection of sayings—quite possibly circulated in one or more written forms, known today as the "Q document"—is especially significant. This constitutes a gathering of sayings of Jesus which are common to the gospels of Matthew and Luke but not found in Mark. Probably Q came from a Greek-speaking community, predominantly Jewish-Christian in outlook, located around the middle of the first century in northern Palestine. Since the sayings vary in content each group at Antioch could find something to support its own position. But because the sayings were thought to come directly from Jesus they could not be dismissed easily. The sayings contain radical moral demands, end-time prophesies, and wisdom sayings.

Still other traditions are more clearly identified with the concerns of the individual groups. Sayings of Jesus rejecting the Gentile mission (Mt

10:5–6; 15:24) would have been important to the extremists of the Jewish wing of the community. The James group which argued for a strict observance of the Mosaic law according to the interpretation of Jesus would have found support in the material in the Sermon on the Mount which does not abrogate the Mosaic law (e.g., Mt 5:21–24, 27–28). The same could be said of the catechesis critical of pagan prayer (6:7–8) and the exhortation to accept the leadership of the synagogue authorities (23:2–3).

The Hellenists and Gentile Christians, we may suppose, were responsible for handing on traditions which favored the Gentile mission and which opposed the Pharisaic emphasis on the law. Important to this group would be the story of the magi, representing the coming of the Gentiles to Christ (Mt 2), and Jesus' mandate for a universal mission (Mt 28:16–20). This group would also have preserved traditions critical of the Pharisees (15:12–24) and those moral teachings of Jesus which revoked parts of the Mosaic law (5:33–37, 38–39a). Thus Hellenists could have shown the group which honored James that they too were concerned about the morality of the community while maintaining nonetheless Jesus' superiority over the law.

Probably the different house communities would have used these various traditions in their liturgies and in their catechesis and apologetics. No doubt these traditions were subject to editorial changes in the process of transmission and use. Further editing would come from the interaction between these various traditions. As the split between the Christian church and the synagogue hardened, some of these traditions would have acquired an anti-Jewish tone.

The presence and development of these various traditions in the Antiochene church has given rise to the hypothesis that, among the Christians in the Syrian capital, a group of scribes or teachers collected and edited these developing Christian traditions and taught them to others. Acts 13:1–2 tells us that there were at Antioch prophets and teachers (*didaskaloi*) who were also involved in the public worship of the community. The gospel may be referring to the same group of preachers and teachers in its reference to the "prophets and wise men and scribes" (Mat 23:34) of the community. There is much to support the thesis that Matthew's gospel has behind it a well-established Jewish Christian scribal tradition which flourished in the Antiochene church. In that context it is very likely that the editorial comment that "every scribe who has been trained for the kingdom of heaven is like a householder who brings out of his treasure what is new and what is old" (Mt 13:52) is an autobiographical hint of the author of the gospel.

Matthew's Gospel and the Church at Antioch

A careful reading of Matthew's gospel adds further details to our knowledge of the Antiochene church. By comparing Matthew's gospel with Mark and Luke we can see how Matthew adapted Mark's gospel and the Q sayings to address the specific situation and the particular needs of his community.

There is much to support the thesis (J. P. Meier) that in the 80s the church at Antioch was undergoing both a crisis of identity and a crisis of authority. The crisis of identity came from the break in the Antiochene community's previous ties with both the Jerusalem Christians and the Jewish synagogue. The sense of drift from the loss of these two anchors was compounded by the presence of increasing numbers of Gentile converts. The crisis of authority came from the desire to present a moral teaching to the many new converts without the help of the synagogue and of those who stood firmly in the Jewish tradition. It was the evangelist's genius to offer to the Antiochene church a synthesis of the new and of the old.

Two theological developments in Matthew's gospel were of decisive importance in helping the church get through its difficulties. The first came in Matthew's reflection on God's plan of salvation, allowing for Jesus' restricted mission among the Jews, yet providing for the current Gentile mission. Matthew saw God's plan divided into three parts: the time of prophecy before the coming of Jesus, the time of Jesus' fulfillment of God's plan, and, in the evangelist's day, the time of the universal mission of the church. The turning point came in the death and resurrection of Jesus. Matthew incorporates into his accounts of both the death and resurrection of Jesus the mention of an earthquake (27:51–54; 28:2–4), a symbol of the new age dawning with these events. In this way the community could find an explanation for both the limits of Jesus' mission (10:5) and the new openness of the mission after the resurrection (28:16–20). To Mark's parable of the tenants who are entrusted with the care of the vineyard but who prove unfaithful (Mk 12:1–12), Matthew adds to Jesus' words the important instruction: "Therefore I tell you, the kingdom of God will be taken away from you [the Jewish people] and given to a nation producing the fruits of it" (21:43). This was a further help in the community's transition to a predominantly Gentile church.

Matthew's second major theological theme follows the first: the risen Christ is the foundation of the new community and the ground and norm of its moral code. Matthew can preserve the memory of the Jewish Christian respect for the authorities of the synagogue (23:1–3a) but the ultimate authority after the resurrection belongs to the risen Christ: "All authority in heaven and on earth has been given to me. Go therefore and make disciples of all nations" (28:18–19a).

Within this framework (following still the hypothesis of J. P. Meier) we can understand two important developments in the Matthean community: its stance vis-à-vis the synagogue and its tentative moves toward the development of institutional structures.

Matthew's church is becoming ever more distant from the synagogue. The use of the expression "their [your] synagogue(s)" (Mt 4:23; 9:35; 10:17; 12:9; 13:54; 23:34), the harsh judgment against institutional Judaism (Mt 23), and the recognition of an organizational autonomy within the Christian community all suggest a growing rupture with Israel. Indications of Jewish reaction surface in the gospel: propaganda against Jesus' resurrection (28:15) and hints of a charge that Jesus was not legitimately born (1:18–19; cf. Jn 8:41b). Yet in spite of increasing separation and polemics, Matthew's community maintained vestiges of respect for its Jewish past: there may even have been a Christian observance of the sabbath (24:20); Jerusalem, though forsaken and desolate (23:38), remained "the holy city" (27:53).

Matthew's gospel is also valuable for what it tells about the development of institutional structures within the Antiochene community. Such a development is not surprising, given the community's efforts to come to grips with its own sense of identity, its need to provide guidance for new members and to deal with pressures coming from both the synagogue and the civil government.

Unlike the other three gospels, Matthew's gospel uses the term "church" (*ekklēsia*) and does so three times. Once it is used of the universal church (16:18) and twice of the local community (18:17). Both passages use the term in situations which speak of authoritative binding or loosing. In the second passage especially the gospel writer understands the term "church" as implying a visible structure with authoritative officials and authoritative functions.

The Role of Peter in the Antiochene Church

The first of the two uses of "church" comes in the famous scene of the commission given to Simon Peter at Caesarea Philippi (Mt 16:13–19). Contrary to a pre-critical approach to the church's beginnings, current scholarship does not regard this text as a strictly historical reminiscence. (The parallel passages in Mark 8:27–33 and Luke 9:18–22 lack mention of a commission to Peter.) The Matthean passage probably has its basis in the tradition of an appearance of the risen Jesus to Peter immediately after the resurrection (see 1 Cor 15:5; Lk 24:34). Quite probably Matthew builds on that tradition and develops it as part of his effort to deal with the problems of the church in Antioch around A.D. 85. In this hypothesis (based on the work of J. P. Meier), Matthew also drew upon the memory of the mediating role Peter played among the representatives of the various tendencies present at Antioch in the 40s and 50s. He appealed to that memory to make the figure of Peter and the position he represented the moderate center of the Antiochene church in the 80s, promoting thereby a unity between the Jewish Christians of the James group and those identified more closely with Paul or the Hellenists. Indeed, in the concern to meet the needs of the church for which he was writing, Matthew presents Peter as the chief teacher of the universal church ("the supreme rabbi," in the words of B. H. Streeter, though the words are not used in the gospel text).

Note that the Caesarea Philippi passage is immediately preceded by a scene where Jesus rejects the teaching of the Pharisees and Sadducees (Mt 16:12). In the Caesarea Philippi scene Peter is portrayed as having for the universal church (not just for the local church at Antioch) the authority to teach what is licit or illicit according to the teaching of Jesus. Matthew presents Peter as the moderate center and norm of the whole church, and in so doing opposes as norm any one-sided interpretation of the traditions which came from James or Paul or the Hellenists.

> There is no evidence that any one individual in the mid-80s actually functioned in this Petrine role for the universal church either at Antioch or anywhere else. (Available evidence suggests that Rome at this time did not have any one such leading figure.) It seems clear that Matthew saw the Petrine role as a symbolic one for the universal church. This was consistent with the symbolic roles exercised by Peter and the Twelve in the decades after the resurrection. Only in succeeding centuries did the Petrine role become institutionalized. Catholics hold that the institution of the papacy as a ministry for the good of the universal church developed from its New Testament roots under the guidance of the Spirit. (Along with Matthew 16:17–19, Luke 22:31–32 and John 21:15–17 are also very important texts. There are other Petrine texts as well.)

Life and Order in the Church at Antioch

The second passage in Matthew's gospel which mentions "church" (Mt 18:15–20) is found in the context of a collection of sayings and teachings attributed to Jesus, a collection which has often been called the "Discourse on Church Life and Order" (Mt 18:1–35). Here the term "church" refers to a local church, presumably Matthew's church. The passage in question deals with the problem of sin in the church. When a sinner refuses to accept the correction of another person, or that of two or three others, then the local church is to hear the case and make a decision. If the sinner persists and refuses to accept the decision, then the church is to regard that person as "a Gentile and a tax collector." Such a formula, probably coming from the Jewish roots of the community, would be the equivalent of an excommunication. If that is the case we have here a picture of a local church exercising a formal disciplinary action. But the saying might also mean that the sinner is to be the special concern of the community, following the example of Jesus who reached out to tax collectors and was charged with being their friend (Mt 9:11; 11:19). (The exhortation to forgiveness which follows in 18:21–22—introduced by a question from Peter—serves as a check on the disciplinary action of the local church.)

However one interprets the text of Matthew 18:17 it is the local church as a whole which makes the decision. The evangelist does not appeal to a local leader or group of leaders to act for the community. All the members of the community are called to share in an important decision concerning one of its members. In the analysis of a passage such as this, one must ask whether the evangelist has described what *actually* was happening or whether he is saying what *should* happen in that church. In either case, that the issue is raised at all indicates the presence of a question that called for a response.

While there is no mention of a local leader or group of leaders in the above case, there are clearly designated officials in the Matthean church. We have seen that Antioch seems to have had designated prophets and teachers from the beginning (Acts 13:1). At the time of the gospel's composition there seems to be a collective leadership exercised by a group of prophets and teachers (and/or wise men or scribes; Mt 13:52; 23:34). These charismatic preachers and teachers probably also presided at the liturgical gatherings of the community. Further, in Matthew's version of Mark's story of the healing of the paralytic (Mk 2:1–12), Matthew edits the conclusion to show that there are some in the church who share Christ's power to forgive sins (Mt 9:8). We cannot say precisely who these people are. But nowhere do we have evidence that at Antioch at the time of Matthew's gospel there was one leader presiding over the entire community.

The fact that the evangelist does not look to or promote an authoritative figure in the local church (which is not inconsistent with his arguing for the symbolic role of Peter as the figure on whom the church was built) may have come from abuses or fears of such. In the guise of a tirade against the Jewish scribes and Pharisees, the evangelist speaks against those who seek recognition through showy religious clothing, places of honor in social and religious gatherings (23:5–6) and special titles (23:7–10). The titles to be avoided, rabbi, father, and master, suggest that the teachers of the community were the cause of the evangelist's concerns. Here we may have a good example of a church struggling with its own transition. For his part, the evangelist sees the need for the church to develop institutional means to provide guidance and leadership, yet he knows also that their presence may involve abuses and excesses. (Though Matthew issued strong warnings in the 80s against the use of titles by officials within the community, it is interesting to recall that Paul in the 50s likened himself to a "father" of the Christian community; see 1 Cor 4:15.)

The "discourse" on church life and order in Matthew 18 contains other indications of life in the community at Antioch. With increasing numbers of adherents, it is to be expected that all members of the community would not have been equally devoted to the standards of the community. Matthew 18:15–20 tells us of the evangelist's concern about the sinner who does not accept the call to repent. Matthew also sees the need to warn against giving scandal (18:5–9) or despising the little ones of the community (18:10). He understands as well the need to show special pastoral concern for those who stray (18:12–14). The conclusion of the discourse, the account of Peter's question about how many times one should forgive one's brother or sister and the parable about forgiveness (18:21–35), are further expressions of the author's concern that forgiveness be a hallmark of relationships in the community.

One final word about Matthew's community: several indications in the gospel tell us that some, at least, were well-to-do. Where the Markan Jesus instructs the twelve as they leave on mission to take with them "no money in their belts" (Mk 6:8), the Matthean Jesus commands the disciples to take no "gold, nor silver, nor copper coin" (10:9). In a parable drawn from the Q source, where Luke has the nobleman giving each of his servants ten minas (Lk 19:13; modern translations use different terms for this coin), Matthew's version has the nobleman giving talents to the servants (Mt 25:15). A talent was worth approximately fifty times as much as a mina. More familiar is the Matthean "Blessed are the poor in spirit" (Mt 5:3) in contrast to the Lukan "Blessed are you poor" (Lk 6:20). These and other textual differences indicate the more comfortable financial situation of the Matthean community. Matthew's treatment of the rich differs from the harshness of Luke's treatment, though Matthew does record Jesus' warning that riches can choke off the fruitfulness of God's word (Mt 13:22) and Jesus' assurance that in God even the rich can enter the kingdom of heaven (19:23, 26). Matthew's references to money and his treatment of the wealthy members of the community speak against the oversimplified view that most or all the members of the early communities were among the poorest classes of society.

We have looked now at two gospels as sources for our understanding of the development of the early church. Luke's gospel will not serve as a comparable source of information. Whereas Matthew and, even more, the author of the fourth gospel weave their understanding of the church's post-resurrectional experiences into their accounts of Jesus' ministry, Luke does not approach his gospel account in the same way. Of course, Luke has a second volume, the Acts of the Apostles, in which he gives his "account" of the beginnings of the church, from the ascension of Jesus to Paul's arrival at Rome in the early 60s. Recognizing Luke's strong theological concerns even in the Acts' account, we have tried to draw what historical knowledge Luke does give us about the early church and have made use of that in earlier chapters.

Probably Luke's two volumes were written ca. A.D. 80–85. The most recent full-length study of Luke's gospel (J. A. Fitzmyer) says that we cannot do more than guess about where the two volumes were written. Luke's gospel and his Book of Acts present us with one of the major theological understandings of church in the New Testament; a discussion of that ecclesiology is beyond the scope of this study.

The Church in the Pastoral Letters

Another valuable source for our understanding of the development of the early church comes to us in the first and second letters to Timothy and the letter to Titus. Since the early eighteenth century these writings have been known as the "pastoral letters" because of their dominant concern to give "pastoral" ("shepherding") guidance to the churches and church leaders. The language, the style of the letters, and the historical situation they presuppose lead the great majority of biblical scholars today to attribute these letters to someone other than Paul. That position is adopted here. Following R. H. Fuller and Burton Scott Easton, we will call the unknown author the pastor. The letters are commonly thought to have been written (perhaps even as a collection) sometime in the 80s or 90s. If this is the case, they are roughly contemporary with Matthew's gospel. (Some scholars—W. G. Kummel, N. Perrin, R. J. Karris—prefer to date the letters in the early second century.)

It is difficult to say where the letters were written: Ephesus may be their place of origin, or possibly Rome. In either case the pastor wrote with the conviction that Paul's authority would be an important factor in helping the churches deal with the problems facing them. It may be that Timothy and Titus and the places associated with them, Crete and Ephesus, really serve a representative function. The epistle to Titus may have been intended for small congregations of Jewish Christian believers such as those found on Crete. The first epistle to Timothy may have been directed to Gentile converts in congregations which developed as a result of Paul's mission to Asia Minor. Ephesus may have been seen as a symbol of these congregations. The second letter to Timothy is drafted as if it were Paul's last will and testament to all communities which stood indebted to him as their founder.

The pastoral epistles have sometimes been viewed as the New Testament's voice for "law and order" in the church. In fact, they do make a strong case for the importance of church organization and structures. But this development must be understood in terms of the church of the 80s, a period of transition from the apostolic period to a time when the guidance of the apostolic leaders was no longer available.

The term "apostolic period" strictly speaking applies to the second third of the first century, during which time the apostolic leaders gave direct guidance to the early church. The "sub-apostolic" period may be used to describe the last third of the first century (roughly A.D. 70–100). It was during this time that most of the New Testament texts were written, some of them in the name of one or another of the apostles. The "post-apostolic" period designates the time of the third generation, after A.D. 100.

The principal challenge facing the churches for which the pastorals were written was the presence of false teachers (Tit 1:10–11; 1 Tim 4:1–2; 2 Tim 3:6) and the confusion resulting from the spread of their teachings. Because the pastorals are more given to exhorting than refuting erroneous teaching, we lack a clear understanding of the errors in question. It seems more likely that the letters are dealing with a type of gnosticism influenced to some extent by Jewish Christianity (see 1 Tim 1:7; Tit 1:10). The pastor speaks against those who give heed to "Jewish myths" (Tit 1:14) and who engage in speculation about "endless genealogies" (1 Tim 1:4) instead of holding steadfastly to the faith. A major theme centered on the error that "the resurrection is past already" (2 Tim 2:18). This idea may reflect the gnostic position that by the possession of knowledge (*gnosis*) one already enjoyed the fullness of salvation (resurrection). The other side of the coin of such a teaching is that bodily and worldly existence are of no significance or, perhaps, of negative significance. This may explain the pastor's references to those who forbade marriage and called for abstinence from certain foods (1 Tim 4:1–5). All the various positions opposed by the pastor are united by the common theme that salvation is beyond this world, that the created world and people's lives within it are of little moment.

In the pastor's view the most effective check to such false teachings comes in strong and effective church leadership. For this reason much in the letters is directed to Timothy and Titus and the ministers of the local church. While we do not have clear job descriptions of these local leaders, we find throughout the pastoral letters, and most especially in Timothy, many comments about the responsibilities of those who have official positions in the church. Leaders are called first of all to teach, but also to preach, to rule and to exhort. A special emphasis is placed on the responsibility of Timothy to care for and to preserve the "deposit" (1 Tim 6:20; 2 Tim 1:12, 14) which had been entrusted to him and which he was to transmit to those who were called to be leaders in the church. The latter are to regard the care and transmission of the "deposit" as a basic responsibility of their ministry.

The pastor does not make explicit what this deposit is, but it is reasonable to assume that it consisted of creedal formulae and hymns (see 1 Tim 3:16) which gave expression to the apostolic tradition. Some have thought that this "deposit" and the role it played in the life of the community was a static one: a body of propositions to be handed intact from one generation to the next. Perhaps it is more accurate (following R. J. Karris) to view the deposit in a figurative way and to see the transmission of the deposit as a call to preserve and pass on the memory and vision of Jesus in the new circumstances in which these communities find themselves. The pastor, however, does not exhibit the creativity we see in the letter to the Ephesians, also written in the name of Paul.

The churches addressed by the pastor are in the process of settling down, not engaging in a vigorous missionary program. Church members need to live their faith in the ordinary demands of everyday life and to resist the temptation to live one's religious life in another world, neglecting the cares and demands of life in this world. This is clearly reflected in the qualifications the pastor recommends for those who would be *episcopoi*, overseers/supervisors, and *presbyteroi*, elders, in the church. (The lack of distinction between the two terms is characteristic of this period, the last third of the century. Only in the next generation does a clear distinction between the two roles emerge.) The qualifications are appropriate for those called to guide the church in a period of stabilization (Tit 1:5–9; 1 Tim 3:1–7). The model of the church leader is the *paterfamilias,* the head of the household. (Paul himself would not have met the qualifications set forth by the pastor, for Paul was an apostle at the cutting edge of the mission to the Gentiles.) What was needed now were managers, administrators, leaders able to hold the community fast to the faith and to consolidate the community in a common and ordered life.

The roles of overseers/supervisors and elders seem to have their roots in two strains of Judaism which were adapted by the early church. From the synagogues of Pharisaic Judaism the Christian church seems to have received the tradition of a group of elders (in Greek: the *presbyteroi*) who served as a council which set policy for the community. From the Dead Sea Community may have come the inspiration for the figure of a supervisor or overseer (in Greek, the *episcopos*) who had the responsibility of pastoral oversight for the elders and all the other members of the community. While there may have been some overlap in the two roles as they were adapted by the Christian church, it seems that not all elders assumed the role of supervisor. Elders who ruled well and who were engaged in preaching and teaching (i.e., who had a supervisor's role) were to be given double compensation (1 Tim 5:17).

There are indications in 1 Timothy which suggest the presence of women office-holders in the community, though some of the evidence is ambiguous. Clearly there is an order of widows (1 Tim 5:3–16). Given the social system of the Greco-Roman world and the lack of security for women deprived of the support of a family, the lot of widows was difficult. The Jewish tradition, of course, had a very strong concern for "the sojourner, the fatherless, and the widow" (Dt 27:19). It was probably this Jewish tradition which stands behind the Christian order of widows. The passage in Timothy insists that only those who had reached the age of sixty were eligible to be a part of this group. It also underscores the care and respect which the community was to have for those who met the requirements of the order. The widows were to give themselves to a ministry of prayer; they may also have had other such duties as helping to raise children, giving hospitality, "washing the feet of the saints," caring for the afflicted and conducting pastoral visits.

A reference to what may have been an order of women deacons is less clear. The passage on deacons in 1 Timothy 3:8–13 includes a directive on women which technically could mean either women deacons or the wives of deacons. Because these women are given the same directives as (male) deacons, they clearly seemed to have served as deacons. There may be another reference to women deacons in 1 Timothy 5:2: the term *neoterai* (younger ones, feminine form) is elsewhere interchangeable with *diaconos* (see Lk 22:26). (Yet in 1 Timothy 5:11 and 14 the same term *neoterai* refers to younger women who are widows.) While the evidence is not without ambiguity, it is plausible that there were men and women deacons in the churches of the pastorals. This is not the only possible reference to women deacons: Romans 16:1 refers to Phoebe as a deacon of the church at Cenchreae.

The Pastor's Attitude Toward Women

It is important to read the pastorals in the light of both the situation of the churches for which these letters were written and the strategy of the pastor insofar as we can reconstruct it by a careful reading of the texts. It is in this framework that we understand the pastor's rather negative attitude toward women. This attitude surfaces in the severe restrictions placed on women and the rationale given in 1 Timothy 2:11–15, but also in the mistrust of young widows in 1 Timothy 5:11–13 and the disdainful attitude toward women in 2 Timothy 3:6–7.

The overarching problem troubling the churches of Timothy and Titus came from false teachings which, in part, were markedly disparaging toward marriage, sexuality, and procreation. If the pastorals give us an accurate picture, a number of women in the congregations of Crete and Ephesus accepted these false teachings. In this context the pastor, who has a tendency to use (what are for us) stereotypes in his exhortations (see 2 Tim 3:1–9), gives his harsh comments about women. In the process of his efforts to correct the erroneous teaching, the pastor gives a strong reaffirmation of the traditional role of women in the only way he knows how: by reasserting that women, who are to understand their lives in terms of their domestic responsibilities, are to be seen and not heard.

A second factor may further explain the pastor's stance. We see several indications in early church writings of the apologetic attempt to deflect possible negative criticism that might be leveled at the Christian community and to present the community in such a way that it might be more publicly acceptable to its non-Christian neighbors. Paul's call for believers to be respectful toward civil authorities and to be diligent in paying taxes (Rom 13:1–7) was likely inspired by this apologetic motive. If the text in 1 Corinthians about women keeping silent in the churches (14:34b–36) comes from Paul himself, and not from a later editor, this might be another indication of this same apologetic concern. This concern seems to have been a factor in the use of the "household" codes in the letters to the Colossians and to the Ephesians. This same apologetic was probably at play in the pastor's mind as well. But we shall see when we look at the Johannine community that the outlook of the pastor was not shared by all.

The Community of the Beloved Disciple

The city of Ephesus in Asia Minor may be the place of origin of the pastoral letters; it is quite likely that the same city was home to the fourth gospel. But the picture of the church in the fourth gospel and the letters of John is quite different. For this reason these writings have an important place in our efforts to understand the development and diversity of the early church.

Each of the gospels is, of course, an attempt to tell the story of Jesus, but each does so as a guide to the community for which the gospel was written. In so doing the authors may indirectly tell us a good deal about the story of the community for which the gospel was intended. In no other case is this so clearly true as in the fourth gospel. A great deal of research on this gospel in the last thirty years has resulted in a pronounced shift in our understanding of the gospel text and the community with which it was associated. An important segment of recent studies of the fourth gospel centers on reconstructing the history of this particular community through a careful examination of the text. This reconstruction contains a good deal of scholarly guesswork, but scholars are confident that a major part of this historical picture will probably hold up.

The fourth gospel professes to be the witness of the disciple whom Jesus loved (Jn 19:35; 21:24) and suggests that it was even written by him. Nowhere is that disciple identified. Two of the foremost commentators on the fourth gospel, R. Schnackenburg and R. E. Brown, concur in the view that the beloved disciple is the authority behind the gospel, though they think it is very improbable that he wrote the gospel or that he was one of the Twelve. The later tradition that the fourth gospel was written by John, the son of Zebedee, has little hard evidence to support it. Many writers who refer to the fourth gospel as the gospel of John or speak of the Johannine community hold to the positions of Schnackenburg and Brown on the question of authorship.

The history of the Johannine community may be outlined in broad strokes. The original nucleus of the community was made up of Jewish believers and included some who were once followers of John the Baptist. Quite likely this number included the one who was to become the leader of the community, the beloved disciple. There is no reason to think that this group was at the beginning any different from other disciples of Jesus. In the early years after Pentecost, though, the group to which the beloved disciple belonged was joined by another group of Jews; the latter were also followers of Jesus but, like the Hellenists of Acts 6, had more radical views on the place of the temple in their own religious self-understanding. This second group was perhaps instrumental in the conversion of a party of Samaritans (see Jn 4:4–42). In turn, the presence of the Samaritans may have been a catalyst in the community's development of a way of seeing Jesus which put less emphasis on his status as Davidic Messiah and more stress on his importance as Savior of the world, the one who came from God and who spoke for God. (Alienated from Jerusalem and from other Jews generally, the Samaritans distanced themselves from the hopes of a Davidic Messiah. They hoped for a prophet like Moses, who spoke with God and who spoke for God.)

Inevitably, this group—with its Samaritan converts (Jn 4:39), its different and more exalted understanding of Jesus (5:16–18), and its opposition to the temple cult (4:21)—provoked the hostility of more traditional Jews. The gospel stories of the sick man by the pool of Beth-Zatha (Bethesda) in chapter 5 and of the man born blind in chapter 9 are thought to reflect the historical situation of the Johannine community. Jewish religious authorities understandably rejected the exalted claims the community made about Jesus and excluded from the synagogue those who held them (9:22; 16:22). For their part, the Johannine Christians portrayed the Jewish leadership as "blind" (9:39) and obdurate in their opposition to Jesus. The harsh language of the fourth gospel reflects the acute tensions between the Johannine community and the Jewish synagogue during these years.

To the growing Johannine community there was added yet another group—Gentile converts. We may have a hint of this in John 12:20–23 where the arrival of "some Greeks" becomes a sign that Jesus' ministry has come to an end. It may be that the influx of the Gentiles into the Johannine community led to a move of the community, or at least part of it, from Palestine to a location in the diaspora. Scholars ask if the question of the Pharisees in 7:35, asking if Jesus is to go to the diaspora to teach the Greeks, is the evangelist's way of hinting at such a relocation. The presence of the Samaritans in the early life of the community and the accurate references to Palestinian places and customs in the gospel argue for a Palestinian origin of the Johannine community, though external evidence—the context of the diaspora and persecution by synagogue authorities—supports the unanimous voice of ancient tradition that the gospel was written at Ephesus.

The incorporation of the Jewish believers of an anti-temple outlook and the Samaritan converts took place in the 30s and 40s. The period during which the distinctive outlook of the Johannine community was formed probably extended from the 50s to the late 80s. One supposes that the distinctive character of Johannine christology took some years to

mature. The final development of the Johannine high christology con-
curred with Jewish opposition to the Johannine community in the 80s.

Opposition to the Johannine Community

The next identifiable phase in the development of Johannine Christianity coincided with the writing of the gospel, ca. A.D. 90. Here we see a
community feeling very isolated, experiencing opposition and tension
from several quarters.

The gospel's frequent pejorative references to the "world" tell us that
the community saw itself generally alienated from the world, a stranger
to those around it. We are told that Jesus' coming is a judgment on the
world (Jn 9:39; 12:31) and that the world hates Jesus and those who
follow him (7:7; 15:18–19). The true home of the community is to be
found not in this world but in the world to come (14:2–3). Yet even if
the fourth gospel and the Book of Revelation were both written in the
vicinity at Ephesus, we do not detect in the gospel the intensity of
confrontation with the world so evident in the Book of Revelation. The
gospel's treatment of Pilate and the emperor also lacks the bitterness so
characteristic of Revelation. Perhaps difficulties from Roman civil authorities alluded to in Revelation occurred when tensions flared up between the synagogue and the Christian community.

Quite clearly the Johannine community which so insisted on its distinctive faith was opposed by synagogue authorities trying to avoid the
sectarianism that marked Jewish life earlier in the century. The Johannine community's stress on the divinity of Jesus would have been more
than sufficient cause for vigorous opposition to its claims. Evidence from
the Book of Revelation that there were hostile synagogues in the nearby
cities of Smyrna and Philadelphia supports the case for Ephesus as the
location of the Johannine community.

There seem to be indications of tensions, too, between the Johannine
Christians and some followers of John the Baptist. The many statements
in the gospel which argue for the secondary role of John the Baptist in
God's plan (see Jn 1:8; 1:15, 30; 1:19–23; 3:28–30; 10:41) may indicate
the presence of those who were disciples of John the Baptist but who did
not follow Jesus. (We know from another source, Acts 18:24–19:5, that
there were disciples of John the Baptist at Ephesus who had little or no
knowledge of Jesus.) The fourth gospel is peppered with arguments
about John the Baptist's inadequacy yet lacks any direct attacks on him.
Perhaps Johannine Christians were hopeful for the conversion of the
Baptist's followers.

The Johannine Community and Other Christian Groups

Recent studies have pointed to possibly three Christian groups who may have been in some type of interaction with the Johannine community. Virtually all scholars see in John 12:42–43 an indication that there were Christian Jews who believed in Jesus but who did not openly profess their faith lest they be expelled from the synagogue. If the story of the blind man in John 9 is a story of the Johannine community, as seems quite likely, we may guess that there was little tolerance in the community for those who did not openly profess an adequate faith in Jesus. These "crypto-Christians," as they have been called, may well have objected to the high christology of the Johannine group that led to conflict with the synagogue authorities. This group may have shared something of the outlook of those to whom the epistle to the Hebrews seems to have been directed, Jewish Christians who wanted to preserve the pre-eminence of Moses and to retain the cultic heritage that was associated with the Mosaic tradition.

Some scholars see indications in the fourth gospel of yet another group of Christians in contact with the Johannine Christians, though scholarly recognition of this group is not so widespread. According to one hypothesis (R. E. Brown) there was a second group of Jewish Christians who were not a part of the synagogue and who were publicly known as Christians but whose faith fell short of the beliefs of the evangelist and his community. A text supporting this hypothesis occurs just after the "Bread of Life" discourse in John 6 where Jesus is presented as the bread of life, either as God's revelation come from heaven or as flesh and blood giving life to his followers. "Many of his disciples," the gospel tells us, found those teachings, especially on Jesus' flesh and blood, difficult to accept. As a result, they "drew back and no longer went about with him" (6:66).

Another possible indication of Jewish Christians whose faith was thought to be inadequate comes in the comment that "even his [Jesus'] brothers did not believe in him" (7:5). Written at the end of the century, such a statement may indicate the author's frustration with Jewish Christians for whom the memory of James, the brother of the Lord, was very important. This group was probably regarded as rigidly conservative on such issues as understanding the full teaching about Jesus and the Christian relation to Judaism and opposed to developments in the understanding of the eucharist. We know that some Jewish Christians in the second century came to be treated as heretics. Theological developments in the Johannine community may have led even in the 90s to opposition between that community and such Jewish Christians.

Finally, there are signs of yet other Christian groups related to the Johannine community. These were the groups represented by Peter and the Twelve and which may be called the "apostolic churches." (The author of the fourth gospel never uses the term "apostolic." But the group we are now describing might have used such a term in their self-understanding: from the other gospels and the author of Revelation we know that the notion of Twelve apostles was common coin among Christians in the last third of the first century.)

We have one indication that a group represented by the memory of Peter and the Twelve was seen as a distinct group in the evangelist's account of the "Bread of Life" discourse. The gospel tells us that some Jewish Christians drew back from following Jesus. But the Twelve, of whom Peter is the spokesman, held fast to their faith in Jesus (Jn 6:67–69). Further, the inclusion of Peter and other members of the Twelve at the Last Supper and in Jesus' final discourse and prayer (13:31–17:26) indicates a basic acceptance of this group. But the apostolic Christians are not altogether one with the Johannine Christians. In a half-dozen instances, Peter and the beloved disciple, the leader of the Johannine community, are contrasted one with another, with Peter always being put in a less favorable light (in 13:23–25, the Last Supper scene; in 18:15–16, the scene at the court of the high priest; in 20:2–10, the scene at the tomb; in 21:7, at the Sea of Tiberias after Jesus' resurrection; in 21:20–23, concerning Peter's question about the beloved disciple; and, implicitly, in 19:26–27, where the beloved disciple stands at the foot of the cross after Peter has fled).

The differences between the Johannine Christians and the apostolic Christians probably centered on two areas—the understanding of Christ and the understanding of the church. In the early part of the gospel, Andrew, Peter, Philip, and Nathaniel (not one of the Twelve) profess, as did the earliest nucleus of what would become the Johannine community, that Jesus is the Messiah, the one who fulfills the law and the prophets, and the Son of God (1:41, 45, 49). Yet Nathaniel is told that he will see greater things (1:50). Philip is rebuked at the Last Supper because he does not yet understand that Jesus is one with the Father (14:8–9). In time the Johannine Christians, by contrast, came to grasp the mystery of the pre-existence of Jesus and of his origins in God (1:18; 8:42, 58). The gospels of Matthew and Luke, both written only about ten years earlier, clearly teach that Jesus is the Son of God, but neither gives any indication of his pre-existence with God. Both of these gospels, of course, give an important place to Peter and the Twelve as leaders and guides of the faith of the community.

The second difference between the Johannine Christians and the apostolic Christians may have centered on the understanding of church. The fourth gospel shows no interest in the category of "apostle" (the term as such never appears in the gospel) but puts great emphasis on the category of "disciple." Continuity with Jesus comes not through the apostles, but through the beloved disciple (Jn 19:35; 21:24). At approximately the same time as the church is moving toward greater institutionalization and a growing emphasis on church offices (Matthew, Luke/Acts, the pastorals), the fourth gospel stresses unity with Jesus and, in its use of disciple as the basic Christian category, relativizes all church offices. It is in this context that we can appreciate the meaning and role of the Paraclete-Spirit (14:16–17, 26; 15:26; 16:7–13), the post-resurrectional presence of Jesus with his disciples now that he is no longer bodily on earth but with the Father in heaven. There is no reason to suppose that the author of the fourth gospel is totally opposed to the increasing emphasis on apostolic succession or the development of church structures and offices which we see in the other New Testament writings of this time. But the evangelist does give voice to the different experience and tradition of his own community and serves notice that what is most important is that the church be a community of disciples remaining in unity with Jesus through the presence of the Paraclete-Spirit.

Christianity Becomes a New Religion

Two other distinctive features of the Johannine community deserve to be mentioned before we look at the group's final years. The first of these is the Johannine church's self-understanding vis-à-vis Judaism. The story of the community of the beloved disciple is unintelligible apart from its relation to Judaism and the dissolution of that relationship. For all his earlier polemics with Judaism and with Jewish Christians, Paul comes to state in the letter to the Romans his belief that Gentile Christians are but the wild shoot grafted on the olive tree that is Israel (Rom 11:17). The post-Pauline letter to the Ephesians affirms that in the death of Jesus, Jew and Gentile are reconciled and both in one Spirit have access to the Father (Eph 2:13–18). But the Johannine Christians have an altogether different perspective: here the Christian community replaces Judaism.

This theme of replacement is expressed most especially in the gospel's attitude toward the temple and the feasts of the Jewish cult. The temple of Jerusalem has been replaced by the body of Jesus (Jn 2:19–21). The sabbath and the great Jewish feasts are reinterpreted or replaced by Jesus (ch. 5, the sabbath; ch. 6, the Passover; ch. 7, the feast of tabernacles; ch. 10, the feast of the dedication of the temple). In effect, in the Johannine community Christianity has become a new religion separate from Judaism. For the Matthean community at Antioch, Christianity has become the fulfillment of Judaism; for the Johannine community, probably at Ephesus, Christianity has become a new religion. This position was a result of the entire history of the Johannine community, but most especially, perhaps, a result of the development of its distinctive christological teaching.

The Role of Women in the Johannine Community

In the pastoral letters, presumably written in the 80s or 90s, there are indications that the pastor sought to curtail the role of women in the ministry of the church. The attitude of the fourth gospel and the Johannine community is quite different.

While the beloved disciple is the principal authority in the community, women are credited with functions vital to the community's life and growth. It is through the word of the Samaritan woman, for example, that many people of the city come to believe that Jesus is the Messiah (Jn 4:39–42). In the same context the Samaritan woman is recognized for her role in the missionary harvest of the apostles (4:38). In the story of Lazarus (ch. 11) it is Martha who is given prominence. It is to her that the mystery of resurrection and life in Jesus is revealed (11:25–26). And it is her profession of faith, "I believe that you are the Christ, the Son of God" (11:27), that is the closest gospel parallel to Peter's solemn profession of faith described in Matthew's gospel, "You are the Christ, the Son of the living God" (Mt 16:16). The same Martha is said to serve (*diakonein*) at table in the story of Jesus' anointing at Bethany (Jn 12:2). The Johannine passage is more significant when seen in relation to the office of deacon (*diakonos*) which appears in the pastorals and in Paul's letters (Rom 16:1; Phil 1:1). We also may recall that the task of waiting on tables was a specific function of the appointed officials in Acts 6.

Mary Magdalene is yet another important figure in the tradition of the Johannine community. In the fourth gospel it is not to Peter but to Mary Magdalene that the risen Jesus first appears (20:11–16) and it is she who is sent to bring the news of his resurrection to the disciples (20:17–18).

The fourth gospel says practically nothing about offices in the church, in part because discipleship was its most important category. Yet the positive manner in which it spoke of women (at about the same time when the pastorals were speaking in a very different manner), ascribing to them evangelizing roles which other New Testament writings ascribe to men, testify to the rich diversity of the early church at this time.

The Johannine Community at the Turn of the Century

A strictly chronological order would leave until the next chapter a look at the Johannine church(es) as we see them in the letters of John. But the historical development of the community as well as the inner connection between the gospel and the letters make it appropriate that we take up the topic at this time.

The three letters of John were likely written ca. A.D. 100, a decade after the writing of the main body of the fourth gospel (John 21 will be dealt with shortly). During this decade members of the community had become involved in a schism because of differing interpretations of some of the traditions of the community, if not of the text itself of the fourth gospel. We learn most about the conflict of interpretations through the first of the letters.

The first letter of John is less a letter than a treatise in which the author tries to rally the members of the Johannine community against a group which had broken away and was trying to win more adherents to its views. For the author the break was a dramatic one. He uses apocalyptic language to describe it: those who have seceded from the main body of the Johannine community are "false prophets" who act in the spirit of the "anti-Christ" (1 Jn 2:18; 4:1–6). Apparently the author's opponents have met with considerable success: perhaps even a majority of the community has followed them (see 1 Jn 4:5).

The errors of the secessionists centered on two topics: the understanding of Christ and the approach to ethical responsibility. While we know of the secessionists only through the Johannine letters, it appears that those who left the community were so preoccupied with the preexistent and the divine in Jesus that they paid little heed to his humanity or to his historical life, particularly his death on the cross (see 1 Jn 4:2–3, 10; 5:6; see also 2 Jn 7). Further, because they held that believers already had eternal life, they saw little value in doing good deeds or in observing the commandments (1 Jn 1:6, 8, 10; 2:3; 3:24).

A careful reading of the letters and of the gospel supports the view that the secessionists could well have believed that they were but drawing out the implications of the teaching present in the gospel. But the author of the letters believes, not without reason, that it was he who was faithful to the message of the gospel. In effect, what is at issue here is a difference of interpretation of the fourth gospel or its pre-written tradition.

The second letter of John, written by one who calls himself the elder (presbyter), seems to be directed to a single community in the provinces. This particular church is warned not to welcome members of the secessionists who might wish to visit them (2 Jn 10). The third letter is written by the presbyter to Gaius (in yet another town?), who is thanked for having received missionaries in the past (vv. 3, 5–8) and is asked to receive Demetrius who is about to come (v. 12). We are told that the presbyter has already written to this church, but that Diotrephes refuses to welcome anyone into the church and opposes those who do. It may be that both Gaius and Diotrephes are living in the same provincial town but belong to different house churches. Having failed in his attempts to gain welcome for his emissaries in the house church of Diotrephes, the presbyter may be trying to get Gaius to welcome Demetrius. There is no evidence to suggest that Diotrephes was a member of the secessionists.

The situation which comes to light in the Johannine letters is a complex one. First, the letters suggest a principal Johannine community composed of several, perhaps even many house churches in a large center (Ephesus?) with satellite Johannine communities in provincial towns not far away. (These letters are one of the reasons for the present scholarly view that most of the churches in the first century were located in the chief cities on the major trade routes. Only at the end of the century was Christianity spreading into the outlying villages.) Second, we see a serious split in interpreting a common tradition. This is not the first instance of sharp differences in the understanding of basic issues, but here we witness an actual schism within a particular community. And we have evidence that the breach was never healed. Both sides could appeal to the guidance of the Paraclete-Spirit (see 1 Jn 2:26–27), but the gospel says nothing about what happens when differences of interpretation cannot be resolved. The author of 1 John could only counsel: "Do not believe every spirit, but test the spirits to see whether they are of God" (4:1).

Third, we see a community where there were clashing views: emphasis on the discipleship of all the members (with a concurrent deemphasis on offices) versus an emerging leader of another local community (and all that might imply). Diotrephes was such a leader. He may have faced the prospect of a visitation by emissaries from both the presbyter-author of the letter and from the secessionists. Rather than leave it to the community to decide on authentic interpretation, Diotrephes may have decided that the interpretation of tradition was best left to the local leadership of the church. The author of 3 John understandably opposes this because this represents a break with the Johannine tradition concerning the Paraclete and the basic equality of all disciples. For his part, Diotrephes may have seen his approach as the only practical way to deal with conflicting interpretations of the original tradition.

Peter Becomes a Shepherd of the Johannine Community

The movement toward a more authoritative local leader in the Johannine community which we see in 3 John comes into sharper focus in the final chapter of John's gospel (chapter 21). Generally regarded as an appendix written by a final redactor, the chapter is thought to have been added to the gospel text about the same time the letters were written. A community for whom Jesus himself was the shepherd (Jn 10) is now asked to accept the pastoral authority of Peter (Jn 21:15–17). The dignity and memory of the beloved disciple is preserved in this added chapter, and Peter, in the threefold question about his love of Jesus, is made subject to the Johannine criterion of genuine discipleship. But Peter, not the beloved disciple, is made the shepherd of the community. The final editor knows that this goes against the grain of the Johannine tradition, so the proposed change is put in the form of a story in which Jesus authorizes Peter's role.

The story of this commission to Peter is perhaps a symbol of the Johannine community's history. Second century records show no further traces of the community as a distinct group. One can only surmise that the Johannine communities became consolidated with the apostolic churches. But if the Johannine community ultimately accepted the structure of the apostolic Church, it was able to preserve the christological insights which stood at the core of its identity. Had the community looked ahead, it would have seen its christology becoming the dominant interpretation of Jesus in the centuries which followed.

For their part, the secessionists also leave without any further record. It is likely that they gradually became one with the gnostics. Their teaching that Jesus only appeared in a human form but was not really one with us led to their exclusion from the main body of the church.

The Church in Northern Asia Minor:
The First Letter of Peter

There are two other New Testament sources of information about the church in Asia Minor during this period. We will look now at the first letter of Peter; the Book of Revelation will be discussed in the next chapter.

The majority of contemporary scholars hold that 1 Peter was written by an unknown author, a disciple of Peter, ca. A.D. 80. Most probably the letter was written at Rome. The letter is addressed to "the exiles of the diaspora in Pontus, Galatia, Cappadocia, Asia, and Bithynia" (1 Pet

1:1). It is not clear whether almost all of Asia Minor is meant or only the more precise areas of northern Asia Minor. The latter view is favored. If this is so, we are dealing with churches which were not part of the Pauline mission.

That a letter sent from Rome in Peter's name would have authority for these churches may be explained by the hypothesis that the churches of northern Asia Minor were evangelized by missionaries from Jerusalem, representatives of the moderately conservative Jewish Christian wing of the early church represented by Peter. Among the Jerusalem Christians, it was Peter more than James who was open to the Gentile mission. We know that Jewish Christians of an even more conservative character were active in the southern region of Asia Minor, among the Gentiles of Galatia (Gal 2:12). If, as we saw in Chapter Five, the Roman church was characterized by a moderately conservative Jewish Christian stance, it would make sense that a letter from "Peter" at Rome should be sent to these churches of Asia Minor. They and the church at Rome may well have shared a common type of Christianity that had its origins in Jerusalem. The Jewish themes in 1 Peter add support to this hypothesis.

Before looking at this Jewish imagery we may note three other features of the churches of northern Asia Minor which come to light in this letter. The first of these concerns the communities to which the letter was addressed. The author speaks of "the fiery ordeal" which comes to a people "reproached for the name of Christ" (1 Pet 4:12, 14). In the past such language led to the conclusion that the church was experiencing a persecution at the hands of the Roman government. We have similar examples in the local persecution of Christians at Rome under Nero (ca. 64), in the scattered persecutions which took place in the later years of the reign of Domitian (the 90s), or in the repressive measures which Trajan imposed in Bithynia (ca. 112). But a strong case has been made (J. H. Elliott) that the language of 1 Peter, however dramatic, reflects the social and religious hardships of the community. The addressees, spoken of as "aliens and exiles" (1:1, 2:11) may have felt alienated on two counts. First, as foreigners or migrant workers, they may have experienced restrictions in their political, legal, and social rights. These communities may also have felt themselves excluded because of their adherence to a religious belief which separated them from the pantheism and syncretistic spirit of their neighbors. To be called a "Christian" (4:16) was to be outside the mainstream of social life and regarded as a potentially disloyal, disruptive element in society.

It was in response to this disheartening situation that the author put forward his understanding of the church. This is the second feature we should notice. In face of these tensions and conflicts, the Christians could adopt either of two positions. They could yield to the pressures before them and, at least on one count, become one with their neighbors by adopting the pagan religions of the state. The intensity of 1 Peter's arguments suggests that some members of the church were, in fact, taking this option. The other option, proposed by the author, is that the Christians remain firm in their faith and find consolation and support in knowing that they are God's elect (1 Pet 1:2), a "chosen race, a royal priesthood, a holy nation, God's own people" (2:9), a new household in the Spirit (2:5).

It is this last image and the context we have been describing that may also be the key to interpreting the use of the household code in 1 Peter (see 2:18–3:8). The use of household codes in Colossians and Ephesians may be explained at least in part by the apologetic motive of showing Christian conformity to important features of the social and political system of the Greco-Roman world so as to avoid suspicion and mistrust. But here it may be (again, J. H. Elliott) that the author of 1 Peter uses the familiar code as a way to build up the church's cohesion and identity in the face of an unfriendly world. This is accomplished in conjunction with the letter's many references to baptism and to its use of symbols associated with that rite. In effect, this homeless people is being called to see the church as their home. The good order that is called for by the use of the codes would also serve to allay the suspicions that society might have of these foreign Christians.

A third feature of these northern Asia Minor churches comes to light in the author's exhortation to the elders (presbyters) of the community (5:1–4). The call to exercise the ministry "not by constraint but willingly" implies that the office was conferred by some type of designation or election. The reminder that the ministry is not to be seen as a source of "shameful gain" indicates that elders were paid a salary (see 1 Tim 5:17). Such injunctions suggest that leadership roles in the early communities had by this time undergone a considerable degree of development. The third element of the exhortation is no less significant: elders are not to be "domineering over" the community but are to be examples to the flock. The Greek word for "domineering" is the same word used in Jesus' instruction on the exercise of authority in Mark 10:42, a passage which has parallels in Matthew and Luke. Further, there are affinities between these texts and the footwashing scene in John 13 and the charge to Peter in John 21. The frequent and varied expression of this tradition indicates that the proper exercise of Christian ministry was an important concern in the early church.

The Church at Rome

The first letter of Peter is a valuable source of information about the church in northern Asia Minor. But it also sheds light on the church at Rome in the last third of the first century. This light shows how strongly Jewish was the Christianity at Rome. The first letter of Peter seeks to bolster the spirit and morale of Christians in Asia Minor by appealing to what was important to them and important as well to the church from which the letter was sent. The author in the first part of the letter (1 Pet 1:3–2:10) gives a baptismal instruction (drawn possibly from a baptismal liturgy or baptismal confession) that is steeped in the Jewish heritage of Christianity. We see the themes of exodus, passover, and the desert wandering applied to Gentiles who have been converted to Christ. In the same section the author employs the language of the ancient Jewish cult to describe Christ and the Christian church. The letter shows that even after the destruction of the temple and the end of Jewish temple sacrifice, the symbolism of Jewish worship was a powerful element in Roman Christian thought. We will see more of this when we look at the letter to the Hebrews.

Two other items call for attention. That a letter attributed to Peter is sent from Rome to churches in Asia Minor may be a telling indication that the church at Rome was beginning to assume a pastoral role toward other Christian churches. One notes, too, the strong appeal that Christians subject themselves to every human institution, whether it be the emperor or the governor (1 Pet 2:13–17). The text in 1 Peter recalls Paul's similar counsel in Romans 13:1–7. No doubt both texts indicate the authors' desire to silence critics of the church who argue that Christian belief makes the church hostile to the good order of the state.

The Letter to the Hebrews

Over the centuries the letter to the Hebrews has generated a great deal of speculation as to its author, its place of origin, and its destination. Though in the second century some attributed the letter to Paul, this attribution was even then seriously challenged. Almost universally today scholars hold that the author was someone other than Paul. Perhaps the best that can be said is that the letter—really a written sermon and one of the finest written documents of the New Testament—is the work of a second generation Christian (see Heb 2:3 and 13:7) who was not a well-known authority in the early church. We assume the latter from the fact that the message of the author was not well heeded.

The Lectionary for Mass of the revised Roman Missal generally (but not consistently) omits Paul's name from the title of the readings from the letter to the Hebrews.

Scholars generally conclude from internal evidence (13:23–24) that the letter was written to Christians in Rome. Indications within the text itself (for example, 2:3 and 13:7), the internal argument of the letter, and its citation by Clement ca. A.D. 96 date reasonably the writing of the letter between A.D. 75 and 90.

A recent study of the church at Rome (R. E. Brown) advances as plausible (it is difficult to do more than that with Hebrews) that not only was the letter written to the Christians at Rome but that its message was really meant as a corrective to the Roman church's outlook reflected in 1 Peter. More precisely, the heavily Jewish character of Roman Christianity is challenged by the author of the letter to the Hebrews.

We have seen above (Chapter Four) that the earliest believers in Jerusalem saw themselves as Jews, the nucleus of an Israel renewed by Jesus the Messiah in whom the end-time had been inaugurated and the covenant promises of God fulfilled. We saw too (Chapter Five) that the church at Rome was likely founded by missionaries from the Jerusalem church and that the Jewish and Gentile Christians of Rome retained strong ties to the Jewish Christianity exemplified by James and Peter. If our analysis of the letter to the Romans is correct, Roman Christian sympathy with its Jewish roots was still very strong in the late 50s when Paul wrote his letter. Probably, then, both Jews and Christians at Rome were affected by the defeat of Jerusalem and the destruction of the temple in the Jewish War of 66–70.

The Jews of Rome must have felt the burden of Roman propaganda after the war. After all, the war was a revolt in a minor province, but victory eluded Rome for several years and the empire's wounded pride needed to heal. A triumphal procession of the victor Titus, with the vessels of the temple displayed as military booty, occurred the year after the war ended. Roman coins into the 90s were inscribed with a reminder of the Jewish defeat (*Iudaea capta*). At the end of Titus' reign in the early 80s, the great arch celebrating Titus' victory and Jewish defeat was erected in the Roman Forum. Jews who had once paid a tax for the support of the Jerusalem temple were now forced to pay a "Jewish tax" for the support of the new temple to Jupiter built in the Roman capital. Yet for all the reminders of defeat, Jewish literature of the period records that some Jews—recalling the reconstruction of the temple after the defeat of Jerusalem in the sixth century B.C.—expected some type of restoration.

Perhaps some of the Roman Christians may have expected that in God's plans a Christian sanctuary might arise, replacing the Jewish levitical cult with its sacrifices and priesthood. Christians had in their tradition the memory of Jesus' statement that the Jerusalem temple would be replaced by another temple "not made with hands" (Mk 14:58). (In that passage the statement is put on the lips of false witnesses, it is true, but variants of this tradition surface in Matthew 26:61 and John 2:19–21). The variety of interpretations of this saying possibly indicates that some may have expected a Christian sanctuary as a successor to the temple. Indirect support for this may have come from the view that the Roman temple to Jupiter was Rome's replacement of the temple in Jerusalem.

As we know, the Essenes regarded themselves as faithful preservers of authentic temple traditions, as opposed to (in their view) the adulterated practices and impure priesthood of Jerusalem. They may even have practiced some form of cult in their desert communities as an expression of a renewed temple community. The use of strong exodus symbolism in the first part of 1 Peter shows that Christians, quite likely at Rome, shared a similar type of thinking.

Possibly Christians at Rome began to think that the levitical cult and sacrifices of the Jerusalem temple were to continue in some form in a spiritual Israel in the diaspora. We noted that Jewish and Gentile Christians in Rome took an intermediate position between Christians who wanted to preserve circumcision and those who rejected the Jewish law altogether. Roman Christians may have looked for a mediate position between the early Jerusalem believers who continued to worship at the Jewish temple and the Hellenists who rejected the temple and its cult.

This background may render intelligible two of the basic teachings of the letter to the Hebrews. The first part of the letter (Heb 1:1–4:13) insists that God's definitive word has been spoken in the Son and that his word has a priority over any communication made through angels or through Moses. The second part of the letter (4:14–10:31) teaches that Jesus is the eternal high priest whose sacrifice on the cross has atoned for sin once and for all, establishing the new covenant between God and humankind. The first (Mosaic) dispensation has been abolished, the author announces, and the second has been established (10:9). The letter to the Hebrews is really a Hellenist sermon seeking to dissuade Roman Christians (or a group of them) from their attraction to levitical cult and sacrifices, even if those were to be seen in a Christian context and exercised in a spiritual way. The author of Hebrews is really more radical than Paul; there is only one tabernacle and that is in heaven (8:1–2; 9:24); the law and priesthood have been changed (7:12); and the new covenant has made the old one obsolete (8:13). Though in its first decades the church could profess its faith in Christ and still remain within the fold of Judaism, the author of Hebrews no longer sees that as a possibility. (In this, the author of Hebrews adopts a position similar to the fourth gospel.)

In this view, the community to which this letter is addressed is not (as has sometimes been claimed) a church whose members are returning in discouragement to Judaism. Rather, the author of the letter to the Hebrews is arguing against a movement toward a conservative form of Jewish Christianity; leaning to some form of the levitical cult, this movement saw Jesus in continuity with the angels and with Moses. Whereas the author of 1 Peter advances the position that a spiritual continuation of the levitical cult is continued in the Christian community, the author of Hebrews rejects such an idea and argues against any sanctuary on earth.

We will see in the next chapter that the letter to the Hebrews was not successful in its efforts to alter the direction of Roman Christianity. However, this letter and John's gospel point to the continuing struggle of the early church (even toward the close of the century) to come to terms with its Jewish roots.

Two other New Testament writings evidence the continuing vitality of the wing of early Christianity for whom James was the chief authority. The first comes in the letter of James, generally thought to be the work of an anonymous author writing under the mantle of the brother of the Lord, leader of the Jerusalem church. The letter—really a homily—is written in a good Greek style by one who was evidently well educated. The author deals with the relationship between faith and action in the world, possibly against libertines who interpreted Paul's teaching on faith in an irresponsible way. (The letter seems to presuppose an awareness of Galatians 3 and Romans 4.) The letter of James really stands in the tradition of Jewish wisdom literature; in its social concern it is easily the peer of Israel's prophetic tradition (G. S. Sloyan). A recent study (S. Laws) suggests that probably James comes from the Jewish-Christian circles of Rome. Unlike the teaching of the letter to the Hebrews, the letter of James witnesses to the conviction that Christianity involves a belief in Jesus and an intensification of Jewish values, not a break with Judaism.

A second text, the letter of Jude, is also a pseudonymous writing, claiming the authorship of Jude, the brother of James (and therefore a brother of the Lord; see Mk 6:3). The work seems to come from the milieu of a Christianity very conscious of its Jewish roots. Internal evidence—the reference to the apostles in the past tense (v. 17), for example—and the fact that the letter was known by the author of 2 Peter places its writing in the latter part of the first century. The letter of Jude is a polemic against libertine gnostic teachers creating dissent within the church, though we have no indications where the church was located. The author draws upon Jewish and Christian apocalyptic; with the Book of Revelation it shows that apocalyptic was still a living force in the church even as institutional structures were developing. The end of the letter (vv. 20–21) cites a formula which was probably taken from the liturgy of the church.

Chapter Eight

The Church at the Turn of the Century

In the previous chapter we continued our account of the church's development by means of a geographical overview which, after a look at events associated with Jamnia in Palestine, moved to Antioch, then to Crete and Asia Minor, and finally to Rome. In this chapter we will reverse our direction and begin with the church at Rome and end with the church at Antioch. Our present time frame takes in the final years of the first century and the first decades of the second. This period coincides with the beginning of the third Christian generation.

The Church at Rome: Pastoral Care for Other Churches

Our understanding of the church at Rome during this period comes principally from two non-biblical sources, the letter of Clement of Rome to the church at Corinth (ca. A.D. 96) and the letter of Ignatius of Antioch to the church at Rome (ca A.D. 108–117). Both letters stand clearly within the post-apostolic period; they were composed by persons who wrote in their own name and on their own authority and not under the mantle of an apostolic leader.

These letters and other contemporary documents make it clear that the church at Rome was at this time exercising a pastoral care that extended beyond its own community. This may not have been the only church engaged in a broader pastoral mission, but it seems to have done so more than any other. The church at Jerusalem ceased to exercise its leadership after the flight of the Christians from the Judean capital at the time of the Jewish War. Perhaps the church at Rome felt called to a wider concern for other churches because of its location in the imperial capital, though that circumstance was never invoked. That the memory of Peter and Paul was often called to mind suggests that religious motives were far more important.

In an earlier day Catholic scholars spoke of this extended pastoral care of the Roman church at the end of the century as a "primacy" (Altaner, 1960) or as a "universal ecclesiastical supremacy" (Quasten, 1950). Today Catholic scholars regard Rome's solicitude at this time differently: it was a continuation of the apostolic care and guidance once associated with Peter and Paul but exercised in the last decades of the first century through the community most closely identified with the two principal leaders of the early church.

A Move Toward Christian Priests and Levites

Looking primarily at the letter of Clement but also at the letter of Ignatius, we can identify several important features in the church at Rome at the turn of the century. The first is the tendency to describe church officials in terms of a divinely ordered pattern and as a parallel to Jewish cultic roles. Clement's letter tells us of these developments. The letter was drafted to deal with a problem at the church in Corinth.

A radical group at Corinth had removed from liturgical office presbyters whose lives and ministry were evidently without fault. They created thereby a schism in the church (1 Clem 44 and 47). The cause of the conflict is unknown to us. Perhaps there was a struggle between charismatic leadership and a more established order. It may be that a youthful group rebelled against the elders of the community. Or there may have been simply a struggle between different groups trying to get control of church offices. Clement lamented the "jealousy and envy" that led to such an action (1 Clem 4–6); these same attitudes, he noted, led to the persecution and death of Peter and Paul decades earlier in the city of Rome (see above, Chapter Six). As part of his argument against the Corinthians who acted in this way, Clement invoked the divinely ordered pattern of the temple worship which consisted of high priest, priests, levites, and lay people (1 Clem 40:1–5; 41:2).

1 Clement 40:5 gives us the first instance of the use of the term laity, *laikos,* in Christian literature. The word *laikos,* "belonging to the people," comes from the word *laos* (people). Even the earliest New Testament writings, e.g., 1 Thessalonians show an awareness of different roles among the people of the church, but only gradually does the early church develop the vocabulary to express these differences within the basic unity of the baptized. From this development we get the words *laity* and *clergy* (from *klerikos,* "belonging to the inheritance," a reference to the Levites whose only inheritance was the Lord (Num 18:20).

Just as the Jewish cult had a divinely ordered pattern, so now, Clement taught, there was a divine pattern in the Christian community: apostles, presbyter-bishops, and deacons. The community's ministry was seen as the Christian equivalent of the Jewish levitical structure that prevailed until the fall of the temple.

In this development Clement was taking up a theme that appeared in 1 Peter and in the letter to the Hebrews. In 1 Peter there is a movement toward a spiritualization of the levitical cult and its application to the Christian community. The author of Hebrews discouraged such a development by teaching that Christ's one offering rendered the levitical cult and its repeated sacrifices obsolete. Clement does not accept the outlook of Hebrews but pursues the direction set by 1 Peter and even advances it: Clement uses the Jewish cultic order of high priests, priests, and levites as a way of describing Christian ministry. In fact Clement never speaks of eucharist nor does he speak of presbyters (elders) as priests. But he does speak of the "sacrifices proper to the episcopate" (44:4) and initiates a tendency that became even stronger in the course of the second century, that bishops, priests, and deacons were seen as Christian high priests, priests and levites because of their role in the eucharist as the Christian sacrifice.

With this development we have in place all the elements of what would become the traditional understanding of eucharist. By the end of the first century Christians saw themselves as a religious body distinct from Judaism. They saw the eucharist as an unbloody sacrifice replacing the sacrifices once offered in the Jewish temple. And those who presided at eucharist were soon called priests. This understanding of the development of priesthood and eucharist as a sacrifice obviously calls us to modify the view that Jesus instituted the priesthood at the Last Supper. The understanding presented in the account of this book affirms the legitimacy of the developments we have just summarized, and affirms that the priesthood and eucharist have a basis in the ministry of Jesus. But it also recognizes that the traditional understanding only emerged over the course of several decades in the life of the early church.

The Church and the Roman Government

Another element surfaces in Clement's letter which had great significance for the future of the church. To sustain his call for good order in the Corinthian church, Clement appeals not only to the example of a divine order in the levitical priesthood but to the order of the created universe (1 Clem 20) and to the ordered structure of the imperial government (1 Clem 37; see also the prayer formula in 60:4–61:2). Clement calls for obedience to civil authority because this is part of God's plan for the created universe.

In this Clement takes up a theme that was present in earlier texts associated with the Roman church: we find similar advice in Paul (Rom 13:1–7) and in 1 Peter (2:13–17). All three authors, we should note, were aware that the government of the empire could also be a source of harassment and persecution for the church. In the beginning of his letter (1 Clem 1:1) Clement alludes to the persecution which the church had experienced in the later years of the reign of Domitian (A.D. 81–96) and which had probably ended just before the letter was written.

However, Clement gives a new twist to his concern for Christian observance of public order. Even if the church was troubled by occasional persecution at the hands of Rome, Clement shows a positive admiration for the Roman system of organization and even draws a parallel between obedience to the presbyters and obedience to civil and military leaders. Of course, Clement was not the first in the church to see in civil structures and in Jewish tradition models that could be used to good advantage in the church's effort to order its own life and direct its mission. But the esteem that Clement and others had for the organizational structures of the empire, and their readiness to draw parallels between the empire and the church, had momentous consequences for the church in the centuries to follow. On the positive side, the Christian church became organizationally a powerful vehicle for evangelization. However, the negative side meant an uncritical acceptance of some organizational structures and styles which at times sadly hindered the witness and mission of the church.

Roman Presbyters at the Turn of the Century

In Clement's letter there are several glimpses of Roman church life and its presbyteral structure at the end of the first century. The house church was still an important structure of the Roman Christian community. Indirectly this is shown in the attention to house order given at the opening of the letter (1 Clem 1:3) and in the concern for ordered relationships in what is probably a house community (1 Clem 21). The emphasis on the virtue of "hospitality" (1 Clem 11:1; 12:1, 3) may be another indication of the importance of the house church.

Roman house churches were probably presided over by presbyter-bishops as in the churches of the pastorals and 1 Peter, but with a greater emphasis given to the cultic role of the church leader. By contrast to the church structure described in the letters of Ignatius, there is no clear distinction between presbyters and bishops in the Roman church; rather, we see here a twofold order of presbyter-bishops and deacons just as we see it in the pastorals. There is no indication that the church at Rome, comprised of several house churches, was governed by a sole individual. All the evidence seems to point to a collective leadership of the house-church presbyter-bishops in the city of Rome. This arrangement lasted until ca A.D. 140–150. Interestingly when Ignatius of Antioch wrote letters to various churches in Asia Minor and at Rome, his letter to Rome is the only one which fails to mention a bishop who is head of the entire local church community.

The leaders whose names are found in later lists of successors to Peter at Rome were probably the prominent presbyter-bishops of the city, some of whom may have exercised leadership concurrently. These lists come from a later period in which authors simply assumed that the structures of their day were also in place in the earlier hundred years of Roman Christianity. In the context of this understanding, Clement may well have been the presbyter-bishop assigned to write a letter to the Church at Corinth on behalf of the collective leadership of the Roman church.

One further point about presbyters-bishops in Clement's letter is noteworthy. In yet another aspect of his effort to restore and support good order in the Corinthian church, Clement proposed that the ejected presbyters had a pedigree that began with the apostles. The passage (1 Clem 44:1–2) is a famous one:

> Our apostles, too, were given to understand by our Lord Jesus Christ that the office of the bishop would give rise to intrigues. For this reason, equipped as they were with perfect foreknowledge, they appointed the men mentioned before [bishops and deacons], and afterward laid down a rule once for all to this effect: when these men die, other approved men shall succeed to their sacred [liturgical] ministry.

Clement's picture of apostolic succession is clear and simple, but other evidence from the period suggests that the matter of appointment and succession was far more complicated.

Our earliest New Testament document, 1 Thessalonians, written ca. A.D. 51, a few months after Paul founded the community in that city, refers to those who have a type of oversight with regard to others (1 Thes 5:12). Probably Paul himself had a part, at least, in designating the community's leaders.

The author of Acts records (14:23) that Paul and Barnabas in their early missionary journeys in Asia Minor appointed "elders" in the local churches they founded. We have no indication of an order of elders in any of Paul's letters, although, apart from Galatians, Paul's letters are not addressed to churches in Asia Minor. Certainly there were elders in the churches when Acts was written several decades later. There must have been some means of selection or appointment of church leaders, though we cannot say or assume that there was a uniform procedure in all churches. In the pastoral letters the apostolic degelate Titus is told to appoint elders in every town (Tit 1:5). But the Didache (possibly written around the same time as 1 Clement) instructs the people to appoint for themselves bishops and deacons worthy of the Lord (Didache 15:1). And nowhere in the New Testament do we have any evidence that the Twelve appointed others or laid hands on them to designate them as successors. Clement's portrayal, then, is an oversimplification and no doubt generalizes an occasional practice by some of the apostles (understood in the broader sense of the term).

In effect, Clement provided a divine sanction for what he believed to be the most orderly system of governance. In so doing, he provided a parallel to the two models cited earlier: the levitical priesthood, which was hereditary, and the empire whose two most successful periods coincided with the Julio-Claudian dynasty (Augustus to Nero, 27 B.C.–A.D. 68) and the Flavian dynasty (Vespasian to Domitian, A.D. 69–96).

This point is significant. On the surface Clement's view supports a pre-critical approach to the church's beginnings. A historically critical study recognizes a more complicated development, though we can easily understand how and why Clement advanced his view.

Readers familiar with Vatican II's Dogmatic Constitution on the Church (*Lumen gentium*) will recognize the Clementine picture of apostolic succession in chapter 3, article 20, of that text. Vatican II cited the letter of Clement along with certain texts from Acts and the pastorals. The intent of the council in this article was to reaffirm the ancient teaching that the bishops are the successors of the apostles and that this is part of God's plan for the church. The work of modern biblical scholarship supports that ancient teaching. But the council's presentation in this instance lacks the refined sensitivity to modern critical studies that we find elsewhere in the council documents; for the council did show a careful appreciation of the historical complexity of the development of ministry in the church, as we shall see.

The Church in Asia Minor

Our focus now moves from the city of Rome to the region of Asia Minor. (Through the letter of Clement we have seen something of the church in the Greek city of Corinth and need make no further comment on the church in that city.) Our principal source is a difficult one, the Book of Revelation, but one which gives important details to our picture of the church.

The Book of Revelation is a powerful poetic tableau which uses the distinct type of writing known as "apocalyptic." Writings of this genre use images and symbols to convey a message of hope to a people facing great dangers or persecution. The author purports to share with his audience (the text was clearly meant to be read to a community: see Rev 1:3) a vision which describes the situation of the hearers in mythical and symbolic language and promises that those who persevere will emerge victoriously from the present trials. We have many examples of this type of writing: in the Book of Ezekiel, in Zechariah 9–14, and most clearly in Daniel 7–12. In visual form we have what might be called a modern-day example of apocalyptic in Pablo Picasso's masterful "Guernica."

Several times in the text (Rev 1:1, 4, 9; 22:8) the author identifies himself as John. In antiquity and even today there are those who assume that this is John the son of Zebedee and the author of the fourth gospel. However, there are good reasons, among them the marked differences in language and patterns of thought, which support the view that the author of Revelation was an otherwise unknown prophet who wrote in his own name. A comment in the text suggests that John may have been the head of a prophetic school (see Rev 22:9). His self-described exile (Rev 1:9) to the Aegean island of Patmos off the coast of Asia Minor has the ring of plausibility. People who proved troublesome were often banished to such islands by the Romans.

The Book of Revelation was probably written ca. A.D. 90–95, toward the end of the reign of Domitian and thus at most a few years before the letter of Clement. Under Domitian Christians for the first time were persecuted by the government on religious grounds, though this persecution took place in some regions more than others. At issue was the imperial cult to which increasing attention was given throughout the period of the Flavian emperors: Vespasian (69–79) and his sons Titus (79–81) and Domitian (81–96). The cult of the emperor was especially fostered in the provinces. Proclaiming Domitian as "Lord and God" and participating in the state religion became a sign of political loyalty. Christians who proclaimed Jesus "Lord and God" could find themselves subject to banishment, torture, or even death, especially when the local government insisted on the imperial cult.

The situation of the Christians was aggravated because, increasingly separated from the synagogue, they were denied the protection accorded to Jewish religion by Roman law. Specifically, Christians no longer shared Jewish exemption from worship of the emperor and military service under the imperial banner. If the local authorities decided to press the issue, Christians were easily vulnerable to a charge of disloyalty. Apparently there was no all-out persecution of Christians prior to the second century, but sporadic incidents did take place and the increasingly totalitarian character of Domitian's reign made the future look very ominous. John himself had been exiled and could easily assume that the persecution that affected him could affect any or all of the churches of Asia Minor.

One way to avoid a confrontation with the empire was to compromise. Such was the position of the Christian prophets who are named in three of the letters to the churches with which the Book of Revelation begins. The church at Ephesus is praised because it rejected the itinerant Nicolaitan prophets (Rev 2:6); the church at Pergamum is faulted for allowing the same group a foothold in that community (2:15). A similar charge is placed against the church at Thyatira (2:20–23) where a woman prophet whom the author called Jezebel (see 1 Kgs 16:31; 2 Kgs 9:22, 30–37) won adherents among the community and taught the acceptability of eating food offered to idols. The Nicolaitans and the school of Jezebel could easily have argued that idols were of no account and that eating food offered to them had no religious significance. (We recall that a similar argument was used by certain members of the Corinthian church; see 1 Cor 8.) A believer might argue that insistence on a religious deference to the emperor was but a means of promoting political loyalty. Could not one honor the emperor (see 1 Pet 2:17) and participate in the ceremonies of the imperial cult without abandoning one's faith in the one who was truly Lord and God?

The author of Revelation entirely rejects such an argument. For him nothing less was at stake than two rival claims, those of the empire and those of the kingdom of God and of Christ. The struggle on earth was but part of a cosmic drama played out earlier in the heavens. In the apocalypse proper of Revelation 4–22, the author describes this struggle between the power of God and that of the empire. Jesus Christ alone is "King of kings and Lord of lords" (Rev 19:16). The seer rejects totally any Christian acceptance of Roman political power or of the imperial cult.

The Book of Revelation is but one voice in the early church, but it speaks a word which is very different from rendering to Caesar what belongs to Caesar and to God what belongs to God—a saying which the author of the first gospel attributes to Jesus (Mk 12:17). It differs also from the words of Paul (Rom 13:1–7), or the author of 1 Peter (2:13–17), or Clement of Rome. An awareness of the varied situations of the early churches helps us understand the diverse views expressed in the writings of the period.

Letters to Seven Churches

In addition to the more general information which the Book of Revelation gives us about the church in Asia Minor in the early 90s, we have at the beginning of the book (cc. 2–3) letters to seven churches in Asia Minor: Ephesus (the first named and possibly the author's own church), Smyrna, Pergamum, Thyatira, Sardis, Philadelphia, and Laodicea. The presence of such letters in an apocalyptic writing is remarkable; probably the great impact of Paul's letters on the early church explains the use of the letter form.

Each letter is written in a similar pattern: there is a word of praise for the church's accomplishment, followed by a statement of the church's shortcomings, and finally a word of warning. While each letter alludes to local circumstances, the letters were meant for the entire church of the region. Besides the teaching of the prophets mentioned earlier, other problems were a cause of concern. Some of the churches were showing a loss in their original fervor (Rev 2:4; 3:1, 15–16). There was some difficulty with a Jewish group whom we cannot otherwise identify (2:9; 3:9); perhaps this group was thoroughly Hellenized and saw no hesitancy in participating in emperor worship. It may be that some of its members brought charges against the Christians—leading to persecution by state officials. Finally, there is the problem of responding to persecution (2:3, 9; 3:8, 10). To all of these churches the seer calls for renewed allegiance to the Lord as the best way of facing oppression.

Two final observations on the Book of Revelation: the first concerns the author's emphasis on the role of the twelve apostles in the "new Jerusalem" which descends from heaven at the climax of God's victory over all the forces of evil (Rev 21:9–14). In this symbolic new city there will be twelve gates on which the names of the twelve tribes of the sons of Israel will be written. The walls of the city will have twelve foundations; on these will be written the names of the twelve apostles. This view preserves the symbolic end-time role associated with the Twelve in the gospel saying which appears in Matthew 19:28 and Luke 22:28–30 (see above, Chapter Three).

A second observation: for all the evidence of institutional structures because the church would exist for an extended period of time (an expectation especially evident in the pastorals and 1 Clement), the Book of Revelation shows how lively still the expectation of Jesus' coming remained. Three times in the epilogue of the book, the Jesus who guarantees the oracles contained in the prophet's words proclaims that he is soon to come. The third of these proclamations and the author's response are well known: "He [Jesus] who testifies to these things says, 'Surely I am coming soon.' Amen. Come, Lord Jesus!" (Rev 22:20).

The Church at Antioch

We end this chapter with another glance at the churches of Asia Minor and a final look at the church at Antioch. In doing this we will draw upon another non-biblical source, the letters of Ignatius, a leader of the church at Antioch.

Ignatius was probably of Syrian origin and a convert from paganism. He emerged as a leader of the church at Antioch and, for reasons unknown to us, was tried and sentenced for an offense punishable by death. He was sent from Antioch to Rome, where, the historian Eusebius (died ca. A.D. 340) tells us, he suffered death during the reign of the emperor Trajan (98–117). On his way to Rome he was taken to Smyrna, a large and important commercial center about midpoint on the western coast of Asia Minor. Here he was given an honorable welcome by Polycarp, the bishop of Smyrna, and by representatives from neighboring Christian communities. At Smyrna he wrote letters to the church at Ephesus, to the churches of the nearby cities of Magnesia and Tralles, and to the church at Rome. From another stop at Troas, further north on the western coast of Asia Minor, he wrote letters to the churches at Philadelphia (an inland city in western Asia Minor) and at Smyrna, and a letter to Polycarp, the bishop of Smyrna. The letters are commonly thought to have been composed between A.D. 108 and 117.

The seven letters of Ignatius are personal testimonies to the author's deep faith in Christ and his readiness and even eagerness to see the culmination of his discipleship in the execution that awaited him. In his letters he encourages the various churches to unity and steadfast faith. But through the letters we see that Antioch and the churches to which he wrote were facing a twofold challenge. First, there was a Judaizing movement that was exerting an influence on the churches, both in theology and in matters of cult (Magnesians 8–10; Philadelphians 6). Second, a threat came from Docetists who minimized Jesus' life in the flesh and held that Jesus' human nature was not real but only an appearance. For some, this denial of Jesus' humanity extended to a rejection of the Eucharist (Ephesians 7–9; Magnesians 11; Trallians 9–11; Smyrneans 1–7; Polycarp 3). We noted above (Chapter Seven) that a type of docetist teaching was also the view of the Johannine secessionists.

To meet the challenge of these erroneous teachings, Ignatius places a great emphasis on the leadership of the churches. In this context we learn of an important development in church structure which took place at Antioch at this time. Unlike the loose structures of prophets and teachers in the Antioch of Matthew's gospel (Mt 23:34; see Acts 13:1) or the two-tiered structure of presbyter-bishops and deacons evident in the letter of Clement of Rome, we see in Ignatius' letters a clearly distinguishable three-tiered structure of one bishop, a group or council of presbyters (a *presbyterion*), and a group of deacons (Philadelphians 4; Magnesians 2–3, 13). In the letters the leadership role of the bishop is highlighted: the bishop is the chief teacher in the church; obedience and "every mark of respect" (Magnesians 3) are to be shown to him; nothing should be done in the church, no baptism or eucharist undertaken, without reference to the bishop (Smyrneans 8). Oversight and direction under the leadership of the one bishop has been called a "monarchical episcopate," but in this case the term must be used carefully: in Ignatius' letters the one bishop presided in a collegial manner.

There is no mention of prophets or teachers, possibly because these roles have been absorbed into that of the bishop in union with the council of presbyters. Other church ministers presumably became deacons and the diaconate itself became a hierarchical office subordinate to the bishop. (Ignatius gives no indications that women held any of these roles. We do have evidence from the third and fourth centuries that women deacons played a subordinate role in church ministry.)

Two factors account for the change in structure. First, the church needed to counter growing threats to the integrity of the faith. Such threats came from gnostic teachings, especially those which minimized the humanity of Jesus and, by extension, the reality of the eucharist. A Judaizing group also needed to be dealt with, though this was not cause of so intense a concern. Perhaps the church at Antioch still had within it some of the tensions which Matthew's gospel sought to address. Second, the spread of even intermittent persecution at the hands of the government, of which Ignatius himself was a victim, may have led to further consolidation within the church community. The effort to provide a stronger leadership evidently met with success: when Ignatius reached Troas he learned that peace had been restored to the church at Antioch (Philadelphians 10:1; Smyrneans 11:2; Polycarp 7).

The organizational shift represented in Ignatius' letters was a dramatic one, but should not be exaggerated. The whole church of Antioch might have been the size of a present-say parish (J. P. Meier), with the bishop serving the role that would correspond to a pastor today. Further, this particular structure probably emerged quite naturally when one singularly gifted prophet-teacher at Antioch—Ignatius himself perhaps—assumed first place in the college of leaders from which he came. The change at Antioch may have been a logical fusion of charism and office for the good of the church. And the office, in Ignatius' mind, was to be conducted in a collegial manner. Yet the evangelist Matthew might not have regarded such a change as a happy development: he did not look kindly on those who sought the chief place in the community (Mt 23:6).

The shift to this three-tiered structure must have been recent, for Ignatius' insistence may imply that it was an innovation and was meeting some resistance. The transition to this new form of governance at Antioch took place ca. A.D. 100. This date allows sufficient time after Matthew's gospel for the change to occur, and sufficient time for the change to become so customary at Antioch that Ignatius took it for granted in his letters. It is this three-tiered hierarchical structure described in Ignatius' letter which has been a characteristic of many Christian churches ever since.

The bishops at Vatican II recognized this development of church structure and did so in a very interesting way. The Council of Trent, in its twenty-third session (1563) dealing with the sacrament of order, added to its statement of doctrine the following canon: "If anyone says that in the Catholic Church there is not instituted a hierarchy by divine ordinance, which consists of bishops, priests and ministers, let that person be anathema." Vatican II, in chapter 3 of its Dogmatic Constitution on the Church, took up the issue of the hierarchy; in article 28 it referred to the canon of Trent. But in the transmission of the teaching of Trent, Vatican II showed a careful sensitivity to the complex historical development we have been reviewing.

This is the statement of Vatican II: "Thus the divinely instituted ecclesiastical *ministry* is exercised in different degrees by those who even *from ancient times* have been called bishops, priests and deacons" (italics added). There are three changes in the text. First, where Trent used the term hierarchy, Vatican II spoke of ecclesiastical ministry. In a section dealing with the early history of ministry, Vatican II wished to recognize that the term hierarchy is not found in the New Testament writings. Second, where in Trent the distinctions between the offices were said to be instituted by divine ordinance, Vatican II spoke simply of a divinely instituted ecclesiastical ministry. The recent council recognized that ecclesiastical ministry is part of the divine plan for the church; but it was aware that the triad of episcopate, priesthood, and diaconate is never mentioned as such in the New Testament. Finally, Vatican II states that the three orders mentioned are *very ancient,* implying that they may not have been in place from the beginning.

Trent did not intend to make a pronouncement on the historical beginnings of the church's ministry; it intended to teach that a structured ministry in the church was part of the divine plan for the church. Vatican II wished to preserve that teaching, but did so in a manner that took account of recent biblical scholarship. The representatives of the theological commission of the council explicitly pointed out that this was their intent.

The Second Letter of Peter

The writing which is commonly thought to be the last written text of the New Testament is the second letter of Peter. This text takes us to the outside edge of the time frame of this study, but since it is one of the canonical writings, mention of the text is appropriate. While the letter makes the claim to have been written by the apostle Peter (2 Pet 1:1, 16–18), even in antiquity this claim was challenged. It is generally accepted today that the work was written by a third or even a fourth generation Christian, possibly as late as A.D. 125. The letter is written in the style of a final testimony of a great leader to the community of his followers or, possibly, of a civil decree in which a benefactor recalls his services to the recipients with a view of eliciting a response from them (F. W. Danker). Because the letter refers to the first letter of Peter it may be that this letter was also written at Rome to the same general region of northern Asia Minor, but this is only an educated guess.

Two items in the letter are of interest. The first is the fact that, again, the community was threatened. But this threat came not from the imperial government as in Revelation nor from a hostile environment as was the case in 1 Peter. The threat came rather from those within the community who preached a false gospel and led lives of self-indulgence that contradicted their Christian commitment (2 Pet 2:1–22).

One of the teachings questioned was the belief in the second coming of the Lord (2 Pet 3:3–4). This denial was accompanied by the thought that life and history were without any final destiny. The author of 2 Peter strongly reaffirmed the traditional teaching in the face of this skepticism. But he did so in a way which indicates that the expectation of the Lord's return had become very weak: "Do not ignore this one fact, beloved, that with the Lord one day is as a thousand years, and a thousand years as one day" (2 Pet 3:8). The teaching is affirmed as a dogmatic principle, but it is not a strong influence on daily life.

The second point of interest is the indication that Paul's letters have by this time achieved an almost official status and are clearly regarded as "scripture" for the community (2 Pet 3:15–18). Evidently the false teachers within the community were appealing to Paul's letters and using them as a support for their teaching. The author of 2 Peter, in the name of Peter, rejects such an abuse and gives his approval to the letters of his "beloved brother Paul." The memory of the earlier tensions between Peter and Paul (recall Gal 2:11–14) has been replaced by the view of later decades that Peter and Paul were the two principal figures of the early community.

Chapter Nine

The Beginnings of the Church—Today

The Swiss missionary theologian Walbert Bühlmann tells the story that at the close of the 1974 Synod of Roman Catholic Bishops—on the theme of evangelization in the modern world—Pope Paul VI handed each of the participants as they left a copy of the Acts of the Apostles. It was a symbolic gesture on the pope's part: a reminder that this early account of the church retains its importance almost two thousand years after it was written, and an expression of his belief that the Spirit which guided the church of the first century guides the church still (W. Bühlmann, *The Church of the Future*). It is in that same perspective that we might reflect on how a knowledge of the church's beginnings could be a resource for us today.

More important than a historical study of the early church is the abiding value of the scriptures as God's word, calling us and guiding us in who we are and what we do as church. But a clearer historical understanding of our beginnings can also serve us as a guide, an encouragement, and a challenge.

We rightfully do not expect from the history of the early church a blueprint for the church today. But a better understanding of our past can give the church a boldness and a freedom—and a word of caution as well—as we look to the last years of this century and the beginning of the third millennium. Seven themes seem especially important. The considerations which follow are influenced by the Roman Catholic experience of the author and, no doubt, by his personal interests as well. It is hoped that these reflections may be a stimulus to all Christians as they engage in reflecting on the church of Christ.

Development in the Church

Certainly one of the striking features that emerges from a study of the church's beginnings is the very phenomenon of development. The Christian story began simply enough with Jesus and his disciples. Through the events of Jesus' death and resurrection and the presence of his Spirit, through the interaction between Hebrews and Hellenists and between Jewish Christians and Gentile converts, the group which followed Jesus gradually developed into a new religious community with its distinctive beliefs, its own worship, and its own form of life. ("Community" is put in the singular to give expression to the sense of *koinōnia* so frequently expressed in the New Testament as binding together diverse Christians and their leaders.) Such development did not take place without tensions and misunderstandings, nor did it unfold uniformly in every location. But there were developments in every major area of the life of the early church. We simply cannot see the early church correctly apart from an awareness of this phenomenon.

Christians have not always been very sensitive to this aspect of the church's life. The outlook of many Christians, Catholic and Protestant alike, was quite ahistorical in the period following the Reformation, whether or not they realized it—and understandably so since they did not have the methods or tools for deep historical research. In the nineteenth century a new interest in history generally, and studies on the history of the church in particular, led the churches to deal more directly with the phenomenon of their own historicity. The dialogue between the churches and the historians, if it occurred at all, did not go smoothly. Perhaps this was especially true of Catholics.

Almost simultaneously with his becoming a Catholic John Henry Newman published his own probings into the historical reality of the church in his *Essay on the Development of Christian Doctrine* (1845). But Catholics were suspicious of the book; only in the 1930s and 1940s did they give the book widespread positive recognition. The bishops at Vatican I (1870), drawing upon nineteenth century Catholic apologetics, stated that the church's "unconquered stability" was one of the external factors which constituted an "irrefutable witness" to her divine mission (Dogmatic Constitution on the Catholic Faith, chapter 3). In the early part of this century official Roman Catholic reaction to the modernists allowed little room for the notion of development. It was Catholic scholarship in the 1940s and 1950s and most especially the Second Vatican Council which helped Catholics meet head-on the factor of development in the life of the church.

Today more and more we recognize and accept the phenomenon of development in the church's history and particularly in the special period in which the church began. This recognition may do us good service in the decades ahead when we may be challenged to accept new developments in the life of the church.

Unity and Diversity in the Church

Unity and diversity were inseparably a part of the phenomenon of development in the early church. The more the New Testament and the early church are studied with the use of historical-critical methods, the more we come to see the rich and perhaps surprising diversity that was present in first century Christianity. In the early part of the twentieth century scholarly critics argued that there were two basic forms of early Christianity, a Palestinian Jewish Christianity and a Hellenistic Gentile Christianity. We have long since come to see that such an analysis is woefully inadequate in face of the evidence. On the sole issue of the church's relation to Judaism there were Jewish Christians and Gentile converts who alike took various positions on a spectrum that ranged from those who wanted to maintain the full observance of the Mosaic law to those who saw no need for circumcision, Jewish cult, or many of the Jewish observances. There was a marked variety, too, in the way different communities and writers understood Christ, the Spirit, and other aspects of Christian life.

The diversity of the early church is reflected still in the writings of the New Testament. By accepting the twenty-seven books of the New Testament as her canon (rule) of scripture, the church has chosen to live with diversity and with the tensions which sometimes come in the wake of diversity. No single understanding of Christ and no one expression of church fully exhaust the mystery of Christ or the richness and variety of life that come when the Spirit dwells among Christ's followers.

But diversity is only one element; throughout the early church the strong concern for unity prevented diversity from degenerating into chaos or disintegration. The early Christians struggled to preserve a unity of faith and a community in the Spirit. Some segments of the church—the Ebionites, the Gnostics, the Docetists—did not preserve the basic faith, and eventually they went or were made to go their separate ways. But Peter, Paul, and James strove to preserve communion, even in the midst of their differences. Among these three leading figures, there is ample evidence that Peter became a stabilizing force for unity amidst diversity. In the decades after his death the memory of Peter served as a moderating influence among those who, in the name of either Paul or James, would have pushed to extremes. The presence of diversity in the early church and the conviction of the need for a basic unity were not easily maintained. But both had and have still an essential and—let us say it clearly—a God-given place in the life and mission of the church.

There are several areas where the example of the early church in its unity and diversity can be a guide for us. It is no secret that there are strong differences within the Roman Catholic Church, for example, in these decades after Vatican II. It is very salutary for all Christians to see and keep before them the early church's conviction that there is and must be both unity and diversity in the church. When the tension to preserve both these elements gives way to a single-minded interest or advocacy of either one or the other, something very basic to the reality of the church is neglected and the church as a whole suffers from such neglect.

The issues of unity and diversity also bear upon the relationships that Christians have with each other. Here too the New Testament and the early church have something to say to us. There was a time when various Christian churches tended to grasp one of the different New Testament perspectives on church and use that perspective to justify a particular outlook or church structure against other Christian bodies. Happily there seems to be much less of that approach today. Perhaps the recognition of a likeness between one's own Christian church and one or another emphasis of the New Testament churches may help Christians today to appreciate the value of their particular tradition and its fidelity to some part of the legacy of the early church.

But there is more to be considered. Put very starkly, we cannot use the New Testament or the early church to support or justify Christian division. Diversity within a basic unity, yes; division, no. Our awareness of the complementary features of unity and diversity in the early church challenges us to do all we can, under God and in the Spirit, to overcome Christian disunity. It is a blessing, surely, that many Christians today are more appreciative of the partial unity among us that is founded on shared faith and a common baptism. But that unity is not complete. The communion of the early churches prompts us to seek a full visible unity among Christians. The diversity in the early church and the New Testament writings may be telling us that in that unity there may well be room for greater diversity than was once thought possible.

There is yet a third area in which the church, in years to come, may give witness to unity and diversity. Roman Catholics, for one, have recently become far more respectful of the different cultures in which the Christian faith may take root. Such respect can enable the church to draw from the customs, the wisdom and traditions, and the arts of diverse peoples those things which can promote the life and mission of the church.

Vatican II, in its Decree on the Church's Missionary Activity, promoted such an outlook among Catholics. Since then this same theme was taken up in the 1974 Synod of Bishops and in Pope Paul VI's remarkable document, "On Evangelization in the Modern World," issued the following year. More recently Pope John Paul II, in his fourth encyclical, "Apostles of the Slavs" (1985), proposed as models for the church the ninth century missionaries Cyril and Methodius. Their work of evangelization is put forward as a paradigm of "inculturation," the incarnation of the Gospel in native cultures, and the introduction of those cultures into the life of the church. The more such a principle of evangelization is allowed to shape the growth and expression of the church in Africa, Latin America, and Asia, the more we may come to see new expressions of diversity within the unity of the church.

Christianity in the Greco-Roman World

One of the remarkable features of the early church was its transition from a Jewish Christianity to a Gentile Christianity in the Greco-Roman world. Jesus himself, of course, was a Jew, deeply rooted in the faith and traditions of his people. The earliest believers after the resurrection were Jews, natives of Palestine and inhabitants of the diaspora. But it was not long before there were evangelizing efforts among those who were not Jews. Missionary efforts were soon taking place in the cities along the important trade routes of the Greco-Roman world.

In the course of the first century the Christian church moved from its Jewish Christian beginnings to become a new and distinct religion, predominantly Gentile, seeking to find a place in the Greco-Roman world. The Gospel of Luke and the Book of Acts stand out among the New Testament writings in their effort to situate Christianity in the broader context of the world of the Roman Empire. In the following centuries Christianity became the dominant religion of the Greco-Roman world. With the passing of the Roman Empire Christianity became the faith of Europe and of the Byzantine East.

This transition of the church from its Jewish milieu to the Hellenistic and European world marks the first epochal change in the church. Christians generally and Roman Catholics in particular may now be entering another transition which rivals in significance the shift that took place in the first century. The late Jesuit theologian Karl Rahner advanced the thesis that Christians are now passing into the third great epoch of the church's history. The first period, though very brief, was that of Jewish Christianity. The second was the period of the church as the religion of Hellenism and of European culture and civilization. And the third period which we are now entering is the period of the world church.

In what has generally come to be recognized as a key interpretive essay on Vatican II, Rahner (*Concern for the Church,* chapter 6) says that the council was in a rudimentary way the Roman Catholic Church's first official self-actualization as a world church. This is seen, in part, in the worldwide episcopate—a novelty in the history of the Catholic Church—which made up the council. The acceptance of the vernacular in the liturgy and the council's concern for the entire family of humankind are further indications which, Rahner maintains, support his thesis. The council's desire to respect regional diversity in the church and to relate to other Christian churches and to other religions are added signs of this shift.

Rahner's thesis—and specifically the parallel between the early transition from a Jewish Christianity to a Gentile church (which was, we have seen, a very complex process) and the transition now from a church of Europe (and of countries heavily influenced by Europe) to a burgeoning world church—has been adopted by others. Walbert Bühlmann (in the work cited earlier in this chapter) points to demographic factors which in the year 2000 will make Christianity (and Catholicism even more so) a church in which more than two-thirds of its members will come from Latin America, Africa, and Asia. He suggests that the transition the church now faces finds its closest counterpart in the church of the first century. We do not know what exactly all this will mean, though it will inevitably involve the inculturation mentioned in the previous reflection. It will also include development, the struggle for unity and diversity, and likely the tension that is inevitable in so significant a transition.

The Local Church

One very striking feature of first century Christianity is the fact that the early church was really many local churches, each with its distinctive beginning, its own make-up and, at times, with problems and challenges which were proper to itself. When we speak of the beginnings of the church we are often speaking of the beginnings of the church at Jerusalem, at Samaria and at Antioch, at Thessalonica and Corinth, at Rome. The specificity of the early churches consisted not merely in their geographical location. There were differences in theological understanding and pastoral practice as well: the church at Jerusalem in the 30s and 40s was quite different from the church at Antioch in the 80s. One of the major results of recent New Testament studies is precisely the awareness of the variety of early local churches and the distinctiveness of each.

This awareness coincides with an important development in recent Roman Catholic theological reflection on the church. Since the sixteenth century, Roman Catholics generally have thought of church as a universal church with its center in Rome. The bishops at Vatican II preserved that universal dimension, but they sought to complement it with a recognition of the importance of the local church and its priority in the lived experience of most believers. It was recognized that the basic "building-blocks" of the church are local people who believe in Jesus and seek to live in a given time and place according to God's word and God's Spirit; who enter the community through baptism and celebrate its life at eucharist; who seek to carry on the church's evangelizing mission. So the local church must be given a new importance, preserving always the bonds of communion with other churches and the unity of the local church with the universal church.

It is precisely this shift of focus that has been likened to a "Copernican revolution" in recent Roman Catholic understanding of church. No longer do Catholics look primarily at the universal church and its center and see the local church as a portion of the whole. Rather, they are increasingly coming to see the local church as their primary experience of church. From one point of view, the universal church is a communion of local or particular churches. A study of the early church enhances this perspective.

Within the particular churches of the first century certain elements stand out, perhaps because developments in the churches of our day make us especially sensitive to them. First, in the letters of Paul, most especially in the First Letter to the Corinthians and in his Letter to the Romans, it was taken for granted that each member of the community had a charism, a gift, to be used for the good of the entire group. To be sure, there were difficulties that came from the presence of these varied charisms. The need for a mutual recognition of these gifts and their coordination for the good of the entire body could become a pressing pastoral concern. But for Paul these gifts were an expected and indispensable element of the community's composition.

Among Christian churches the Roman Catholic Church in particular has come to have a new appreciation of the plurality of gifts in each local community, even if the word charism is not always used. The presence of these gifts and their place in the renewal and growth of the church were given official recognition at Vatican II (Dogmatic Constitution on the Church, articles 4, 12). The experience of the early church may be an encouragement for Catholics to seek out and to recognize the presence of these gifts; it may also offer guidance as to their use.

One cannot avoid being struck by another feature in the life of the early churches—the frequent threat that came from teachings which were incompatible with the basic message of the gospel. The danger posed by such teachings was a serious one and many times there was a critical need to preserve the community's fidelity to the Lord and to his basic message. Here we must be careful not to oversimplify our reading of the New Testament or draw a one-sided conclusion from the experiences of the early church. In dealing with the questions of normative teaching and authoritative teaching supervision in the church, different Christian churches since the sixteenth century have made much of one or another element of the New Testament writings or of the early church. Some have looked to the presence of authoritative leaders in the community; others, to the belief that the Spirit is present in all the members of the church. Here especially there may be a temptation to choose one element to the neglect of another; we can find no support for such an approach in the canon of the New Testament writings. The struggle to preserve a fidelity to the Lord, the presence of authoritative teachers in the community, and the need to understand the teaching of the Lord in the light of new situations and new circumstances—all are abiding factors in the life of the church. The challenge to give each of these elements its due is a great one, but it is a challenge that cannot be avoided.

Ministry in the Church

Another of the results of contemporary biblical scholarship is our better appreciation of the development and diversity of forms of ministry among the first Christian generations. In the Jerusalem church there were the Twelve, the Hellenist leaders, and James and the elders. In the Christian mission were Paul, Barnabas, Apollos, co-workers Sosthenes, Euodia, Synteche, Andronicus, Junia. There were the heads of household in the various house churches: Prisca and Aquila are perhaps the most notable among them. There were the apostolic delegates, Timothy and Titus, and the presbyter-bishops of the pastorals. Mention must be made, too, of the beloved disciple in the Johannine community, of the presbyter who wrote at least two of the letters of John, and of Gaius and Diotrephes.

In giving form to the leadership roles in their communities, the early church drew from different sources—from the structure of synagogue leadership, for example, or from models such as those of the Dead Sea community at Qumran. Moreover, adaptations were made as needs became apparent. Diversity and development are present throughout.

There are several ways in which our knowledge of the ministry of the early church might bear on our approach to ministry today. An appreciation of the diversity of ministry in the early church may lead to a greater acceptance of variety in forms of church ministry in the future. This might be especially true in a reunited Christian church which, we fervently hope, will be a reality before too long. The presence of those who preside over (*episkopein*) the community in a serving leadership is quite clearly an essential part of the structure of the church. But the exact shape of other forms of church ministry may be open to greater variety than we had come to expect in times past.

Catholics may be drawn to another consideration. By almost every assessment, one of the most significant changes within the Roman Catholic Church since Vatican II has been the great increase in the number of those engaged in various types of ministry in the church and in the world. At first—and for some this is still the case—ministries of the laity were seen as a fill-in for fewer numbers among the clergy or religious. Vatican II itself, it may be said, reflects something of this attitude. More recent statements (e.g., the statement of the U.S. Catholic bishops, "Called and Gifted: Catholic Laity 1980") see ministries founded in part on the share given to each of the baptized in the mission of the church.

As our experience and understanding of new and developing ministries has grown over the years, we have come to appreciate the experience of the early church as an exemplar and encouragement in this matter. Pope Paul VI, in his statement "On Evangelization in the Modern World," pointed to a twofold guide in the contemporary development of ministries: the writings of the New Testament and the present needs of humankind and of the church. As a church Catholics are making their way in this area: the story of the early church tells them that they ought to proceed with good order, but also with creativity and imagination.

The Role and Ministry of Women

Current interest in the role of women in the church leads us to ask if a study of the church's beginnings offers any guidance to the church of our day as we deal with this important issue.

A careful reading of the New Testament texts shows that women had a greater place and role in the early church than many of us had at one time thought. Perhaps there is a parallel between our appreciation of development in the early church and our appreciation of the role of women. In the past many views of the church's development were greatly influenced by the picture of the church that comes to us in the Book of Acts. Impressed by the somewhat idealized picture given in that source, we tended to miss the intensity and complexity of some of the struggles that took place in the early years of the church. In a similar way, some Christians, at least, have probably been influenced in their view of the role of women in the church by the picture of the church in the pastorals, for example, and perhaps by their own experience up to fairly recent times of women's roles in the church—roles that reflected the position of women in secular culture. As a result many of us tended not to give full attention to the prominence of women in the early church.

A more attentive reading corrects this neglect; we are helped to see aspects of the picture which were overlooked. Our present knowledge of the early church does not give us a blueprint of how women today should take part in the life and mission of the church. But a more complete knowledge of the early church does support current efforts to explore the role of women in the church and in its ministries.

All agree we must take full account of all the evidence of the New Testament texts on the role of women in the early church. Some scholars, however, argue that these texts have an in-built patriarchal bias which obscures the place which women actually held in the early church. A patriarchal world-view is one which assumes and accepts the dominance of men in the structures of government, in the economy and the military, and in institutions of culture and religion. By contrast, a feminist perspective views all patriarchal forms of domination as unjust; today women and men should seek to recognize the positive contributions of all persons and seek to establish equality between the sexes. Feminist exegetes note evidence of a patriarchal attitude in some New Testament writings (e.g., the pastorals) and argue that this same attitude in subtle ways has influenced the writing of other biblical texts so as to give a distorted picture.

To remedy this deficiency, feminist exegetes offer their own reconstruction of the beginnings of the church (see, for example, the work of Elisabeth Schüssler Fiorenza). They try to appreciate fully all the evidence that touches upon the role of women in the early church. But they also try to read between the lines—with tentative methods which have not won wide acceptance and which are still being refined—to produce what they believe to be a more accurate picture of the role of women in the church of the first century.

The account given in this book has tried to give a faithful representation of the role of women in the early church as we can draw it from the texts themselves. Reconstructions making use of more speculative methods offer other readings.

Judaism and Christianity

The last of our reflections, on the relationship between Christianity and Judaism, brings us back, literally, to the beginning, but also looks to the future. The historical and theological relationship between Christianity and Judaism is a complex one, but it can draw light from a knowledge about Jesus and the beginnings of the church.

One of the unmistakable results of contemporary biblical and historical studies is the realization of the Jewishness of Jesus and of the early church. There were elements in the teaching and ministry of Jesus which were distinctive to him, to be sure, but these fit within the context of his Jewish background. Overall, Jesus' life and ministry are unintelligible apart from his Jewishness and the Jewish milieu in which he lived. Jesus conducted his mission as one who proclaimed the dawning of God's kingdom and who sought to bring Israel to the core, as he saw it, of its religious faith. Even if very soon after the resurrection some of his followers pushed to new frontiers and began a mission to the Gentiles, the early church can only be seen correctly if we see its Jewish roots.

The story of the evolving relationship between Judaism and emerging Christianity in the first century does not permit easy summarization. Relations between Judaism and the first three generations of Christians were at times stormy. Reflections of the sometimes bitter tensions between the two groups are a permanent record in several of the New Testament writings. The polemics in some of these texts had a role in encouraging in later centuries a reprehensible anti-Semitism that at times seriously compromised the Christian element of the history between the two groups.

We cannot deny that in some regions in the first century Christians were excluded from the synagogue. Nor can we fail to recognize that at the end of the New Testament period segments of the early church came to see themselves as Israel's replacement in God's plan. Yet even at the end of the New Testament period there was no single Christian assessment of the relationship between the church and the synagogue that was universally held. We have only to think of the views of the fourth gospel and the Letter to the Hebrews and of 1 Peter, James, and 1 Clement.

Roman Catholics since Vatican II have become much more mindful of the bonds between Christians and Jews. The bishops of the council made use of the biblical symbol of the people of God as one of the chief symbols of their teaching on the church. It was inevitable that questions should be asked about the Jewish people of God and relations between Judaism and Christianity, in the past and at present.

Many voices in recent years have urged that the common spiritual heritage between Christians and Jews foster a mutual understanding and appreciation. Today Jews and Christians cannot solely by the biblical texts or by a history of the early church resolve all the questions and the difficulties that are present in our complex relationship. But a more widespread understanding of the Jewishness of Jesus and the Jewish roots of the early church may help promote a better relationship between Christians and Jews in our time and in the years to come.

Suggested Further Reading

GENERAL WORKS

Brown, Raymond E., S.S., *The Churches the Apostles Left Behind* (New York/Ramsey: Paulist Press, 1984).

Brown, Raymond E., S.S., and John P. Meier, *Antioch and Rome: New Testament Cradles of Catholic Christianity* (New York/Ramsey: Paulist Press, 1983).

Conzelmann, Hans, *History of Primitive Christianity* (Nashville: Abingdon Press, 1973).

Dunn, James D.G., *Unity and Diversity in the New Testament: An Inquiry into the Character of Earliest Christianity* (Philadelphia: Westminster Press, 1977).

Interpreter's Dictionary of the Bible, George Arthur Buttrick *et al.,* editors. 4 vols. (Nashville: Abingdon Press, 1962).

Jerome Biblical Commentary, R.E. Brown, S.S., J.A. Fitzmyer, S.J., R.E. Murphy, O.Carm., editors (Englewood Cliffs, N.J.: Prentice-Hall, 1968). A new edition of this work is being prepared.

Keck, Leander E., *The New Testament Experience of Faith* (St. Louis: Bethany Press, 1976).

Kümmel, Werner Georg, *Introduction to the New Testament* (Nashville: Abingdon Press, 1975; revised edition).

Meyer, Ben F., *The Early Christians: Their World Mission and Self-Discovery* (Good News Studies, 16; Wilmington: Michael Glazier, 1986).

Perrin, Norman, *The New Testament: An Introduction* (New York: Harcourt Brace Jovanovich, 1974).

Rome and the Study of Scripture (St. Meinrad: Grail Publications, 1958; Sixth Edition).

Schillebeeckx, Edward, *The Church with a Human Face: A New and Expanded Theology of Ministry,* Parts 1 and 2 (New York: Crossroad, 1985).

Introduction and Overview (Chapter One)

Brown, Raymond E., S.S., *Biblical Reflections on Crises Facing the Church* (New York/Paramus: Paulist Press, 1975).

Brown, Raymond E., S.S., *The Critical Meaning of the Bible* (New York/Ramsey: Paulist Press, 1981).

Brown, Raymond E., S.S., *Biblical Exegesis and Church Doctrine* (New York/Mahwah: Paulist Press, 1985).

Fiorenza, Francis Schüssler, *Foundational Theology: Jesus and the Church*, Part II (New York: Crossroad, 1984).

Fitzmyer, Joseph A., S.J., *A Christological Catechism: New Testament Answers* (New York/Ramsey: Paulist Press, 1982). The Appendix of this volume contains the text of the Pontifical Biblical Commission's 1964 Instruction on the Historical Truth of the Gospels and a commentary on the Instruction by the author of this volume.

The World of the New Testament (Chapter Two)

Freyne, Sean, *The World of the New Testament* (New Testament Message, 2; Wilmington: Michael Glazier, 1980).

Lohse, Eduard, *The New Testament Environment* (Nashville: Abingdon Press, 1974).

Reicke, Bo, *The New Testament Era: The World of the Bible from 500 B.C. to A.D. 100* (Philadelphia: Fortress Press, 1974).

The Ministry of Jesus (Chapter Three)

Aulén, Gustaf, *Jesus in Contemporary Historical Research* (Philadelphia: Fortress Press, 1976).

Bornkamm, Günther, Article "Jesus Christ," *The New Encyclopedia Britannica*, Vol. 10, pp. 145–155 (1974).

Bornkamm, Günther, *Jesus of Nazareth* (New York, Evanston, and London: Harper & Row, 1960).

Dunn, James D.G., *The Evidence for Jesus* (Philadelphia: Westminster Press, 1985).

Jeremias, Joachim, *New Testament Theology: The Proclamation of Jesus* (New York: Charles Scribner's Sons, 1971).

Lohfink, Gerhard, *Jesus and Community: The Social Dimension of Christian Faith* (Philadelphia: Fortress Press, and New York/Ramsey: Paulist Press, 1984).

Schweizer, Eduard, *Jesus* (Richmond: John Knox Press, 1971).

Senior, Donald, C.P., *Jesus: A Gospel Portrait* (Cincinnati: Pflaum Standard, 1975).

Vermes, Geza, *Jesus the Jew: A Historian's Reading of the Gospels* (New York: Macmillan, 1973).

The Early Communities (Chapter Four)

Dunn, James D.G., *Jesus and the Spirit: A Study of the Religious and Charismatic Experience of Jesus and the First Christians as Reflected in the New Testament* (Philadelphia: Westminster Press, 1975).

Haenchen, Ernst, *The Acts of the Apostles: A Commentary* (Oxford: Basil Blackwell, 1971).

Hengel, Martin, *Acts and the History of Earliest Christianity* (Philadelphia: Fortress Press, 1979).

Lohse, Eduard, *The First Christians: Their Beginnings, Writings, and Beliefs* (Philadelphia: Fortress Press, 1983).

The Pauline Churches (Chapter Five)

Betz, Hans Dieter, *Galatians: A Commentary on Paul's Letter to the Churches in Galatia* (Hermeneia Series; Philadelphia: Fortress Press, 1979).

Bornkamm, Günther, *Paul* (New York and Evanston: Harper & Row, 1971).

Fallon, Francis T., *2 Corinthians* (New Testament Message, 11; Wilmington: Michael Glazier, 1980).

Getty, Mary Ann, R.S.M., *Philippians and Philemon* (New Testament Message, 14; Wilmington: Michael Glazier, 1980).

Keck, Leander E., *Paul and His Letters* (Proclamation Commentaries; Philadelphia: Fortress Press, 1979).

Marrow, Stanley B., *Paul: His Letters and His Theology: An Introduction to Paul's Epistles* (New York/Mahwah: Paulist Press, 1986).

Meeks, Wayne A., *The First Urban Christians: The Social World of the Apostle Paul* (New Haven and London: Yale University Press, 1983).

Murphy-O'Connor, Jerome, O.P., *Becoming Human Together: The Pastoral Anthropology of St. Paul* (Good News Studies, 2; Wilmington: Michael Glazier, 1982; revised edition).

Murphy-O'Connor, Jerome, O.P., *1 Corinthians* (New Testament Message, 10; Wilmington: Michael Glazier, 1979).

Murphy-O'Connor, Jerome, O.P., *St. Paul's Corinth: Texts and Archaeology* (Good News Studies, 6; Wilmington: Michael Glazier, 1983).

Orr, William F. and James Arthur Walther, *1 Corinthians* (Anchor Bible, 32; Garden City, N.Y.: Doubleday, 1976).

Osiek, Carolyn, R.S.C.J., *Galatians* (New Testament Message, 12; Wilmington: Michael Glazier, 1980).

Perkins, Pheme, *Ministering in the Pauline Churches* (New York/Ramsey: Paulist Press, 1982).

Reese, James M., O.S.F.S., *1 and 2 Thessalonians* (New Testament Message, 16; Wilmington: Michael Glazier, 1979).

Thompson, William G., *Paul and His Message for Life's Journey* (New York/Mahwah: Paulist Press, 1986).

Colossians, Ephesians and Mark (Chapter Six)

Best, Ernest, *Mark: The Gospel as Story* (Studies of the New Testament and Its World; Edinburgh: T. & T. Clark, 1983).

Ephesians, Colossians, 2 Thessalonians, The Pastoral Epistles, J. Paul Sampley, Joseph Burgess, Gerhard Krodel, Reginald H. Fuller (Proclamation Commentaries; Philadelphia: Fortress, 1978).

Harrington, Wilfrid, O.P., *Mark* (New Testament Message, 4; Wilmington: Michael Glazier, 1979).

Hengel, Martin, *Studies in the Gospel of Mark* (Philadelphia: Fortress Press, 1985).

Kee, Howard Clark, *Community of the New Age: Studies in Mark's Gospel* (Philadelphia: Westminster, 1977).

Lohse, Eduard, *Colossians and Philemon: A Commentary on the Epistles to the Colossians and to Philemon* (Hermeneia Series; Philadelphia: Fortress Press, 1971).

Matera, Frank J., *What Are They Saying About Mark?* (New York/Mahwah: Paulist Press, 1987).

Rogers, Patrick V., C.P., *Colossians* (New Testament Message, 15; Wilmington: Michael Glazier, 1980).

Swain, Lionel, *Ephesians* (New Testament Message, 13; Wilmington: Michael Glazier, 1980).

Transition and Consolidation (Chapter Seven)

Balch, David L., *Let Wives Be Submissive: The Domestic Code in I Peter* (Society of Biblical Literature, Monograph Series, 26; Chico, CA: Scholars Press, 1981).

Brown, Raymond E., S.S., *The Community of the Beloved Disciple* (New York/Ramsey/Toronto: Paulist Press, 1979).

Cohen, Shaye J.D., "The Significance of Yavneh: Pharisees, Rabbis, and the End of Jewish Sectarianism," *Hebrew Union College Annual* 55(1984), 27–53.

Elliott, John H., *A Home for the Homeless: A Sociological Exegesis of 1 Peter, Its Situation and Strategy* (Philadelphia: Fortress Press, 1981).

Elliott, John H., *1 Peter: Estrangement and Community* (Chicago: Franciscan Herald Press, 1979).

Karris, Robert J., O.F.M., *The Pastoral Epistles* (New Testament Message, 17; Wilmington: Michael Glazier, 1979).

Kingsbury, Jack Dean, *Matthew* (Proclamation Commentaries; Philadelphia: Fortress Press, 1977).

Meier, John P., *Matthew* (New Testament Message, 3; Wilmington: Michael Glazier, 1980).

Meier, John P., *The Vision of Matthew* (Theological Inquiries; New York: Paulist Press, 1979).

Perspectives on First Peter, edited by Charles H. Talbot (Special Studies Series, 9; Macon: Mercer University Press, 1986).

Senior, Donald, C.P., *1 and 2 Peter* (New Testament Message, 20; Wilmington: Michael Glazier, 1980).

Senior, Donald, C.P., *What Are They Saying About Matthew?* (New York: Paulist Press, 1983).

The Turn of the Century (Chapter Eight)

Collins, Adela Yarbro, *The Apocalypse* (New Testament Message, 22; Wilmington: Michael Glazier, 1979).

Fiorenza, Elisabeth Schüssler, *The Book of Revelation: Justice and Judgment* (Philadelphia: Fortress Press, 1985).

Fiorenza, Elisabeth Schüssler, *Invitation to the Book of Revelation* (Garden City, N.Y.: Doubleday & Co., 1981).

Hebrews, James, 1 and 2 Peter, Jude, Revelation, Reginald H. Fuller, Gerard S. Sloyan, Gerhard Krodel, Frederick W. Danker, Elisabeth Schüssler Fiorenza (Proclamation Commentaries; Philadelphia: Fortress, 1977).

Pilch, J. J., *What Are They Saying About the Book of Revelation?* (New York: Paulist Press, 1978).

SPECIAL STUDIES

Brown, Raymond E., S.S., *Recent Discoveries and the Biblical World* (Wilmington: Michael Glazier, 1983).

Feminist Perspectives on Biblical Scholarship, edited by Adela Yarbro Collins (Society of Biblical Literature: Biblical Scholarship in North America, 10; Chico: Scholars Press, 1985).

Fiorenza, Elisabeth Schüssler, *In Memory of Her: A Feminist Theological Reconstruction of Christian Origins* (New York: Crossroad, 1985).

Gager, John G., *Kingdom and Community: The Social World of Early Christianity* (Englewood Cliffs, N.J.: Prentice-Hall, 1975).

Harrington, Daniel J., S.J., *The Light of All Nations: Essays on the Church in New Testament Research* (Good News Studies, 3; Wilmington: Michael Glazier, 1982).

Kee, Howard Clark, *Christian Origins in Sociological Perspective: Methods and Resources* (Philadelphia: Westminster Press, 1980).

Malherbe, Abraham J., *Social Aspects of Early Christianity* (Baton Rouge and London: Louisiana State University Press, 1977).

Meeks, Wayne A., *The Moral World of the First Christians* (Library of Early Christianity, 6; Philadelphia: Westminster Press, 1986).

Osiek, Carolyn, R.S.C.J., *What Are They Saying About the Social Setting of the New Testament?* (New York/Ramsey: Paulist Press, 1984).

Peter in the New Testament, edited by Raymond E. Brown, Karl P. Donfried, and John Reumann (New York/Paramus/Toronto: Paulist Press, and Minneapolis: Augsburg, 1973).

Theissen, Gerd, *Sociology of Early Palestinian Christianity* (Philadelphia: Fortress Press, 1978).

Theissen, Gerd, *The Social Setting of Pauline Christianity: Essays on Corinth* (Philadelphia: Fortress Press, 1982).

Index